Collaborative Practice

Collaborative practice is a method of dispute resolution, used mainly in family law matters. By taking a non-adversarial approach, it challenges the strictly positivist view of the lawyer as 'zealous advocate' for the client. As such, it has received much criticism from the established Bar and legal profession.

This book provides a doctrinal and empirical analysis of collaborative practice with a view to assessing its place within the dispute resolution continuum and addressing whether this criticism has been justified. It begins by establishing the theoretical underpinnings of conflict and differing approaches to conflict resolution, the impact of the comprehensive law movement and therapeutic jurisprudence. The origins and development of the collaborative process and the framework it provides for a multidisciplinary approach to conflict resolution is outlined. The book addresses the examination of the process undertaken in the lead up to the enactment of the Uniform Collaborative Law Rules/Act in 2010, now regarded as a model of best practice. Finally, through an examination of empirical research undertaken in the US, Canada and in England and Wales, and in presenting the results of the first known empirical research into the process in an Irish family law context, the book concludes with an evidence-based analysis of the process from the perspective of couples who chose to use the collaborative model to resolve the issues surrounding their relationship breakdown and views from collaborative lawyers and lawyers who do not advocate a non-adversarial approach.

As such this book provides a valuable insight into the process which will be of interest to: academics; practising lawyers; members of the judiciary; researchers in the fields of conflict resolution and family law and for students studying alternative dispute resolution (ADR).

Dr Connie Healy is a lecturer in law at the National University of Ireland, Galway. Having practised as a solicitor for over 15 years, she returned to academia in 2010 and was awarded a PhD for her thesis entitled *Resolution of Conflict in Family Law Matters: An Alternative and Child-Inclusive Approach* in 2014. Her research has attracted funding and awards nationally and internationally from bodies such as the Irish Research Council and the European Commission on Family Law.

Collaborative Practice

An International Perspective

Connie Healy

Routledge
Taylor & Francis Group
LONDON AND NEW YORK

First published 2018 by Routledge

2 Park Square, Milton Park, Abingdon, Oxfordshire OX14 4RN
52 Vanderbilt Avenue, New York, NY 10017

Routledge is an imprint of the Taylor & Francis Group, an informa business

First issued in paperback 2019

British Library Cataloguing in Publication Data
A catalogue record for this book is available from the British Library

Library of Congress Cataloging in Publication Data
Names: Healy, Connie, author.
Title: Collaborative practice : an international perspective / Connie Healy.
Description: Abingdon, Oxon [UK] ; New York : Routledge, 2017. | Includes bibliographical references and index.
Identifiers: LCCN 2017006187 | ISBN 9781138948761 (hbk)
Subjects: LCSH: Compromise (Law) | Dispute resolution (Law) | Conflict management.
Classification: LCC K2390 .H49 2017 | DDC 347/.09–dc23
LC record available at https://lccn.loc.gov/2017006187

ISBN: 978-1-138-94876-1 (hbk)
ISBN: 978-0-367-87498-8 (pbk)

Typeset in Galliard
by Taylor & Francis Books

Contents

Acknowledgements

Completing the empirical research for this book would not have been possible without the kind assistance of all of those who gave their time to contribute through interviews or replying to questionnaires/surveys. Thank you very much to all of those that contributed. Special thanks to: Marie McGonagle and Professor Donncha O'Connell (NUI Galway); Professor Shane Kilcommins (University of Limerick); Professor Geoffrey Shannon; Linda Wray of the International Academy of Collaborative Professionals; the members of the Association of Collaborative Practitioners in Ireland and the Galway Solicitors' Bar Association.

Thank you also to Anne McD, Joan, Elaine, Liz and Michael O'Neill. Finally, a special thanks to my mum Rita and my husband Jim for their love, kindness, incredible thoughtfulness and support, and my two wonderful children, David and Anna. This book is dedicated to the memory of my father, Joe Healy.

Table of cases

Banerjee v Bisset 2009 B.C.L.R. 2d. 1808
Conklin v. Hannoch Weisman, 678 A.2d 1060, 1069 (N.J. 1996)
Hartshorne v. Hartshorne, 2004 SCC 22, [2004] 1 S.C.R. *550*
Miglin v. Miglin, 2003 SCC 24, [2003] 1 S.C.R. 303
Roche v Roche [2010] 2 ILRM 1 24
Rosalba Alassini v. Telecom Italia SpA (C-317/08), Filomena Califano v. Wind SpA (C-318/08), Lucia Anna Giorgia Iacono v Telecom Italia SpA (C-319/08) and *Multiservice Srl v Telecom Italia SpA* (C-320/08) ECR [2010] I-02213

Table of statutes

The Family Law (Divorce) Act 1996
The Judicial Separation and Family Law Reform Act 1989
Uniform Collaborative Law Act and Rules 2010
Solicitors Act 1954
Solicitors (Amendment) Act 1994

Abbreviations

ADR	–	Alternative Dispute Resolution
IACP	–	International Academy of Collaborative Professionals
ACP	–	Association of Collaborative Practitioners
LRC	–	Law Reform Commission
UCLA	–	Uniform Collaborative Law Act

Introduction

This book aims to provide an original perspective on a multidisciplinary approach to the resolution of conflict in family law cases. Specifically, it provides a doctrinal and empirical analysis of the concept of collaborative law, also known as collaborative practice or collaborative divorce.

Collaborative practice is an alternative method of dispute resolution which involves a separating party and their lawyer working with the other party and their lawyer, to find the best possible solution to the issue in dispute; one that meets the needs, where possible, of all involved and is tailored to their family circumstances. The process is structured on an agreement in which the lawyers and their clients agree to be open and honest with each other and to negotiate in good faith. Unique to the process is the requirement that, in the event settlement cannot be reached, the agreement stipulates that the parties will have to instruct different lawyers if they wish to take their case before the court. This is known as the disqualification clause or disqualification provision.

In taking a collaborative, non-adversarial approach, the process in many respects challenges the strictly positivist view of the lawyer as zealous advocate for the client. Arguably in doing so, it demands, as proposed by Peppet,[1] a higher standard of legal ethics. As such, it has received much criticism from the established Bar and those who uphold the black letter law approach of winning a client's case regardless of the impact on the other parties involved.

This book begins by addressing the theoretical underpinnings of conflict and conflict resolution. It outlines the origins and development of the collaborative process in the US and its place within the dispute resolution continuum. Now twenty-five years in existence, it assesses the academic commentary and the extent to which collaborative practice has been accepted by lawyers and their clients. In doing so, it considers the ethical opinions issued by State Bar Associations in the US, the American Bar Association and the discussions and debates which led to the enactment of the Uniform Collaborative Law Rules/Act in the US in 2010. The book also addresses the manner in which the Uniform Act has influenced policy making and decisions internationally. For example, the Act was used as a term of reference and a model of best practice by the Law Reform Commission in Ireland in their analysis of the process and, in reaching their conclusion that the process is 'an emerging method of dispute resolution'.[2]

Significantly, this book is also original in that it synthesises the research carried out into collaborative practice in the US, Canada and in England and Wales, and presents the results of the first known empirical research into the process in a family law context in Ireland. Previous books on this subject have been published mainly by American/Canadian authors and many have been from a practitioner's perspective.

The opening chapter of the book will set the theoretical framework for the examination of dispute resolution and the collaborative process and establish its position within the wider field of alternative dispute resolution. In doing so, it shall address questions such as whether there is a need for such a method of conflict resolution and how settlement within this process differs from settlement within the adversarial process and what has traditionally been referred to as 'ordinary lawyer negotiation'. This chapter will also examine the collaborative process as one of the vectors in the comprehensive law movement and the wider field of enquiry that is therapeutic jurisprudence.

Chapter 2 will address what in effect makes collaborative practice unique in the way it is structured. Three main issues will be analysed. Firstly, the Participation Agreement which is signed at the outset and the obligations that arise on foot of such agreement. Secondly, this chapter will examine the disqualification clause and the financial and emotional implications of disqualification for both the clients and their lawyers. Finally, the unique multidisciplinary approach promoted in the collaborative model which encapsulates experts from various disciplines (law, psychology including child psychology and finance) working as part of a team for the benefit of the parties rather than as adversaries is examined.

Members of the International Academy of Collaborative Professionals led the way in drafting a Uniform Collaborative Law Rules/Act in the US in 2010. Chapter 3 will therefore explore the provisions of this legislation. Describing this as both 'a teaching and learning process', this chapter details some of the obstacles encountered during the enactment process and how they were addressed. It assesses the Act as a model of best practice and the extent to which it has been acknowledged as such internationally, focusing on the Irish experience and the recommendations made by the Irish Law Reform Commission.

Chapter 4 will provide an insight into the research that has been carried out into the process by the International Academy of Collaborative Professionals in the US, Professor Julie Macfarlane in Canada and by both Resolution and, more recently, by Professor Anne Barlow and her team as part of the *Mapping Paths to Family Justice Project* in England and Wales. In synthesising the research internationally and undertaking a comparative analysis, this chapter addresses questions as to how effective the process has been for clients in reaching settlement and for collaborative lawyers.

The results of the first known empirical research into collaborative practice in an Irish family law context will be presented in Chapter 5. Through a quantitative study, the research assesses the development of the process, settlement rates and factors which influence clients' and lawyers' decisions to use the process. In addition, through qualitative research it provides an in-depth and robust contextual analysis based on semi-structured interviews undertaken with clients that used the process, collaborative lawyers and also with adversarial lawyers who, to-date, have been critical of the process. It addresses whether these criticisms and those of academics who have written on the process, are borne out through the research findings.

Finally, Chapter 6 will examine another method of dispute resolution which has been born out of the collaborative process, namely cooperative law, and will provide an insight into research undertaken into the cooperative process in the US. The chapter concludes with an evidence-based analysis of the success or failure of collaborative practice and the shift towards embracing the benefits of a multidisciplinary approach to the resolution of conflict. It will assess the impact of these changes for clients, practitioners and crucially for the development of legal education.

Note

1 Peppet, S., 'Lawyers' Bargaining Ethics, Contract, and Collaboration: The End of the Legal Profession and the Beginning of Professional Pluralism' (2004–2005) 90 *Iowa Law Review* 475–538, 479.

2 Law Reform Commission, *Alternative Dispute Resolution: Mediation and Conciliation* (LRC 98 – Dublin 2010) para [6.77] at 121.

1 The theoretical foundations of collaborative law and alternative dispute resolution

Introduction

In beginning to examine the effectiveness of any process, it is important to consider the theoretical perspectives upon which it is based. In the past, much criticism has been levied against 'alternatives' to the courts' system. Twining, for example, commented that the 'the vast bulk of mediation literature is atheoretical.'[1] Many see the paper given by Frank Sander at the Pound Conference in 1976 when he spoke about the idea of a 'multi-door courthouse' as the beginning of a change in thinking.[2] Another important milestone was the publication of *Getting to Yes*[3] in 1981, addressing the potential benefits of negotiating settlement rather than taking an adversarial approach. As Menkel-Meadow[4] notes, however, in taking either of these approaches, we may be:

> failing to pay enough serious attention to earlier 'intellectual' founders of ADR – those who provided the key ideas, concepts or organizing frameworks from which we have built our modern movement of theories, practices, policies, and institutions.[5]

This book, in addressing the origins and development of collaborative practice and in presenting the results of original empirical research undertaken into the process,[6] will begin by examining the theoretical underpinnings of alternative dispute resolution (ADR) and the writings of these 'intellectual founders'. Specifically, this chapter will explore the concept of 'conflict' and the extent to which it can be a positive rather than a negative force.[7] It will highlight the importance of examining the 'ecology of human development',[8] the way in which society forms into 'groups' and the manner in which tensions and hostilities are addressed and disputes transformed, within and between those groups.[9] Next, the importance, if any, of the 'process'[10] used in resolving these disputes and issues surrounding the concept of 'procedural justice' will be discussed. Central to this is the move from more traditional forms of resolution, namely: adjudication by the courts, to 'ordinary lawyer negotiation'[11] within the courts' system; the role that clients and their lawyers play in 'adding to' or 'cooling down' the dispute; and the place of collaborative practice within this dispute resolution continuum. The chapter will conclude by addressing the extent to which collaborative law or collaborative practice can be considered to be part of the 'comprehensive law movement'[12] and the wider 'field of inquiry' that is therapeutic jurisprudence.[13]

The theory of alternative dispute resolution and the importance of understanding conflict

Menkel-Meadow, in seeking to identify the theoretical frameworks from which the field of alternative dispute resolution or conflict resolution emanates, opines that the field of ADR is 'richer for multiple sources of insights and sensitivity to the interactive effects of law and legal institutions with other social institutions.'[14] She notes that alternative dispute resolution is 'situated in the broader intellectual space of the sociology or philosophy of the role of conflict.'[15]

While initial perceptions of conflict may have portrayed it in a negative light, referring to it as having 'disruptive, disassociating and dysfunctional consequences,'[16] Coser, in examining the 'functions' of conflict comments that:

> groups require disharmony as well as harmony, dissociation as well as association; and conflicts within them are by no means altogether disruptive factors … Far from being necessarily dysfunctional, a certain degree of conflict is an essential element in group formation and the persistence of group life.[17]

Simmel and Coser, 'see conflict as variable: sometimes "destructive," but sometimes "constructive" or even creative … an opportunity for learning and growth'[18]; a positive force, enabling problems to be aired leading to creative problem solving. Mary Parker Follett also spoke about 'constructive conflict.'[19] She noted that:

> As conflict – difference – is here in the world, as we cannot avoid it, we should, I think use it. Instead of condemning it, we should set it to work for us … The music of the violin we get by friction … We talk of the friction of mind on mind as a good thing. … we have to know when to try to eliminate friction and when to try to capitalize it, when to see what work we can make it do. That is what I wish to consider here, whether we can set conflict to work and make it *do* something for us.[20]

For Follett there were three ways to deal with conflict: through domination, compromise or integration. She favoured the idea of integration, finding a solution that was conducive to all and not one in which any party would unduly compromise or dominate. In promoting integration, she also highlighted the importance of taking an interdisciplinary or multidisciplinary approach in how issues are resolved.

Significant, also, in Follett's work was her appreciation of the differences that may lie between an individual's 'declared motives' for the conflict and their 'real motives' and the need to 'get underneath all the camouflage, to find the real demand.'[21] She was acutely aware that in some instances this deception may be deliberate but that it may also 'exist unconsciously'[22] to the person in dispute; these 'unconscious' reasons may, in modern alternative dispute resolution terms, be considered the parties' 'interests'. Follett acknowledged the need for differing approaches once such 'motives' have been uncovered: on occasions to break a problem down into its constituent elements and, in other instances, to view it as a whole. Negotiation may then begin by addressing the 'costless' or less important concessions first, before moving on to the more contentious issues with a view to creative problem-solving.[23]

Coser however, cautions that left to their own devices, some social conflicts may be infinite. To 'prevent their struggle from becoming a zero sum game in which the outcome can only be total defeat or total victory,'[24] feuding parties need to have a 'common interest' in agreeing 'explicit provisions' as to what constitutes the end of the conflict.[25] Once these parameters or 'symbols'[26] are in place, '[t] ermination of conflict becomes a problem to be solved by both parties.'[27] It will be argued throughout this work that the ability to appreciate the need for such parameters, and to be able to set realistic goals, effectively determines feuding parties' ability to engage in different forms of dispute resolution mechanisms along the continuum.

The social context

What impacts on disputants' ability to set these parameters? Conflict, as already noted, is a social construct. Thus, in examining its role, it is necessary to explore the societal factors that impact on its development and resolution. Some of these matters are within disputants' control. Others, perhaps not.

An understanding of what Bronfenbrenner describes as the 'ecology of human' development helps to understand the way societies operate, the multi-layered web into which disputants are born.[28] Bronfenbrenner usefully described a series of 'systems' which, in his view, allows humans to develop in a manner similar to a 'set of nested structures, each inside the next, like a set of Russian dolls.'[29] The first system he identified was the 'micro-system'. This, he believed, represented the immediate relationships that people have in their lives. For example, the relationship between a parent and a child, between a child and a teacher. The next level, Bronfenbrenner described as the 'meso-system', namely, the relationships between differing 'micro-systems': the child's home and school environment combined and how they may influence each other. Beyond these immediate relationships, Bronfenbrenner noted how factors outside of an individual's direct environment, what he termed the 'exo-system', may also impact on their lives: a parent's relationship with their work environment may impact on the family, in a situation where a parent, perhaps, becomes unemployed. Losing a job may not be relevant to the immediate issues at dispute but will obviously affect how matters are resolved. Finally, wider social policy and developments, at national or international level, form part of what Bronfenbrenner referred to as the 'macro-system', or society's plan.

In conducting his research, Bronfenbrenner focused on examining human behaviour not in a laboratory-controlled environment, but in a way that explored how people actually live their lives. This corresponds to a phenomenological approach: the study of 'human lived experiences';[30] particularly relevant in family law matters, in which each family's circumstances are unique. Bronfenbrenner was also cognizant of the impact of time. Douzinas, too, as a postmodern legal scholar, notes that the '[t]ime of justice differs from the time of interpretation.'[31] Issues that have caused hurt or conflict when a relationship breaks down may be less relevant when a case comes to a court hearing or settlement.

Coser's work on the functions of social conflict, referred to earlier, is also insightful in understanding the importance of 'groups'[32] that tend to form naturally within these 'systems,' and in understanding the extent to which groups will seek to protect and maintain their members. When a threat arises from something outside of the group, the group tends to mobilise to protect itself.[33] 'Family', with its varying definitions,[34] is possibly the most immediately recognisable 'unit group' within society, and has been recognised as such at national and international level. Recognising that there can be 'a directing of antithetical feeling (affectionate and hostile) toward the same person'[35] within close personal relationships, if the actions of one of the parties threatens the preservation of the group, the conflict is often more deep-seated and difficult to resolve.

Coser argues that hostilities that have been building up within the group will suddenly come to the fore; those that perceive themselves as 'underprivileged' will seek to assert their rights. Felsteiner, Abel and Sarat have also written on this issue of how disputes evolve. In their work on '[t]he transformation of disputes', they, similarly to Coser, note that people may have a certain 'grievance apathy'[36] and will ignore some 'experiences' that occur. In exploring the way in which disputes are formed or 'transformed,' however, Felsteiner, Abel and Sarat's work helps to develop an understanding of how an 'experience', something that causes conflict, develops into a 'grievance' and how this grievance, if not addressed, in turn, becomes a dispute. For a dispute to materialise they refer to the necessity of 'naming' the wrong alleged to have been suffered; the aggrieved person acknowledges the issue by telling someone about it. The next step is 'blaming': attributing blame to the person or organisation believed to have caused or contributed to the wrong; and if this complaint is not dealt with, 'claiming' occurs: making a claim for the wrong suffered. Within relationships, this transformation may take place over a number of years.

Felsteiner, Abel and Sarat[37] acknowledge that the way in which individuals deal with disputes may also be 'a function of personality as it interacts with prior experience and current pressures.'[38] Mayer, likewise, in documenting the many ways people either 'avoid' or 'engage with' conflict, notes that this can have a significant bearing on how disputants choose to deal with issues that arise.[39] Central to this is a recognition of difference,[40] the unique characteristics of a person's 'risk preference, contentiousness, and feelings about personal efficacy, privacy, independence, and attachment to justice (rule-mindedness).'[41] Disputes are further complicated by the fact that they are also subjective and reactive. Each disputant will have his or her own narrative as to how the dispute arose and a view of the parts played by the respective parties.

One common reaction is for separating parties to pursue goals in a representative or collective way, rather than as individuals, with one parent taking on the assumed role as protector of the 'group', in this case the family. Coser argues that this approach often allows disputants to distance themselves from personal issues and to argue or claim 'respectability' in the conflict, portraying an image of fighting for the rights of other members of the group – often the children.[42] The feminist movement has also highlighted this issue, but from the perspective of the impact of what it terms the 'relational' issues, arguing that women, in particular, feel constrained in the decisions they are free to make because of the potential impact of such decisions on the children of the relationship.[43] Menkel-Meadow sets out additional factors to be considered, including: the extent to which the parties are free to choose which resolution method they wish to use or whether this may be court ordered; the visibility of the dispute itself – whether the negotiations take place in public or in private; and what is at stake for the parties.[44] The costs and availability of the various processes can also be relevant in choosing a method of dispute resolution, as can the normative constraints, personalities and values of the negotiators.[45]

Negotiators or third parties with whom the aggrieved person may come into contact are important to the way a dispute may progress. If, for example, the person with whom they choose to discuss a grievance has a calming effect, the disputant may choose to seek peaceful means of resolving the issue. If, on the other hand, the disputant speaks to someone who takes an adversarial approach, they may be more likely to wish to fight their case. Lawyers, therefore, as agents in the dispute-resolution process, have a central role to play and, as the research undertaken for this study will show, often tend to underestimate the influence that their approach or advice may have on the way a dispute is resolved.

Anthropologists also point to the importance of cultural issues in the type of disputing processes that a particular society may adopt. Nader cautions against merely transplanting different frameworks for resolution from one culture to another.[46] She points to the difficulties in, for example, cultures which place a strong emphasis on public knowledge, engaging in mediation or similar processes that are perceived as being 'secretive' or occurring behind closed doors. Again, this will be addressed throughout this work, which aims to assess the impact of collaborative law as an American concept and how it has been accepted in other jurisdictions, and to examine the cultural nuances of how the process has been tailored to adapt. Central to this also is a recognition of the importance of not compromising justice and the rule of law in using what are perceived as more value-laden, peaceful dispute resolution processes.[47]

What then is 'justice' in a family law context?

Questions arise, therefore, as to what 'justice' means in a family law context, and how important procedural and other issues are in making sure that the 'rule of law' is not compromised.

It is outside of the remit of this work to outline all of the theoretical perspectives on what constitutes 'law'; in attempting to define 'family law', however, Diduck describes it as 'the body of law that defines and regulates the family, family relationships and family responsibilities.'[48] More specifically, as noted by Herring, it is the 'law governing the relationships between children and parents, and between adults in close emotional relationships.'[49] Justice, on the other hand, can be more difficult to define. Objectively, it incorporates both substantive justice, to do as the law commands, and procedural justice, which 'requires that a person's rights and duties under the law be determined according to fair procedures.'[50] Both are defined by a set of rules. Subjectively, however, disputants will have quite different views as to what constitutes a 'just' outcome in any particular case. In seeking access to, or remedies within, the 'family law' system, many potential litigants often feel a disparity between what Ratnapala describes as '[j]ustice according to law and justice of the law.'[51]

Difficulties, too, may arise in defining 'procedural justice' in a family law context. Maclean suggests that the family court 'provides a framework within which compromises can be made.'[52] This 'framework' is akin to what Rawls has described as 'background justice': a basic structure for removing 'bargaining advantages' and putting 'all citizens in a position to manage their own affairs on a footing of a suitable degree of social and economic equality.'[53] Equality before the law is a central concept in any justice system. However, equality 'necessarily ignores the specific history, motive and need that the litigant brings.'[54] As noted by Douzinas 'it fails to remove the mask from the face of the person and the blindfold from the eyes of justice.'[55]

Macfarlane notes that lawyers also value this legal framework, following court procedures as the key determinant in obtaining 'justice', rather than placing much, if any, emphasis on the outcomes achieved.[56] Lawyers arguably feel safe in explaining the courts' process to their clients, presenting justice as per the system rather than judging outcomes, which may be 'abstract'. Resistance to 'alternative' methods of dispute resolution may relate to the flexibility of such alternatives, to the fact that they often lack a defined system of rules.

George notes, however, that family law is not straightforward.[57] It interrelates not only with 'many other areas of the law, but also with other academic disciplines and with social policy more broadly.'[58] Within the framework of 'background justice' then, what rules should be followed? Should family law decisions be made purely based on the law itself, or should these wider issues of sociology or psychology be relevant? To what extent should 'extra-legal'[59] concerns be taken into account? Is it only through the established 'framework' that is the family courts' system that justice can be dispensed, or is there any place for less formal mechanisms? These issues will be addressed throughout the book, but at the same time the reality is acknowledged that whereas the courts' process is an important and integral part of the system, and currently provides the 'framework' for dispute resolution, the number of cases that progress to a full hearing before a court are few.[60]

Collaborative practice on the dispute resolution continuum

In adhering to a strict positivist interpretation of justice and the rule of law, there is, as noted by Douzinas, 'an antipathy towards … non judicial methods of dispute resolution.'[61] Positivists view the legitimacy of law as being formulated on rules and reason, with subjective issues or values playing little or no part in how decisions are reached. For some, therefore, alternative dispute resolution methods that offer flexibility and an interests-based approach are inherently dangerous mechanisms, which purport to accommodate the needs of all parties but, under which, the weaker party may suffer at the hands of a more dominant negotiator.[62] A post-modern approach, however, takes a different view, recognising the importance of the individual and the need to provide disputing parties with more participative, tailor-made solutions.[63]

Examining the dispute-resolution continuum, in most jurisdictions the most amicable solution for separating parties is being able to resolve issues themselves, a process often termed 'kitchen table' divorce. At the other end of the spectrum the adversarial court process is, most frequently, used by those who are not in a position to negotiate directly and who prefer to hand the dispute over to lawyers and take an arms' length approach: those who may, as Coser noted, not be in a position to agree parameters for the dispute or what should effectively signal the end of the conflict. Mayer refers to this coping strategy as 'avoidance through surrogates'.[64]

Gulliver describes the courts' process as one:

> where two parties are separated from each other, face an adjudicator who sits in front of, apart from, and often raised above them. They address him, offering information, opinion and arguments. Each seeks to refute the other's presentation and to persuade the adjudicator to favour his own case.[65]

By engaging in this process, '[c]ompulsorily or voluntarily, the disputants surrender the ability to decide for themselves.'[66] The judge, as noted by Douzinas, 'removes the dispute from the domain of interpersonal hostility and places it within the confines of the institution.'[67] Fiss argues that justice can only be achieved through the courts, and that any type of settlement or compromise reached through negotiations or less adversarial methods of dispute resolution is 'a poor substitute for judgement.'[68] He opines that all disputes require the 'thorough presentation promised by the adversary system,'[69] and that 'when a party settles, society gets less than what appears, and for a price it does not know it is paying.'[70] For him, any form of settlement or private negotiation of a dispute raises questions with regard to the equal bargaining power of the parties, whereas the judicial system 'knowingly struggles against those inequalities.'[71] A judge, he believed, can 'supplement the parties' presentations by asking questions, calling his own witnesses, and inviting other persons and institutions to participate as *amici*.'[72]

Lon Fuller, on the other hand, was strongly of the view that the adversarial courts system is not equipped to deal with 'polycentric disputes.'[73] For him, decisions made within the court process were binary in nature and could not accommodate differing perspectives and points of view. By taking an approach that relies on the application of universal rights and legal entitlements, 'the law forgets the difference of the different and the otherness of the other', and in Douzinas's opinion, it therefore 'cannot escape injustice.'[74] Neither did Fuller consider the courts' process to be suitable in situations in which the parties needed to maintain an ongoing relationship. Fuller, described as the 'leading jurisprudential thinker about ADR',[75] viewed law more broadly as a problem-solving activity. He felt strongly about the need for a number of different processes to address different types of disputes, and about the need for purity in each type of dispute process; each has its own characteristics, and processes should not be combined or integrated in any way.

Menkel-Meadow advises that '[s]tudies of legal negotiation must begin with a conception of its purpose. If the lawyer's role is to solve clients' problems, assumptions of competitive gain may be inapplicable if not dysfunctional in some situations.'[76] Gulliver also notes the importance of the clients' interests; if their interests are totally incompatible, or if they require an authoritative third-party ruling, then adjudication is the best route. If, on the other hand, a more 'accommodative' or 'multiplex'[77] solution is required, adjudication may not be the most suitable option.[78] The important questions, therefore, have to be what is it that each client hopes to achieve out of these negotiations and what outcome do they perceive as being a success?

Statistics show, that although court proceedings are issued in a large number of cases, up to 90% never proceed to a full hearing before a judge.[79] Research has also shown that many family lawyers favour settlement over trial.[80] These cases are generally settled by the respective lawyers brokering a deal and negotiating settlement.

Negotiation through lawyers

As noted above, most cases are settled through lawyer negotiation. Hart and Sachs regard a lawyer as 'an architect of social structure.'[81] They were perhaps the first to recognise the importance of lawyers in private disputes, and to point out that their role in negotiation is equally as important as their role within the courts' system.[82] They noted the many skills required of lawyers in negotiation, such as: anticipating probable outcomes; the strengths and weaknesses of each side's argument; and the skills involved in reaching common ground.

Negotiation, has been defined as:

> a process of adjustment of existing differences, with a view to the establishment of a mutually more desirable legal relation by means of barter and compromise of legal rights and duties and of economic, psychological, social and other interests. It is accomplished consensually as contrasted with the force of the law.[83]

Negotiators, following on from their training and experiences in the courts' process, have traditionally been described as falling within two specific categories – competitive negotiators or collaborative negotiators.[84] Zartman and Berman,[85] in examining the psychology of personality types, refer to them as either warriors, seeking their demands at the expense of the other party, or shopkeepers, individuals of good will and limited aims, seeking positive solutions. The legal negotiator most often witnessed within the adversarial system is described by Menkel-Meadow as:

> a consummate game player who maximises gain for clients by engaging in a series of ploys and countermoves designed to mislead the opponent into 'conceding' as much as possible – and to save time and money that might be spent on formal trial.[86]

Negotiations carried out under these circumstances have tended to be positional in nature. Why do clients or their lawyers routinely engage in competitive, positional negotiation? Fisher and Ury argue that for parties and their lawyers:

> [p]ositional bargaining is easy … It requires no preparation, it is universally understood and in some contexts it is entrenched and expected.[87]

As noted earlier, clients, not wishing to negotiate directly, may treat lawyers as 'surrogates'[88] in their disputes. Once positions have been taken, is it then possible to try to settle a case on amicable terms, to take a conciliatory approach to settlement, particularly when the threat of court, 'the force of the law', remains ever present if settlement cannot be 'accomplished consensually'? Lowenthal argues that '[o]ne cannot be competitive and collaborative at the same time, since concepts like trust and suspiciousness, as well as rigidity and flexibility, are functional opposites.'[89] It is understandable and expected that negotiating lawyers will generally hold back during negotiations in case agreement cannot be reached and the matter goes before the court. Cochran, too, notes that '[t]he prospect of litigation defines the framework of traditional negotiation and disclosure and shapes the bargaining strategies. Lawyers, therefore, must engage in a precarious balancing act between litigation and negotiation.'[90]

It also has to be acknowledged, however, that the reality of a client's interaction with his or her lawyers within the adversarial system may be quite different. Not all lawyers see themselves as fitting within these descriptions of either being adversarial or taking a collaborative approach. Many would be of the view that they run a case based on the facts, the parties, or the position taken by the opponent's lawyer, and that they then adapt their approach accordingly. Galanter, in particular, is of the view that there is no division between the adversarial system and negotiation; he asserts that the two processes should not be perceived as alternatives, and that in fact 'there is a single process of disputing in the vicinity of official tribunals that we might call *litigotiation*, that is, the strategic pursuit of a settlement through mobilizing the court process.'[91] Lande refers to what he calls 'ordinary lawyer negotiation' (negotiation within the framework of the adversarial system), and believes that 'lawyers presumably try to get good results for their clients and believe that they are more likely to do so through cooperative conversation than through (either) hard bargaining or systematic analysis of interests and options.'[92]

Negotiation in these situations, frequently at the door of the court, can, however, be perceived by the clients as a 'formless, informal, hidden, and unstructured process.'[93] Is this perhaps why clients have a poor perception of lawyers and the courts' system? Many of the clients interviewed during the course of the research undertaken for this book, for instance, had a perception that the outcome they would achieve through the courts (which they took to include lawyer negotiation) may not be fair or just.[94] Arguably, lawyers may be doing a disservice to themselves too, in that, despite having negotiated well for their client and having obtained the best possible settlement, clients may be left with a sense of uncertainty due to the covert nature of the negotiations. Does this model where cases that are routinely settled at the door of the court therefore accord more closely with Rubin's[95] view that negotiation is, in fact, a matter of settling conflict rather than resolving it?

Interest-based negotiations

What then, in contrast, are 'interest-based' negotiations and how, if at all, can they benefit clients? Fisher and Ury refer to the interest-based approach to negotiation as 'principled negotiation' or 'negotiation on the merits.'[96] They note that '[n]egotiations are not likely to make much progress as long as one side believes that the fulfilment of their basic human needs is being threatened by the other.'[97] The key, therefore, seems to be to remove some, if not all, of the fear involved in the process by outlining for the parties that through interest-based negotiations, the aim is to find shared interests and opportunities for mutual gain, with the parties having more control over the process itself and the outcome. In accordance with a postmodern interpretation of justice, separating parties are treated as 'unique', with the interest-based process recognising not only the context of their dispute but that 'every "context" in itself is a text that needs further interpretation.'[98]

Fisher and Ury explain that there are four basic elements to each negotiation, namely, the people; their interests; the options and the objective criteria. In dealing with the various elements, they propose that negotiators should first 'separate the people from the problem': rather than fighting each other over issues, the parties to a dispute are actively working together on the issue that has caused the problem between them. The parties are then encouraged to focus on their 'interests' and the interests of their family, rather than take a positional stance. In exploring these interests the parties use creativity to accomplish the third element, 'options'; solutions that may work for the mutual gain of both parties are proposed. These 'options' are then tested against 'objective criteria', such as what the likely outcome may be in a court setting, what the norm is in practice, and objective standards like, for example, 'market value' for property.

Parties, it is argued, need reassurance that the decisions they are making are in line with society's norms as 'an agreement consistent with precedent is less vulnerable to attack.'[99] In demanding this 'consistency', are negotiators and their clients still 'bargaining in the shadow of the law'[100]? Mnookin comments that '[t]he legal system affects *when* a divorce may occur, *how* a divorce must be proceeded with and *what* the consequences of the divorce will be.'[101] Regardless of the process used, the legal and statutory requirements remain: the aim of interest-based negotiation is not to change the law but to allow the consideration of a wider, postmodernist interpretation of justice, based on the unique circumstances of the parties involved.[102]

Mediation – an interest-based approach

The most commonly recognised method of 'interest-based' negotiation is arguably the mediation process. Fuller, in his assessment of the various processes available, was the first to recognise the importance of mediation, not only in helping parties reach settlement of their dispute but also for its capacity to 'reorient the parties towards each other',[103] acknowledging the benefits for those who work through their differences and establish a framework for working together in the future. Mediation has been defined as:

> a flexible process conducted confidentially in which a neutral person actively assists parties in working towards a negotiated settlement of a dispute or difference, with the parties in ultimate control of the decision to settle and the terms of resolution.[104]

Defining mediation as a 'flexible process' acknowledges both the variations in the way the mediation process may be carried out and in the models available. Variation will also occur depending on the type of issue that the process is being used to resolve, for example, commercial disputes, employment law issues or family law issues, and also the differences in procedure between various mediation organisations.

The most frequently used models of mediation are the evaluative model, the transformative model and the facilitative model. The evaluative model, most common in the US, is based closely on the traditional legal process and focuses on rights. Therefore during an evaluative mediation process, the mediator is actively involved in evaluating proposals and assisting the parties towards settlement.[105] The transformative model aspires to 'transforming people in the very midst of conflict',[106] with the mediator moving the parties from disempowerment to empowerment, both in their own personal development and in the resolution of their dispute. Finally, facilitative mediation urges mediators to gain an understanding of the issues between the parties and to seek to 'empower the parties to make their own decisions.'[107]

Mediation was heralded as the best way for separating parties to resolve family law matters.[108] Arguments in its favour were that it would assist the parties to maintain an ongoing relationship and would lead to less adversarial settlements.[109] From the courts' perspective, it was also welcomed as a method of removing some of what were perceived as troublesome family law matters from the court list. Those who were less receptive towards mediation warned about the dangers for the spouse who may be in a weaker negotiating position – perhaps being treated unfairly behind 'closed doors'.[110] Concerns were also raised that further victimisation may occur for those who had already been subjected to domestic violence during a relationship.[111]

Issues also began to emerge as to whether mediation should remain a voluntary process or whether there was any role for court-ordered or mandatory mediation. The extent to which parties can be ordered to participate in mediation, or at least to attend mandatory information meetings, varies from jurisdiction to jurisdiction. The courts in examining the issue of mandatory mediation have taken the view that, at worst, it delays, but does not prevent, access to justice.[112] On occasion, parties may engage merely to 'tick the box' and will refuse to participate in any discussion or negotiation. Others, though initially reluctant, may find the process beneficial once initiated.

Collaborative practice as a 'vector' in the comprehensive law movement

Collaborative practice tends to be positioned between mediation, in situations in which the parties may need some outside assistance, and the courts' process, whereby each party is separately represented and the lawyers take over the handling of the dispute. Through the collaborative process, parties have the support and assurance of their legal advisers but are protected or insulated from the polarising atmosphere that may arise if they find themselves sitting on opposite sides of a courtroom. Collaborative practice, similarly to mediation, offers an 'interests-based' approach to dispute resolution.

Pauline Tesler, one of the founders of the collaborative law movement, notes that collaborative law is:

> being recognized among academicians as belonging not only under the rubric of alternative dispute resolution, but also in the realm of two relatively new academic disciplines 'therapeutic jurisprudence' and 'preventative law'[113]

both now described as 'vectors' in the comprehensive law movement. The aim of this movement is to look more broadly at the role of law in society. Susan Daicoff, one of the movement's pioneers, broadly categorises these 'vectors' as consisting of:

- *lenses* through which to view the law: therapeutic jurisprudence, procedural justice, creative problem solving, and holistic justice;
- *processes* in terms of how the law is administered: collaborative law, restorative justice, problem-solving courts, and preventative law; and
- *skills*: active listening, an awareness and understanding of conflict dynamics, self-awareness, and interpersonal skills.[114]

Daicoff does not view processes such as collaborative law as alternative or external to law and legal practice; as one of the 'vectors' of the comprehensive law movement it addresses not only the law but also the 'extra-legal concerns – factors beyond strict legal rights and duties', and it includes a consideration of 'needs, resources, goals, morals, values, beliefs, psychological matters, personal well-being, human development and growth, interpersonal relations, and community wellbeing.'[115]

The comprehensive law movement also stresses the importance of procedural justice and of clients having a voice, being treated with respect, and feeling heard. It was noted earlier that many of the difficulties that can arise with lawyer negotiation do not necessarily arise from the fact that the lawyer may not have negotiated well for the client, but may instead relate to the client having no direct involvement in the process, and so perhaps feeling unsure how the decision was reached. Allowing the client that involvement and giving them a sense of autonomy has been described as a 'rights plus' approach to law.[116] Tyler[117] and Goldberg have both also outlined the importance of litigants or disputants being given an opportunity to speak and be heard, being treated with dignity and respect by the legal professionals that they come in contact with.[118] Collaborative practice, by its nature, is client led.

What is therapeutic jurisprudence and how has it been received?

Central to the comprehensive law movement is the concept of 'therapeutic jurisprudence'. Wexler, one of the founders of the therapeutic jurisprudence movement describes it as:

> simply a way of looking at the law in a richer way, and then bringing to the table some of these areas and issues that previously have gone unnoticed … simply suggests that we think about these issues and see if they can be factored into our law-making, lawyering, or judging.[119]

He stresses that its aim is not to 'trump' the rule of law; it exists merely as a 'lens' through which to view laws and legal actors. He also clarified that:

> In actuality, therapeutic jurisprudence ('TJ') is not and has never pretended to be a full-blown 'theory'. More properly, and more modestly, it is simply a 'field of inquiry' – in essence a research agenda – focusing attention on the often overlooked area of the impact of the law on psychological wellbeing and the like. From the very beginning, however, TJ has sought to work with frameworks or heuristics to organise and guide thought.[120]

Daicoff acknowledges that the adversarial system can prove therapeutic for certain people at various times in their lives. She gives examples of situations in which people may need the public vindication provided through a court hearing, an acknowledgement of a wrong or the need to assert a right.[121] Arguably, therefore, as noted above, the aim of therapeutic jurisprudence is not to detract from the rule of law but to 'concentrate on the law's impact on people's emotional lives and psychological well-being.'[122] King notes that taking a therapeutic approach also allows an element of 'intrinsic motivation' towards 'self-determination' for disputing parties, which 'acknowledges that the individual must confront and solve her own problems.'[123] Brooks and Madden refer to the notion of therapeutic jurisprudence as 'relationship-centred lawyering.'[124] Proponents of a therapeutic jurisprudential approach also highlight the benefits in viewing legal problems in a more global context, with Wexler arguing that it is useful as a method that can transcend legal boundaries.[125]

For many lawyers, the notion of taking a more therapeutic approach, whereby clients have a central, participatory role and autonomy in decision-making, may prove to be an uncomfortable dawn. Lawyers practising within the adversarial system retain a certain element of control over a case and seek, as per their legal training, to minimise exposure to risks for clients. Tesler refers to the 'paradigm shift'[126] in thinking that is necessary for lawyers: thinking more broadly about the needs of the family rather than solely about those of their individual client. While a therapeutic approach is commendable, safeguards must be in place to ensure that clients understand the basis on which they are entering the process.[127] Questions need to be asked as to whether encouraging separating parties to engage in a process in which there may be risks is something lawyers *should do*; such ethical issues will be considered in this book in examining the results of research undertaken internationally and the extent to which this has been considered by the collaborative law movement. Others see the many benefits for lawyers in practising in a new way. Daicoff places emphasis on the benefits for lawyers of portraying an image of 'law as a healing profession', noting that it may address what she refers to as the 'tripartite' crisis in the legal profession – citing concerns over 'deprofessionalism, low public opinion of lawyers and lawyers' distress.'[128]

Critics of therapeutic jurisprudence question its usefulness. Bruce Arrigo argues that there are difficulties in engaging in a therapeutic jurisprudence approach. Firstly, because it starts from a premise that assumes all substantive law is fair, he believes, it cannot apply the law therapeutically when this may not always be the case. He also raises concerns that 'therapeutic jurisprudence promotes a moral, good, and docile individual in a one-size-fits-all law.'[129] Ward, similarly, is critical of what he terms the promotion of the 'good lives' model.[130] Others argue that therapeutic jurisprudence is merely 'old wine in new bottles.'[131] Much concern has been raised about the definitional issues surrounding what is meant by 'therapeutic'; who decides what is therapeutic; and on what basis.

With respect to this being a new way forward for lawyers, Freckelton, in particular, raises concerns about such processes signifying 'intellectual laziness, woolliness, a discomfort with conflict, or the realities of the adversarial system of justice.'[132] An option, perhaps, for lawyers suffering burnout from the adversarial system. Others have expressed concern that it will result in a reversion to paternalism, with lawyers imposing their own values on clients.[133] Coupled with this is the familiar cry of 'This is what a good lawyer does anyway.' Quinn, for example, cautions against criminal law defence attorneys becoming 'rehabilitation change agents', something which she believes would undermine the role of lawyer as zealous advocate.[134]

Daicoff, in response to these criticisms, acknowledges good lawyering may well 'implicitly or unconsciously take those concerns into account – whereas those involved in the comprehensive law movement go a step further by explicitly valuing and promoting such factors.'[135] Cameron describes the difference between practising as a litigator and a collaborative lawyer as that of 'molding the story' to fit within the rules of the adversarial system and 'helping (clients) to build a unified story',[136] taking all of their needs into account. Understanding a person's 'narrative' and 'how they tell their story' embodies a poststructuralist approach, that 'it is useful to focus on contextualised means making, rather than universal truths or all-encompassing reality.'[137] This may help counteract concerns raised by Arrigo. Collaborative practice, by asking the right questions and allowing the parties' narratives to help them reach appropriate solutions,[138] may facilitate unique outcomes rather than promote a 'one-size-fits-all law'.[139]

Many of the concerns raised are somewhat typical of the reaction that new processes are faced with, with allegations being made that proponents of the approach are 'evangelical' or 'self-referential'.[140] Similar criticisms have been made against the collaborative process, with writers like Macfarlane commenting that it is critical to remove the 'taint of ideology' from the process, in effect portraying it as perhaps not just a better way, but the only way, in which disputes should be resolved.[141] More legitimate concerns have been flagged by Diesfield and McKenna.[142] They raise the issue of lawyers embracing this approach by 'talking the talk' without 'walking the walk'.[143] Lawyers, who open the door to engaging with emotional or psychological issues during the collaborative process, without the assistance that mental health experts or family consultants can provide, may not be in a position to deal with the level of emotion involved. Daicoff, too, notes that lawyers 'also need to know when they are in over their heads.'[144] Another issue of concern to be aware of in the lawyer gaining these additional 'skills' as part of the comprehensive law approach is that, in doing so, lawyers may lose some of the objectivity normally required in dealing with a case, inadvertently leading towards countertransference.

Conclusion

As a new and developing dispute-resolution process, collaborative practice draws on a broad theoretical framework that emphasises the need for an understanding of the dynamics of conflict; how it arises, evolves and develops; and the societal and other causes that impact on how it is transformed. As an interests-based method of resolution, collaborative practice aims to reach solutions by enabling parties to engage in a participative process that provides autonomy, transparency and control. In addition, it purports to take a more holistic view of dispute resolution in family law matters, by interpreting laws 'therapeutically' as an agent for good. With this new approach comes the need for both the lawyers and the clients who are participating to develop new skills.

For the purpose of this book, collaborative practice as a 'process' will be analysed through the 'lens' or 'field of inquiry'[145] that is therapeutic jurisprudence. As noted earlier, a phenomenological approach will be taken, examining the lived experiences of those interviewed for the research underpinning this book. Does collaborative practice provide separating parties with a forum to express their views, akin to having 'their day in court' rather than just a method for settling their case? Does it offer the same structure and authority that clients often seek from the court, and does it serve to allay clients' fears with regard to issues such as fairness and justice? Or is there a sense that negotiations taking place in a private forum are less transparent and therefore inherently more open to abuse by a dominant party?[146] Do these concerns have grounding in practice or are they based on misinformation or a lack of education as to what these processes involve and what they have to offer? Do clients appreciate the change in approach? Why do they choose to negotiate in this way, are they happy with the process and the outcomes? Are the vulnerable protected?

In relation to the lawyers who advocate collaborative practice, are they, as alleged, retreating from the burnout of the adversarial system, and is this an 'easier' way to practise law? Or does this new approach have its own challenges? Do lawyers fully appreciate the ethical issues that may arise in encouraging clients to forgo the safeguards of the traditional system? Or are these new approaches to settlement negotiation merely an acknowledgement of the changing roles of lawyers? Is it simply the case that, as Griswold outlines:

> lawyers deal with people. They deal with people far more than they do with appellate courts. They deal with clients; they deal with witnesses; they deal with persons against whom demands are made; they carry on negotiations; they are constantly endeavoring to come to agreements of one sort or another with people, to persuade people, sometimes when they are reluctant to be persuaded. Lawyers are constantly dealing with people who are under stress or strain of one sort or another.[147]

These questions will be addressed throughout this book as the effectiveness of collaborative practice is explored.

Notes

1 Twining, W., 'Alternative to What? Theories of Litigation, Procedure and Dispute Settlement in Anglo-American Jurisprudence: Some Neglected Classics' (1993) 56 *Modern Law Review* 380–392, 381.
2 Sander, F.E.A., 'Varieties of Dispute Processing', Address Delivered at the National Conference on the Causes of Popular Dissatisfaction with the Administration of Justice (Apr. 7–9, 1976), in (1976) 70 Federal Rules Decisions at 111.
3 Fisher, R., and Ury, W., *Getting to Yes: Negotiating Agreement Without Giving In* (Random House, 1981).
4 Menkel-Meadow, C., 'Mothers and Fathers of Invention: The Intellectual Founders of ADR' (2000) 16 (1) *Ohio Journal of Dispute Resolution* 1–37.
5 Menkel-Meadow, C., 'Mothers and Fathers of Invention: The Intellectual Founders of ADR' (2000) 16 (1) *Ohio Journal of Dispute Resolution* 1–37, 2.
6 Using Ireland as a case study and comparing the results to research undertaken internationally.

7 Simmel, G., *Conflict*. Wolff K. H., *et al.* trans., (Free Press, 1955) at 13; Coser, L., *The Functions of Social Conflict* (Free Press, 1956); Deutsch, M., *The Handbook of Conflict Resolution: Theory and Practice* (Jossey-Bass, 2000).

8 Bronfenbrenner, U., 'Ecological systems theory', in Ross Vasta (ed.), *Six Theories of Child Development: Revised Formulations and Current Issues* (Jessica Kingsley Publishers Ltd, 1992).

9 Felsteiner, W., Abel, R., and Sarat, A., 'The Emergence and Transformation of Disputes: Naming, Blaming, Claiming…' (1980–1981) 15 (3–4) *Law and Society* 631–654.

10 Fuller, L.L., *The Principles of Social Order: Selected Essays of Lon L. Fuller*, Winston, K., (ed.) (Bloomsbury, 1981).

11 Lande, J., 'Teaching Students to Negotiate Like a Lawyer' (2012) 39 *Washington University Journal of Law and Policy* 109–144, 118.

12 Daicoff, S., 'Law as a healing profession: The comprehensive law movement' (2005, Fall) 6 (1) *Pepperdine Dispute Resolution Law Journal* 1–63. NYLS Clinical Research Institute Paper No. 05/06–12.

13 Wexler, D.B., 'From Theory to Practice and Back Again in Therapeutic Jurisprudence: Now Comes the Hard Part' (2011) *Arizona Legal Studies* Discussion Paper No. 10–12 at 1.

14 Menkel-Meadow, C., 'Mothers and Fathers of Invention: The Intellectual Founders of ADR' (2000) 16 *Ohio Journal of Dispute Resolution* at 1–37, 3.

15 Ibid. at 6.

16 Parsons, T., 'Racial and Religious Differences as Factors in Group Tension' in Bryson, L., Finkelstein, L. and MacIver, R. (eds) *Approaches to National Utility* (Harper Bros, 1945) at 182–199.

17 Coser, L., *The Functions of Social Conflict* (Free Press, 1956) at 31.

18 Menkel-Meadow, C., 'Mothers and Fathers of Invention: The Intellectual Founders of ADR' (2000) 16 *Ohio Journal of Dispute Resolution* at 1–37, 6.

19 Davis, A. M., 'An Interview with Mary Parker Follett' (1989) *Negotiation Journal* 223–235.

20 Parker Follett, M., *Prophet of Management: A Celebration of Writings from the 1920s* Pauline Graham (ed.) (Harvard Business School Press, 1996) at 67–68.

21 Parker Follett, M. *The New State: Group Organization, the Solution of Popular Government* (Pennsylvania University Press, 1918/1998).

22 Ibid.

23 Gehani, R., and Gehani, R., 'Mary Parker Follett's Constructive Conflict: A "Psychological Foundation of Business Administration" for Innovative Global Enterprises' (2007) 30 *International Journal of Public Administration* 387–404.

24 Coser, L.A., 'The Termination of Conflict' (Dec., 1961), 5 (4) *The Journal of Conflict Resolution* 347–353, 347.

25 Ibid.

26 Ibid.

27 Ibid.

28 Bronfenbrenner, U., 'Ecological systems theory', in Ross Vasta (ed.), *Six Theories of Child Development: Revised Formulations and Current Issues* (Jessica Kingsley Publishers Ltd, 1992).

29 Ibid. at 201.

30 This is an appropriate theoretical framework for the research undertaken for this book, examining the effectiveness of collaborative practice; how conflict arose for the research participants and how they reacted to the conflict; whether it was perceived as destructive or constructive and how they chose to resolve issues.

31 Douzinas, C., *Law and Justice in Postmodernity* (Cambridge University Press, 2015) at 218.

32 Coser, L., *The Functions of Social Conflict* (Free Press, 1956) at 35.

33 Simmel, G., *Conflict*, Wolff, K. H., *et al.* trans., (Free Press, 1955) at 43–44; Coser, L., *The Functions of Social Conflict* (Free Press, 1956) at 67.
34 Article 7 of the European Charter of Fundamental Rights, Article 8 of the European Convention on Human Rights, Article 10 of the Universal Declaration on Human Rights, Article 16 European Social Charter.
35 Freud, S., *A General Introduction to Psychoanalysis* (Garden City Publishing Co., 1938) at 370.
36 Felsteiner, W., Abel, R. and Sarat, A. 'The Emergence and Transformation of Disputes: Naming, Blaming, Claiming…' (1980–1981) 15 (3–4) *Law and Society* 631–654, 636.
37 Ibid. at 631.
38 Ibid. at 640.
39 Mayer, B., *The Dynamics of Conflict Resolution: A Practitioner's Guide* (Jossey-Bass, 2000) 31–33.
40 Douzinas, C., *Law and Justice in Postmodernity* (Cambridge University Press, 2015) at 214.
41 Felstiner, W., Abel, R., and Sarat, A., 'The Emergence and Transformation of Disputes: Naming, Blaming, Claiming…' (1980–1981) 15 (3–4) *Law and Society Review*, 631–654, 640.
42 Coser, L., *The Functions of Social Conflict* (Free Press, 1956) at 113.
43 Mackenzie, C., *Relational Autonomy: Feminist Perspectives on Autonomy, Agency and the Social Self* (Oxford University Press, 1999); Bryan, P., '"Collaborative Divorce", Meaningful Reform or Another Quick Fix?' (1999) 5(4) *Psychology, Public Policy and Law* 1001–1017.
44 Menkel-Meadow, C., 'Mothers and Fathers of Invention: The Intellectual Founders of ADR' (2000) 16(1) *Ohio Journal of Dispute Resolution* 1–37.
45 Lowenthal, G.T., 'A General Theory of Negotiation Process, Strategy and Behaviour' (1982–1983) 31 *University of Kansas Law Review* 105–111.
46 Nader, L., 'Forums for Justice: A Cross Cultural Perspective' (1975) 31(3) *Journal of Social Sciences* 151–170.
47 Delgado, R., *et al.*, 'Fairness and Formality: Minimizing the Risk of Prejudice in Alternative Dispute Resolution' (1985) *Wisconsin Law Review* at 1359–1404, 1396; Grillo, T., 'The Mediation Alternative: Process Dangers for Women' (1991) 100 *Yale Law Review* 1545–1610, 1603.
48 Diduck, A., 'Family Law and Responsibility', in Bridgeman, J., Keating, H., and Lind, C., (eds), *Responsibility, Law and Family* (Ashgate, 2008) at 262.
49 Herring, J., *Family Law* (5th edn, Pearson, 2011) at 15.
50 Ratnapala, S., *Jurisprudence* (2nd edn, Cambridge University Press, 2016) at 367.
51 Ibid. at 356.
52 Maclean, S., *Legal Aid and the Family Justice System* (Legal Aid Board Research Unit, 1998) at 101.
53 Rawls, J., *Justice as Fairness: A Restatement* (Harvard University Press, 2011) paragraph 42.3.
54 Douzinas, C., *Law and Justice in Postmodernity* (Cambridge University Press, 2015) at 213.
55 Ibid. at 213.
56 Macfarlane, J., *The New Lawyer* (University of British Columbia Press, 2008) at 57.
57 George, R., *Ideas and Debates in Family Law* (Hart, 2012) at 7.
58 Ibid.
59 Daicoff, S. 'Law as a healing profession: The comprehensive law movement' (2005, Fall) *Pepperdine Dispute Resolution Law Journal.* NYLS Clinical Research Institute Paper No. 05/06–12, 3–4.
60 Davis, G., Cretney, S., and Collins, J., *Simple Quarrels: Negotiating Money and Property Disputes on Divorce* (Clarendon Press, 1994) at 253; Eekelaar, J., Maclean, M.

and Beinart, S., *Family Lawyers: The Divorce Work of Solicitors* (Hart Publishing, 2000).

61 Douzinas, C., *Law and Justice in Postmodernity* (Cambridge University Press, 2015) at 199.

62 Fiss, O., 'Against Settlement' (1986) 93 (6) *Yale Law Journal*, 1073–1090.

63 Douzinas, C., *Law and Justice in Postmodernity* (Cambridge University Press, 2015).

64 Mayer, B., *The Dynamics of Conflict Resolution: A Practitioner's Guide* (Jossey-Bass, 2000) 31–33.

65 Gulliver, P.H., *Disputes and Negotiations: A Cross Cultural Perspective* (Academic Press, 1979) at 3.

66 Ibid. at 4.

67 Douzinas, C., *Law and Justice in Postmodernity* (Cambridge University Press, 2015) at 213.

68 Fiss, O., 'Against Settlement' (1986) 93 (6) *Yale Law Journal* at 1073–1090, 1082.

69 Ibid. at 1082.

70 Ibid. at 1085. See also Delgado, R., *et al.* 'Fairness and Formality: Minimizing the Risk of Prejudice in Alternative Dispute Resolution' (1985) *Wisconsin Law Review* 1359–1404 at 1391.

71 Fiss, O., 'Against Settlement' (1986) 93 (6) *Yale Law Journal* at 1073–1090, 1078.

72 Ibid. at 1077.

73 Fuller, L.L., 'Mediation – Its Forms and Functions' (1971) 44 *Southern California Law Review* 305–339, 305.

74 Douzinas, C., *Law and Justice in Postmodernity* (Cambridge University Press, 2015) at 214.

75 Menkel-Meadow, C., 'Mothers and Fathers of Invention: The Intellectual Founders of ADR' (2000) 16 (1) *Ohio Journal of Dispute Resolution* 1–37, 16.

76 Ibid. at 32.

77 Gulliver, P.H., *Disputes and Negotiations: A Cross Cultural Perspective* (Academic Press, 1979) at 15.

78 Ibid.

79 Coulter, C., *Family Law Matters*, No. 1 (1) (Brunswick Press, Spring 2007) at 24. Available at http://www.courts.ie/Courts.ie/library3.nsf/(WebFiles)/593A30194F32754C802572870041333C/$FILE/Family%20Law%20Matters%20-%20Vol.%201%20No.1%202007%20-%20web%20version.pdf Last accessed 5 June 2016.

80 Sarat, A. and Felstiner, W., *Divorce Lawyers and their Clients* (Oxford University Press, 1995). See also Mnookin, R. and Kornhauser, L., 'Bargaining in the Shadow of the Law: The Case of Divorce' (1978–1979) 88 *Yale Law Journal* 950–977.

81 Hart, H.M. Jr. and Sacks, A.M., Preface to the 1958 'Tentative Edition' of Hart and Sacks, *The Legal Process: Basic Problems in the Making and Application of Law*, Eskridge, W.M. Jr. and Frickey, F.P., (eds) (Foundation Press, 1994) at 176; as quoted in Menkel-Meadow, C., 'Mothers and Fathers of Invention: The Intellectual Founders of ADR' 2000 16 (1) *Ohio Journal on Dispute Resolution* 1–37, 27.

82 Ibid.

83 Matthews, R.E., 'Negotiation: A Pedagogical Challenge' (1953) 6 *Journal of Legal Education* 93–101, 94.

84 Lowenthal, G.T., 'A General Theory of Negotiation: Process, Strategy and Behaviour' (1982–1983) 31 *University of Kansas Law Review* 69–114.

85 Zartman, W., and Berman, M., *The Practical Negotiator* (Yale University Press, 1992).

86 Menkel-Meadow, C., 'Legal Negotiation: A Study of Strategies in Search of a Theory' 1983 (4) *American Bar Foundation Research Journal* 905–937 at 911, citing the writings of Bellows and Moulton; see also Edwards, H. and White, J., *The Lawyer as Negotiator: Problems, Readings and Materials* (West Publishing Co., 1977); Meltsner, M. and Schrag, P. G., *Public Interest Advocacy: Materials for Clinical Legal Education* Chapter 13, 'Negotiation' (Little, Brown and Co., 1997).

87 Fisher, R., and Ury, W.,*Getting to Yes* (2nd edn, Random House, 1992) at 157.
88 Mayer, B., *The Dynamics of Conflict Resolution: A Practitioner's Guide* (Jossey-Bass, 2000) at 31–33.
89 Lowenthal, G.T., 'A General Theory of Negotiation Process, Strategy and Behaviour' (1982–1983) 31 *University of Kansas Law Review* 69–114, 92.
90 Cochran, Robert F., 'Legal Ethics and Collaborative Practice Ethics' (2009) 38 *Hofstra Law Review* 537–567, 543.
91 Galanter, M., 'Worlds of Deals: Using Negotiation to Teach about Legal Process' (1984) 34 *Journal of Legal Education* 268–276, 268.
92 Lande, J., 'Teaching Students to Negotiate Like a Lawyer' (2012) 39 *Washington University Journal of Law and Policy* 109–144, 118.
93 Menkel-Meadow, C., 'Legal Negotiation: A Study of Strategies in Search of a Theory' (1983) 8 (4) *American Bar Foundation Research Journal* 905–937, 918.
94 The issue of fairness was mentioned by many participants – both in terms of a fair outcome for themselves and for the other party.
95 Rubin, J.Z., 'The Nature of Conflict and Negotiation', in Breslin, W., and Rubin, J. (eds), *Negotiation Theory & Practice*, (The Program on Negotiation, Harvard Law School, 1999).
96 Fisher, R., and Ury, W., *Getting to Yes* (2nd edn, Random House, 1992) at 11.
97 Fisher, R., and Ury, W., *Getting to Yes* (2nd edn, Random House, 1992) at 50.
98 Douzinas, C., *Law and Justice in Postmodernity*, Cambridge Companions Online (Cambridge University Press, 2015) at 206.
99 Fisher, R., and Ury, W., *Getting to Yes* (2nd edn, Random House, 1992) at 86.
100 Mnookin, R., and Kornhauser, L., 'Bargaining in the Shadow of the Law: The Case of Divorce' (1978–1979) 88 *Yale Law Journal* at 950–977.
101 Ibid. at 951.
102 Douzinas, C., *Law and Justice in Postmodernity* (Cambridge University Press, 2015) at 212.
103 Fuller, L.L., 'Mediation – Its Forms and Functions' (1971) 44 *Southern California Law Review* 305–339, 308.
104 *The CEDR Mediator Handbook* (Centre for Effective Dispute Resolution, 2004; 4th edn) at 26. CEDR is an organisation that trains and accredits mediators.
105 Lehane, N., 'Making Talk Work', in Sweeney, D., and Lloyd, M. (eds), *Mediation in Focus: A Celebration of the Family Mediation Service in Ireland* (Family Mediation Service, 2011) 99–112, 103.
106 Bush, J., and Folger, R., *The Promise of Mediation: Responding to Conflict Through Empowerment and Recognition* (Jossey-Bass, 1994) at 2.
107 Lehane, N., 'Making Talk Work', in Sweeney, D., and Lloyd, M. (eds), *Mediation in Focus: A Celebration of the Family Mediation Service in Ireland* (Family Mediation Service, 2011) 99–112, 103.
108 See for example Bush, J., and Folger, R., *The Promise of Mediation: Responding to Conflict Through Empowerment and Recognition* (Jossey-Bass 1994). See also Boulle, L., and Kelly, K., *Mediation: Principles, Process, Practice* (Butterworths, 1998); Gerami, A., 'Bridging the Theory-and-Practice Gap: Mediator Power in Practice' (2009) 26(4) *Conflict Resolution Quarterly* 433–451.
109 Fuller, L.L., 'Mediation – Its Forms and Functions' (1971) 44 *Southern California Law Review* 305–339, 325.
110 Bottemley, A., *Feminist Perspectives on the Foundational Subjects of Law* (Cavendish, 1996) at 28.
111 Gribben, S., 'Mediation in Family Law Disputes' (1992) 6 *Australian Journal of Family Law* 126, 133; Women's Aid, *Submission to the Family Law Reporting Committee* (January 2009) 5; available at: www.womensaid.ie. Last accessed on 1 June 2016.
112 *Rosalba Alassini v. Telecom Italia SpA (C-317/08), Filomena Califano v. Wind SpA (C-318/08), Lucia Anna Giorgia Iacono v Telecom Italia SpA (C-319/08)* and

Multiservice Srl v Telecom Italia SpA (C-320/08) ECR [2010] I-02213; available at http://eur-lex.europa.eu/LexUriServ/LexUriServ.do?uri=CELEX:62008CJ0317:EN:PDF. Last accessed on 1 June 2016.

113 Tesler, P., *Collaborative Law: Achieving Effective Resolution in Divorce without Litigation* (2nd edn, American Bar Association, 2008) at 19. Preventative law focuses on tailoring solutions in a way which may prevent disharmony in the future.

114 Daicoff, S., 'The Comprehensive Law Movement' (2002–2004) 19 *Touro Law Review* 825–846, 835.

115 Daicoff, S., 'Law as a healing profession: The comprehensive law movement' (2005, Fall) *Pepperdine Dispute Resolution Law Journal.* NYLS Clinical Research Institute Paper No. 05/06–12, 1–61, 3–4.

116 This phrase has been used by Pauline Tesler as one of the founder members of the collaborative law movement.

117 Tyler, T., 'Procedural Justice', in Wexler, David B. and Winick, Bruce J. (eds), *Law in a Therapeutic Key: Developments in Therapeutic Jurisprudence* (Carolina Academic Press, 1996) 3–15.

118 Goldberg, S., *Judging for the 21st Century: A Problem-solving Approach* (National Judicial Institute of Ottawa, 2005) quoted in Babb, B., and Wexler, D., 'Therapeutic Jurisprudence' (2005) *University of Baltimore Legal Studies Research Paper* No. 2014–13 at 2. Available at http://www.joasa.org.za/aricles/Judgingfor21scenturyDe.pdf. Last accessed 1 August 2016.

119 Wexler, D., 'Therapeutic Jurisprudence: An Overview', (2000) 17 (1) *Thomas M. Cooley Law Review* 125–134, 125.

120 Wexler, D., 'From Theory to Practice and Back Again in Therapeutic Jurisprudence: Now Comes the Hard Part' (2011) *Arizona Legal Studies* Discussion Paper No. 10–12 at 1.

121 Daicoff, S., 'Families in Circle Process: Restorative Justice in Family Law' (2015) 53 (3) *Family Court Review* 427–438, 429.

122 Daicoff, S., 'The Role of Therapeutic Jurisprudence Within the Comprehensive Law Movement', in *Practicing Therapeutic Jurisprudence: Law as a Helping Profession,* Stolle, D.P., Winick, B.J., and Wexler, D.B. (eds) (Carolina Academic Press, 2000) at 471.

123 King, M., 'Should problem-solving courts be solution-focused courts?' (2011) Monash University Research Paper, Victoria, quoted in Babb, B., and Wexler, D., 'Therapeutic Jurisprudence', University of Baltimore Legal Studies Research Paper – Paper No 2014–13 at 3.

124 Brooks S., and Madden R. (eds) *Relationship-centered Lawyering: Social Science Theory for Transforming Legal Practice* (Carolina Academic Press, 2010).

125 Wexler, D., 'Therapeutic Jurisprudence: An Overview', (2000) 17 *Thomas Cooley Law Review* 125–134, 125.

126 Tesler, P., *Collaborative Law: Achieving Effective Resolution in Divorce without Litigation* (2nd edn, American Bar Association, 2008) at 36–37.

127 Section 14 of The Uniform Collaborative Law Act and Rules 2010, places a statutory obligation on lawyers to ensure informed consent. This will be addressed further in Chapter 3.

128 Daicoff, S., 'Law as a healing profession: The comprehensive law movement' (2006) 6 *Pepperdine Dispute Resolution Law Journal* 1–61, 4; NYLS Clinical Research Institute Paper No. 05/06–12 at 4.

129 Arrigo, B., 'The Ethics of Therapeutic Jurisprudence: A Critical and Theoretical Enquiry of Law, Psychology and Crime' (2004) *Psychiatry, Psychology and Law* 23–43.

130 Ward, T., 'Good Lives and the Rehabilitation of Offenders: Promises and Problems' (2002) 7 (5) *Aggression and Violent Behaviour* at 513–528; Ward, T., and Stewart C.A., 'Criminogenic Needs and Human Needs: A Theoretical Model' (2003) 9 (2) *Psychology, Crime and Law* at 125–143.

131 Sales, B.D. and Shuman, D.W., 'The Newly Emerging Mental Health Law', in Sales, B.D. and. Shuman D.W. (eds) *Law Mental Health, and Mental Disorder* 2 (6) (Wadsworth Publishing, 1996). Freckelton, I., 'Therapeutic Jurisprudence Misunderstood and Misrepresented. The Price and Risks of Influence' (2008) (30) *Thomas Jefferson Law Review* 575–596, 583.

132 Freckelton, I., 'Therapeutic Jurisprudence Misunderstood and Misrepresented. The Price and Risks of Influence' (2008) (30) *Thomas Jefferson Law Review* 575–596, at 593.

133 Macfarlane, J., *The Emerging Phenomenon of Collaborative Family Law (CFL): A Qualitative Case Study* (Department of Justice Canada, 2005) at ix.

134 Quinn, M., 'An RSVP to Professor Wexler's Warm Therapeutic Jurisprudence Invitation to the Criminal Defense Bar: Unable to Join You, Already (Somewhat Similarly) Engaged', *Boston College Law Review*, Vol. 48 (2007) 539–595.

135 Daicoff, S., 'Law as a Healing Profession: The "Comprehensive Law Movement"', New York Law School Clinical Research Institute Research Paper Series 05/06 # 12 at 7. Available at http://ssm.com/abstract=875449 Last accessed 1 June 2016.

136 Cameron, N., *Collaborative Practice: Deepening the Dialogue* (Continuing Legal Education Society of British Columbia, 2004) at 106.

137 Combs, G., and Freedman, J., 'Narrative, Poststructuralism, and Social Justice: Current Practices in Narrative Therapy' (2012) *The Counseling Psychologist* 40 (7) 1033–1060, 1036.

138 Ibid. at 1045.

139 Arrigo, B.A., 'The Ethics of Therapeutic Jurisprudence: A Critical and Theoretical Enquiry of Law, Psychology and Crime', (2004) *Psychiatry, Psychology and Law* 23–43, 23.

140 Lande, J., 'An Empirical Analysis of Collaborative Practice' (2011) 49 (2) *Family Court Review* 257–281, 262.

141 Macfarlane, J., *The Emerging Phenomenon of Collaborative Family Law (CFL): A Qualitative Case Study* (Department of Justice Canada, 2005) at 80. Available at www.justice.gc.ca. Last accessed 1st June 2016.

142 Diesfeld, K., and McKenna, B., 'The Unintended Impact of the Therapeutic Intentions of the New Zealand Mental Health Review Tribunal? Therapeutic Jurisprudence Perspectives' (2007) 14 *Journal of Law and Medicine* 566–574, 569.

143 Ibid. at 586.

144 Daicoff, S., 'Law as a healing profession: The comprehensive law movement' (2006) *Pepperdine Dispute Resolution Law Journal* at 55. NYLS Clinical Research Institute Paper No. 05/06–12 at 60.

145 Wexler, D.B., 'From Theory to Practice and Back Again in Therapeutic Jurisprudence: Now Comes the Hard Part' (2011) *Arizona Legal Studies* Discussion Paper No. 10–12 at 1.

146 Fiss, O., 'Against Settlement' (1986) 93 (6) *Yale Law Journal* at 1073.

147 Griswold, E.N., (1956) 37 Chicago Bar Record 199 at 203, cited in Sacks, H., 'Human Relations Training for Law Students and Lawyers', (1959) 11 *Journal of Legal Education* at 316–345, 317.

2 The process and the unique features of collaborative practice

Introduction

With the theoretical underpinnings of ADR and collaborative practice outlined in the first chapter, this chapter will begin with a brief review of the literature, much of which has been written from the perspective of practitioners. Principally, it will address what makes collaborative practice unique in the way it is structured. Three main issues will be analysed: firstly, the participation agreement signed at the outset and the obligations that arise therefrom; second, the disqualification clause and the financial and emotional implications for prospective parties and their lawyers. Finally, the framework the process provides for a multidisciplinary approach that encapsulates experts of various disciplines (law, psychology including child psychology and finance) working as part of a team for the benefit of the parties, rather than acting as adversaries, is examined.

The origins and development of collaborative law

Webb recalls his experience of practising as a divorce lawyer as constantly living under a 'siege mentality, merely waiting for the next battle'[1] to begin. He describes the panic and fear for separating parties trying to find a lawyer that they perceive to be 'tougher' than the one engaged by their husband or wife. This competition often lays the groundwork for how a divorce commences within the adversarial system. However, as noted in Chapter 1, the majority of divorce cases settle without the need for litigators to display their exceptional court skills. Webb describes this approach as 'hiring a contractor to build your house based on his or her experience as a demolitions expert';[2] what is more appropriate in the majority of cases are lawyers' negotiation skills. With this knowledge of how the system works, or rather does not work, Webb saw the need to reduce this pressure, to take a step away from filing motions and sending accusatory letters with often unfounded, but deeply upsetting, allegations and claims. Collaborative practice is therefore what Bederman describes as a 'bottom up' practice, developed to fulfil the need for a new approach by someone practising within the system. This, Bederman notes, is:

> intuitive and appealing for anyone who lives and works within communities of legal actors, and yet deeply unsettling for those who cleave deeply to strongly positivist positions as to the legitimacy and authority of legal rules.[3]

The collaborative law process has been defined as a 'voluntary, contractually based alternative dispute resolution process for parties who seek to negotiate a resolution of their matter rather than to have a ruling imposed upon them by a court or arbitrator.'[4] In contrast to ordinary 'lawyer to lawyer' negotiation, the collaborative process facilitates direct client participation. The separating parties and their lawyers agree not to go to court and to negotiate settlement through face to face meetings. The process is centred around the participation agreement, signed by the parties at the outset, setting out how the negotiations will take place and the rules of engagement. In addition, clients agree to a disqualification clause. If settlement cannot be reached within the process, the lawyers representing the clients are disqualified from acting for them in any future court action relating to the dispute.

For this process, Webb needed a new 'breed of lawyer',[5] one that was trained in negotiation and who adopted a client-centred, inclusive and interests-based approach to settlement. This represented a significant change in a lawyer's traditional approach, the 'paradigm shift' referred to by another pioneering member of the collaborative law movement, Pauline Tesler. Tesler describes this paradigm shift as 'unlearning adversarial behaviours and learning collaborative behaviours', a change in thinking from wanting to win and obtain as much as possible for one's own client, to facilitating a 'win-win' situation for both clients and the family.[6]

Central to this change is the need for lawyers to embrace new *skills* as outlined in Chapter 1, namely, active listening; an awareness and understanding of conflict dynamics; self-awareness and interpersonal skills.[7] Tesler referred to this as 'retooling': retooling the lawyer as a collaborative lawyer in the way they think and speak; retooling the client by listening carefully to what they have to say and encouraging them to concentrate on their goals for the process; retooling the lawyer's relationship with the other party's lawyer from a positional stance to one in which they work together; and, finally, retooling the negotiations to concentrate on conflict resolution and effective management of the process. In cases where a multidisciplinary approach is taken, lawyers also need to learn to work effectively with team members from other professions for the benefit of the family as a whole. Training for collaborative lawyers therefore concentrates on taking a more holistic approach to the client's needs and re-examining and reflecting on the lawyer's role as an agent in the dispute resolution process.

The collaborative law model spread quickly throughout the US, Canada and indeed, worldwide. In Northern California in the early 1990s, Peggy Thompson[8] began to offer clients an interdisciplinary model in which mental health experts/coaches, child specialists and financial specialists were employed to assist couples through the emotional and financial, as well as the legal, aspects of the divorce. This model is referred to interchangeably as collaborative practice or collaborative divorce. While the option for separating parties to retain such experts was already available within the adversarial process, rather than both sides employing their own experts to give evidence and to contradict each other's assertions, collaborative practice provides a framework under which experts work together, for the benefit of the separating couple and the family as a whole.

Cameron, a proponent of collaborative practice, describes divorce as:

> dreams unfilled, or dreams that have run their course. It may be profound grief and it may be bittersweet freedom. It is about families restructuring: financially, emotionally and practically. It is both conflict and resolution. It is pain and it is relief.[9]

Engaging with these 'extra-legal'[10] concerns is something that the adversarial system has arguably strived to avoid, to remove any interpersonal issues.[11] Collaborative practice, in contrast, acknowledges that separation or divorce may often require more than a legal solution.

This chapter continues with a broad overview of the stages involved in a typical collaborative law case. It will examine what Webb has described as the 'essential features'[12] of the process: ensuring that there is an executed client retainer agreement; that the lawyers contact each other in advance of the first meeting to discuss areas of possible conflict and how best to approach these issues and, that the 'other essential process document' – the participation agreement – is executed.[13] While the concept of collaborative practice has been described as simple in its structure and profound in its effect,[14] many questions arise. Collaborative practice is a limited scope representation. What are the necessary requirements in these types of arrangements and what safeguards need to be in place for the clients and the lawyers involved? Is it necessary, feasible or ethical for a lawyer to significantly alter their role as 'zealous advocate'[15] when representing a client within the process and how is a balance to be achieved between a lawyer's duty to one's own client and the concept of taking a 'whole family' approach? Is the participation agreement a 'contractual agreement' and if so, what, if any, duties are lawyers taking on with respect to third parties or their lawyers? And, finally, is the disqualification clause the 'engine that drives collaborative law' and provides the 'positive settlement tone'[16] or is it an inherently dangerous provision that has ethical, financial and emotional implications for lawyers and their clients? The chapter will conclude by examining the multidisciplinary model of collaborative practice and its aim to provide a more holistic solution to relationship breakdown.

The process – a broad overview

Due perhaps to the organic way in which the process developed, there have been a myriad of different approaches taken, both in terms of the sequence of events leading up to the beginning of a collaborative case, and how participation agreements have been drafted. As noted earlier, Webb's view is that the first 'essential feature' of the process, is signing a client retainer agreement. This ensures clients' written informed consent is obtained and that ethical requirements are complied with.[17] The Collaborative Retainer agreement clearly sets out the nature of the relationship between the lawyer and the client; that representation is for a specific and limited purpose. If that purpose comes to an end, so does the representation. It explains the implications of the disqualification provision, the need for disclosure and the importance of the client's agreement to be forthcoming with information. The agreement may also address the issue of engaging additional professionals, if needs be (this to be decided or recommended at the *discretion* of the lawyer)[18] and provides that the lawyer's 'legally enforceable professional obligations are to (their own client) alone.'[19] In many cases, however, it appears that these client retainer agreements are not signed and the scope of each lawyer's representation is set out in the 'four-way' or 'participation agreement.'

Cameron uses 'conception', 'pregnancy' and 'birth' as metaphors for the development of a collaborative case.[20] Tesler describes this as a series of 'Acts'.[21] Having chosen collaborative practice, broadly speaking, Act One begins with the separating parties meeting their respective lawyers, being fully advised as to how the process works and given what Tesler describes as 'the information needed for the exercise of informed consent.'[22] As well as describing the process itself, it is essential that lawyers explain to clients exactly what is expected of them within the process. Clients need to be aware that, in some ways, collaborative practice is more difficult than hiring a lawyer to deal with the negotiations. The clients must understand how the four-way meetings will work; consider their emotional reactions to meeting their ex-partner across a table; how the ex-spouse will behave during the process, whether s/he is likely to furnish discovery as is required and if s/he is likely to co-operate fully within the process. They need to be advised as to whether their lawyer will meet with them privately outside of the four-way meetings, how the lawyer will engage with the 'other side' and how much legal advice they will be given throughout the process. Clients need to be aware of the implications of the disqualification clause; the costs per hour of their collaborative lawyer and other experts engaged: and that if additional experts are engaged, that they will also be responsible for fees in respect of time that these professionals spend discussing and planning their case outside of the actual four-way meetings. Other factors that should be discussed include: how much pressure may be brought to bear to reveal sensitive information or to promote the use of coaches and/or child specialists. In interdisciplinary cases, clients must be willing to give prior consent to the coaches discussing their case with their lawyers, something which would not have been the norm for therapists or indeed, lawyers, under the traditional adversarial model.

In addition, a lawyer must also assess whether clients have the capacity to negotiate within the process; a mind-set of wanting to resolve matters amicably. Cameron lists '[a] client's level of self-awareness, willingness to engage in creative problem-solving, desire to move to resolution, and ability to communicate' as factors which will be relevant.[23] Webb refers to clients not being suitable for the process if they require someone else to make decisions for them,[24] as noted in Chapter 1, to negotiate through surrogates.[25] Additional contraindications as to suitability may include a history of domestic violence or drug/alcohol abuse within the relationship such that the parties may not have the capacity to engage freely or to negotiate on equal terms. Lawyers need to make sure that those who are not suitable are screened out before they sign an agreement to participate. This may be difficult. Issues not evident at the beginning of the process may become apparent at a later stage, when the parties have already signed the participation agreement and are bound by its terms.[26] Proponents of collaborative practice point to the benefits of having two lawyers screening for issues during this process rather than one person as is the case in the context of mediation.[27] They also argue that having lawyers present for the negotiations makes the process a safer option. On the other hand, critics point to the dangers of allowing vulnerable clients into a process whereby they come face-to-face with the more dominant party.[28]

The second of Webb's 'essential features' is that the collaborative lawyers for each party contact each other, prior to the first four-way meeting, to discuss what Tesler refers to as any 'hot buttons',[29] urgent matters that need to be addressed or particular issues that may be a source of contention during the negotiations. This helps to ensure that the process is effective in achieving settlement. Carefully managing the first four-way meeting ensures that 'only matters that have a likelihood of resulting in immediate success'[30] are discussed, thus creating a co-operative atmosphere and giving the parties the confidence required to proceed to negotiate the more contentious issues as they arise. This element of preparation is often missing from negotiations undertaken within positional negotiation, the courts and adversarial lawyers often taking a 'one size fits all' approach which can jeopardise the possibility of reaching settlement. At the end of 'Act One', once clients are happy with the process and the lawyers have screened as to suitability, the parties sign the participation agreement confirming their commitment to the process. Tesler notes that executing these documents in each other's presence has an 'almost ceremonial quality'[31]; signalling the parties' commitment to reaching an amicable solution.

Act Two begins with preparation for and attendance at the second meeting, at which negotiation gets underway. During the four-way meetings, the lawyers take a step back and allow the clients to negotiate directly, to set their goals and priorities for settlement. The lawyer's role becomes one of assisting the clients to reach their own solution, giving the parties autonomy over how their dispute is resolved. Perhaps, even more significant of a 'paradigm shift' for the lawyers is ceding this element of control.[32] Yet, the lawyers' role remains important in managing the process, providing guidance and legal advice as appropriate. While every effort is made to settle, if settlement cannot be reached the parties may end the process, at any time, and take their case to court for determination by a judge.

The meetings continue, in the same manner, until settlement is achieved. The Final Act[33] brings the parties back into a four-way meeting to read over the terms of settlement drafted by the lawyers and to sign the settlement agreement. Collaborative lawyers have spoken about the cathartic effects of this final meeting in helping the parties see what they have achieved in reaching the settlement together and the benefits for their future relationship, especially when they need to continue to co-parent their children.[34]

The participation agreement

In principle, the participation agreement as Webb's third essential requirement, is a straightforward document aimed at setting the rules of engagement; *how* the collaborative process is going to operate and the basis on which the negotiations are being entered into. The terms of the agreement normally provide that the parties will focus their efforts solely on attaining a mutually acceptable solution, through joint negotiations at scheduled, face-to-face, four-way meetings, each party with their own collaborative lawyer present.[35] The negotiations are undertaken in 'good faith' with a commitment from the parties that they will be honest and open in their dealings with each other, that they will provide full details of their up-to-date financial position and that they will focus on their respective interests, and the interests of their children, rather than adopting a positional stance. In addition, the parties agree not to litigate the matter before the court unless there is a breakdown in the settlement negotiations. All negotiations within the process are confidential and cannot be referred to in any subsequent court proceedings, save as agreed between the parties. Often, the parties will agree to preserve the 'status quo' during the currency of the agreement by not making any significant changes regarding their finances, or will not, for example, move children from the family home. Participation agreements may also clarify the role of each collaborative lawyer and provide for fee arrangements. Difficulties may arise when client retainer agreements are not signed in advance. In these situations, the participation agreements will stipulate that 'the respective lawyers are employed by and represent only the party who retained them.'[36]

The participation agreement: a contract or an agreement?

Despite these assurances and provisos, that each lawyer is acting solely for his or her own client, questions arise as to whether 'participation agreements' are to be construed as being 'contractual' in nature or whether they are *merely* 'principles and guidelines' for the process. If these participation agreements are contractual in nature, signed by lawyers and include a disqualification clause, are lawyers exposing themselves to issues regarding privity of contract and in effect, taking on obligations to third parties? There is no doubt about the potential for conflict if lawyers inadvertently take on legal obligations to the other party and arguably, to the third party lawyers; Peppet also highlights the potential effect of the disqualification provision on the lawyers' professional judgment.[37] Indeed, there is no definitive answer to this question without a close reading of the participation agreement in each case to determine whether it can be construed as being contractual or 'hortative' in nature.[38] Contractual agreements raise privity issues between the lawyers and the other party and also between the lawyers themselves. If these agreements are 'contractually based' does this raise ethical issues?

This matter was considered by a number of Bar Associations across the US who considered the process 'generally consistent with the Model Rules of Professional conduct.'[39] Only the Colorado Bar Association raised concerns. Having considered the process, its opinion was:

> the practice of Collaborative Law violates Rule 1.7(b) of Colorado Rules of Professional Conduct insofar as a lawyer participating in the process enters into a contractual agreement with the opposing party requiring the lawyer to withdraw in the event that the process is unsuccessful. The Committee further concluded that pursuant to Colorado Rules of Professional Conduct 1.7(c) the client's consent to waive this conflict cannot be validly obtained.[40]

The lawyer may not seek the client's informed consent unless he or she has first confirmed that they can provide 'competent and diligent' representation. If the lawyer believes that, by signing the agreement, there is a 'significant risk' that his or her representation of their client could be adversely affected by the lawyer's other responsibilities, perhaps to third parties, this conflict 'in effect forecloses alternatives that would otherwise be available to the [lawyer's own] client'.[41] In the Colorado Bar Association's view, lawyers by signing these agreements *were* taking on obligations to third parties and having the client's informed consent was not sufficient to counteract the conflict of interest.[42] However, they were of the opinion that the agreement would be permissible if the participation agreement was signed by the clients only and not by the lawyers. Shortly after this, the American Bar Association (ABA) responded to the Colorado opinion.

Having reviewed the process, the ABA relied on Model Rule 1.2(c) which states:

> [a] lawyer may limit the scope of the representation if the limitation is *reasonable* under the circumstances and the client gives *informed consent.*[43]

The ABA concluded that collaborative practice is a 'permissible limited scope representation' as:

> When a client has given informed consent to a representation limited to collaborative negotiation toward settlement, the lawyer's agreement to withdraw if the collaboration fails is not an agreement that impairs her ability to represent the client, but rather is consistent with the client's limited goals for the representation. A client's agreement to a limited scope representation does not exempt the lawyer from the duties of competence and diligence, notwithstanding that the contours of the requisite competence and diligence are limited in accordance with the overall scope of the representation.[44]

Peppet notes, however that both the Colorado Bar and the ABA's opinions are somewhat limited as they appear to have examined the process based on a contractual, lawyer privity,[45] disqualification, four-way model.[46] If the process was structured as Webb intended with an executed client retainer agreement confirming the limited nature of the representation and by analogy the disqualification once this representation has come to an end, then these issues would not be of concern. Once each party had this in place, the four-way/participation agreement would only be between the prospective parties themselves. He outlines that there are many other ways in which the process could be, and has been, structured that would not lead to these concerns.[47] He was also of the view that the ABA opinion was less than helpful as it did not clarify, or advise upon, whether there should be, as a matter of practice, a separate limited representation client agreement in each case or if it is sufficient to include such limitations as part of the four-way participation agreement.

The prefatory note to the Uniform Collaborative Law Act in the US describes the process as a '*contractually* based alternative dispute resolution process.'[48] At the time of the drafting of the Uniform Collaborative Law Act advices were sought on this issue from a contracts professor, Professor Sher.[49] The question was posed as to whether participation agreements are 'contracts', and if so, what are the implications for lawyers if they sign the participation agreement as parties to the contract. Professor Sher advised that to avoid taking on contractual obligations to third parties, lawyers should not sign participation agreements or four-way agreements as parties to the agreement; they should sign merely to confirm their representation of his or her own client. The prefatory note to the Uniform Collaborative Law Act clarifies that lawyers sign the participation agreement 'simply … to identify the party's collaborative lawyer so that the disqualification provision can be more easily administered.'[50] It does not make the lawyer a party to the agreement, nor does it change the role of the lawyer in representing their own client. Section 13 of the Act also reiterates that lawyers retain their responsibility to their client and their existing standards of professional responsibility.[51]

Under the Act, ensuring informed consent is now also a statutory requirement.[52] It was arguably, however, a missed opportunity to specify in the Act that part of ensuring informed consent requires the prior execution of a written client retainer agreement.[53] While the Act, in many respects, is a model of best practice, it has not been adopted in all US states and therefore, as noted earlier, variations in practice continue. Many jurisdictions have no specific legislation to determine how the process should be governed; therefore the lawyers are arguably still exposing themselves to the risk of suit. The Act is discussed further in Chapter 3.

The disqualification clause

The aim of the 'disqualification clause' is to cement the focus on settlement. As noted earlier, it provides that, in the event that settlement is not reached within the process, the clients' lawyers are disqualified from acting for them in any subsequent legal proceedings arising out of this issue or any related matter. Lawyers are therefore aware from the outset that they will lose their clients, and clients their lawyers, with the financial and emotional consequences that may bring for all. In addition, all lawyers in those particular lawyers' firms are also disqualified from acting for the client in this matter. This is known as 'imputed disqualification'; the aim is to ensure that each client starts out afresh in the court process with new, unbiased representation. This requirement is also supported by the principles of professional responsibility as set out in the ABA Model Rules of Professional Conduct which state that '[w]hile lawyers are associated in a firm, none of them shall knowingly represent a client when any one of them practicing alone would be prohibited from doing so'.[54] It also helps to create what has been described as the 'container' for collaborative practice in that the parties have the reassurance that they can speak freely within the process in the knowledge that they will not face these lawyers in a court situation, should the negotiations fail.[55]

Either party may also choose to terminate the process at any time. It is important to note that lawyers may also terminate the process if they believe that their client is not being forthcoming with information or is not co-operating with the 'good faith' ethos of the process. Collaborative lawyers will highlight the issue of concern to their client and will point out how this is contrary to the ethos of collaborative law. If the client chooses to ignore the advices of his or her lawyer, the lawyer must terminate the process. Tesler describes this as 'constructive' termination.[56] Tesler sets out examples of behaviour that is considered contrary to the *spirit* of the process as:

> the secret disposition of marital, quasi-marital, or nonmarital (sic) property, failure to disclose the existence of the true nature of assets and/or obligations, ongoing emotional or physical abuse by either party, secret preparation to engage in litigation while appearing to participate in a Collaborative Divorce process, or withholding a secret plan to leave the jurisdiction of the court with their children.[57]

This requirement can also place a collaborative lawyer in an ethical dilemma: by continuing to act, he or she is not acting in a collaborative manner, but yet by terminating the process he or she will lose a client. This is an issue that the collaborative lawyer must explain clearly to a client before they agree to engage in the process and it is one of the key requirements in securing the client's informed consent.[58]

In the past, others, including this author, have described the disqualification provision as a 'unique feature' of collaborative practice.[59] However, if it is acknowledged and accepted by all parties, that the representation is limited, is the disqualification provision not as the ABA has noted merely 'consistent with the client's limited goals for the representation'? If so, should it be such a controversial aspect to the process? To use Webb's analogy: if you hire someone as a contractor and they act like a demolitions expert, would you want to hire them to rebuild once the destruction has occurred? Does it not make sense that that lawyer should be disqualified from acting for the client in the future? Webb saw this as a protection for clients. Lawyers will be less likely to conclude negotiations early if this means they lose their clients. Also, it prevents lawyers from acting in a positional or adversarial manner within the process because collaborative lawyers, like all professionals, rely on their reputation.[60] They value and protect their roles within their local collaborative practice group. If a lawyer acquires a reputation for not doing what they were contracted to do, it is likely they will be shunned or excluded from the group.[61]

Depending on your views then, the disqualification provision is either the 'glue' that keeps the negotiations on track and the parties and their lawyers focused on what they are trying to achieve, or the 'glue' that keeps clients stuck in a process that may no longer be working for them, fearful of the financial and emotional consequences of terminating the process. Tesler, as a proponent of collaborative practice describes the disqualification clause as being the impetus for parties to get 'the sleeves get rolled up'[62] when an impasse is reached, rather than immediately moving forward with litigation. She refers to lawyers stepping back and instead of taking control and moving forward, letting the 'silence' on their behalf assist the parties themselves to realise that they need to find a solution. This is in accordance with what King referred to as the 'intrinsic motivation' towards 'self-determination' for disputing parties which 'acknowledges that the individual must confront and solve her own problems'[63] (Chapter 1). Ver Steegh agrees and comments that '[t]he disqualification agreement adds teeth to the parties' commitment to settle in that they will both incur expense and delay if either seeks court involvement'.[64]

Lande on the other hand, raised concerns about the disqualification provision placing excessive settlement pressure on clients.[65] Schwab, too, argues that it 'diminishes the value of both parties BATNA'[66] (best alternative to a negotiated settlement). In effect, he believed the disqualification clause in making litigation more difficult reduces clients' options if the process fails. However, while it may 'diminish' the use of litigation as the best alternative to a negotiated settlement, it does not 'extinguish' it. It is clear that having the disqualification provision in place forces clients to think more carefully before deciding to end the collaborative process and take the matter to court. Does that keep clients in the process longer than they may have remained otherwise due to the additional pressures of losing their lawyers and the costs involved?[67] The research indicates that, on occasion, it does. Sometimes this may lead to a successful conclusion, other times it will lead to disqualification.

Clients' and lawyers' views in relation to the benefits of, or problems with, the disqualification provision will be outlined as we examine the research undertaken in Canada, the USA, the UK and Ireland. At this point, however, suffice to say that indications are that it appears to be more of an issue for the lawyers rather than the clients.[68] Clients in fact, as noted by Macfarlane, are often 'mystified by the lengths to which their lawyers believe they must go to remove the possibility of litigation, and wonder why counsel could not simply be trusted to use their best judgment in this eventuality.'[69] Much of the criticism in relation to this aspect of the process has come from the profession. Arguably, this is because they can foresee the potential dangers or difficulties more clearly than clients due to their many years' experience in practice. However, the question has to be raised as to whether the danger of losing a client and arguably the largest element of a fee, that involving the court hearing is a factor in this critique. Does Gillers, perhaps, address the hub of the issue when he comments that for legal professionals 'financial reward is rarely, if ever, cited as the reason to oppose a rule. A proxy must be found, based in the interests of clients or the true ends of justice'?[70]

The unique elements of the collaborative process

A number of substantial differences are evident between this process and other forms of negotiation. Firstly, the requirement to be represented by lawyers is a unique aspect to the collaborative law process. If clients choose to take their case before the courts, to mediation or to family law arbitration – there is no such requirement; clients may attend without legal representation. Access to justice is a fundamental right.[71] Is this requirement therefore an impediment to that right? Proponents of the process argue that lawyers are necessary because of the need for prospective parties to give their fully informed consent. Difficulties would arise, they assert, if one party is unrepresented within the process, leaving that party vulnerable due to an imbalance of power or perhaps leading to a confusion of roles for the lawyer, who may, inadvertently, become adviser to the unrepresented party.[72] While it may occur that one party may not have representation within the courts' process, the judge acts as arbiter and the lawyer's role is not affected. Critics, however, note that unless both clients can attain legal representation, many potential separating parties may be excluded from using the process because of the imposed costs of engaging lawyers. Key to addressing this issue is the availability of collaborative practice for low-income clients under national legal aid schemes. The argument has been made that collaborative practice is only for wealthy, educated clients.[73] While research has indicated that many who choose to use the process fall within this description, there is little evidence the process is more expensive than engaging in court proceedings.[74]

Secondly, there appears to be a dichotomy between the client retainer and the assertion in Tesler's 'Principles and Guidelines for the Practice of Collaborative Law/ Collaborative Divorce' notably that: 'Each lawyer's *duty is to his or her own client* to provide advice and counsel aimed at constructive resolution of all divorce-related issues'[75] and, the claim by collaborative practitioners to take a 'whole family' approach. Arguably, combining a 'whole family' approach and fulfilling the obligation to fully represent one's own client requires somewhat of a balancing act for lawyers.[76] Indeed, is this not a conflict of interest? Is the lawyer's duty not solely to their own client, particularly when he or she is not receiving instructions from the family? In addressing the dilemma, Tesler takes what may be described as a simplistic view, acknowledging that a collaborative lawyer must remain 'faithful in the representation of the client and zealously represent the client in pursuit of the client's stated goals'. However, instead of doing this in an adversarial way, Tesler contends that:

> [t]his faithful representation includes informing the client about the law and its application to the client's matter on an ongoing basis, preserving confidential communications, and assisting the client to develop approaches, collaboratively with the other participants, to resolving the matter without judicial intervention.[77]

Straightforward as this may appear, how are lawyers to behave when they feel that the best interests of their client may necessitate taking action that may prejudicially affect the family? It appears that this will remain a matter of interpretation for lawyers in each case and may well result in difficult ethical decisions having to be made.

Third is the agreement to negotiate in 'good faith'. The sample retainer provided by Tesler confirms the 'good faith' nature of the process and warns prospective parties that: 'A dishonest or unscrupulous party could take advantage of the Collaborative Divorce process for delay or advantage in litigation.'[78] It states that no collaborative lawyer can 'guarantee' that this will not happen but that the client will be alerted if there is any 'suspicion' and the lawyer will withdraw their representation (enabling the client to engage another lawyer to continue with the process) or terminate the agreement. Good faith, as Lande notes, is like 'mom and apple pie'[79] – difficult to disagree with but, equally difficult to define. Concerns have been raised about how to ensure compliance with this concept, particularly in view of the agreement not to litigate. Not litigating, in this context, does not simply mean that proceedings will not be issued to bring the matter before the court for final hearing but also that the parties will not seek any interim orders which are frequently sought within the adversarial system (orders for maintenance, custody or access) during the currency of the collaborative process.[80] In relying upon the terms of the participation agreement, separating parties also forgo the right to seek an order of discovery (disclosure of information, e.g. financial records) from the court. Many questions have been raised as to whether encouraging clients to agree to such terms may expose clients to risk or be unethical. Cameron, as a proponent of collaborative practice, cautions that '[i]f your client does not know the extent of the family assets and has concerns that the other spouse will not provide full disclosure, then the case should be screened out of Collaborative Practice.'[81] On the other hand, as Hazard acknowledges, we have 'no proof that the adversary system of trial yields truth more often than other systems of trial.'[82] Indeed, as will be detailed later in this book, lawyers interviewed, having reflected on the adversarial approach, are beginning to question their motives for seeking discovery in some cases; is it to ensure full disclosure for the client or to protect themselves from risk of suit?[83]

More difficult to elicit perhaps is the 'extent' of this good faith requirement. Many participation agreements, including the model provided by Tesler, include a provision whereby the lawyers and parties commit to honesty and the full disclosure of '*all relevant information*'.[84] The difficulty is defining '*relevant information*'. In a traditional lawyer-to-lawyer, positional negotiation, there may be certain facts, non-legal issues (future career plans, new relationships, etc.) that would not be discoverable as part of a litigation file, but may have an impact on the way a case is settled. These issues have been described as 'settlement facts',[85] often used in a strategic way to negotiate settlement in the context of positional lawyer-to-lawyer negotiation. The 'spirit' of collaborative practice may however, require these matters to be disclosed upfront, and this needs to be explained as part of ensuring informed consent.

Are collaborative lawyers taking on a higher level of ethical standards?

The 'dominant approach'[86] to legal ethics 'contends, in essence, that there is one uniform legal profession that must be guided by one set of ethical rules and principles, and that those rules and principles must protect the ideal of the lawyer as adversarial advocate.'[87] A lawyer's duty, therefore, is to be loyal to his or her own client and to represent this client to the best of their ability.[88] In practice however, this does not necessarily imply that lawyers merely ponder 'how they can assure that their clients obey the law. Rather, it generally means that lawyers strategize how they can accomplish their clients' objectives to the greatest extent possible without running afoul of the law'.[89] A lawyer will share information strategically, or perhaps fail to correct something that the opposing lawyer may have interpreted incorrectly, if it is to his or her advantage. These decisions frequently involve judgement calls perhaps based on the lawyer's values or what he or she perceives as acting in the best interests of their clients. Occasionally, such decisions may raise ethical issues. The difficulty is, as noted by Professor Gerald Wetlaufer:

> Ethics is different from and more demanding than law, including the law of professional self-regulation. This difference can readily be understood because law, unlike ethics, must be implemented from a perspective external to the individual and must deal with all of the problems related to such implementation ... Accordingly, the law may permit certain deceits that have had little or no effect, or that are difficult or impossible to prove.[90]

Peppet notes that '[a]mending the traditional lawyer client relationship is a serious business.'[91] Collaborative lawyers, argue that they are not seeking to change this relationship. The sample 'Principles and Guidelines for the Practice of Collaborative Law/Collaborative Divorce' provided by Tesler, refers to 'participation with integrity' which, it is explained, means that no professional will 'take advantage of inconsistencies, misstatements of fact or law, or other's miscalculations, but rather to disclose them and seek to have them corrected at the earliest opportunity.'[92] Schneyer notes that this places a higher burden on collaborative lawyers and that they 'may be taking on heavier client-monitoring duties than rules of legal ethics or civil procedure ordinarily impose'.[93] Peppet has argued that there should be an option for lawyers to agree to a higher standard of ethics when bargaining.[94] He proposes a contract model of legal ethics which would allow lawyers to predetermine the standards upon which they choose to conduct their negotiations. This model would not permit lawyers to have complete freedom with regard to their ethical standards; there would continue to be a minimum standard required of all parties, but rather, lawyers could 'opt in' for a higher standard. Collaborative lawyers by using this process appear to be opting in to this higher standard. They need to be aware of the additional undertakings required and be prepared to abide by this self-imposed duty to their clients and to the process.

So why would lawyers agree to engage with this process?

The adversarial approach is what lawyers have been trained to do.[95] Tesler, however, refers to gaining a 'rekindled joy in the practice of law'[96] since becoming a collaborative lawyer. She speaks of the opportunity to integrate 'one's deeply held personal values into one's work', lawyers recognising that they are members of 'a helping and healing profession'.[97] Again, such pronouncements raise concerns about the issue of lawyers imposing their own values on clients, the 'good lives' model, referred to in Chapter 1. Critics of collaborative practice have pointed to the damage that such 'evangelical' approaches can cause to a new and developing process.[98]

This does not necessarily mean that practising collaborative law is an 'easier' option for lawyers. It is 'challenging' to learn new ways of practice.[99] Tesler acknowledges that '[l]earning the craft of collaborative practice involves mastering knowledge and skills that were not taught to us in law school.'[100] Similarly, it is important to acknowledge that practising this way may not be appealing for every lawyer. Cameron notes that many lawyers are 'risk averse' and will not want to practise within a framework that is seen as outside of the tried and tested court process, their default position.[101] Many lawyers may not want to agree to this higher level of bargaining ethics.

This was evident in the findings from across all jurisdictions examined as part of the current research, which will be detailed in later chapters. As busy practitioners, an important element of training as a collaborative lawyer is that move away from what Cameron describes as '[a]utomatism, or not noticing what one does' which is frequently used as 'a defence mechanism that insulates one from self-awareness.'[102] Important also, is developing one's negotiation skills. Lawyers used to the positional model may be concerned about the higher level of engagement requirement during four-way meetings and about the fact that they, and their negotiation skills, are somewhat exposed before their clients and their colleagues.

In answering the question as to why lawyers choose to move out of the 'comfort zone' of positional negotiation to one in which they will be held to a higher standard of professional ethics, the research indicates that lawyers who make this transition do so because they believe that collaborative practice is a better way for clients. Many are experienced family lawyers who have witnessed the difficulties and acrimony within the adversarial system and who see collaborative practice as fulfilling the need for a process with more support than mediation, but without the positional wranglings of the courts' system.[103]

The multidisciplinary model

Justice Susan Denham, as she was then, now Chief Justice of Ireland, in reaching her decision in *Roche v Roche*[104] (a surrogacy case) commented that the role of a court of law is 'to make a legal decision' and 'not about the wonder and mystery of human life.'[105] Collaborative practice is the first process within a legal framework to acknowledge the need for a more holistic approach; to acknowledge or allow some acceptance of the 'wonder and mystery of human life'; and to facilitate some consideration of the 'ecological' and social factors that may impact on individuals' views. In contrast to both mediation and ordinary lawyer negotiation, it offers separating parties the opportunity to engage additional experts who are specifically trained to work with the legal framework of the process, experts who may add depth to the overall settlement achieved in terms of the parties' ability to rebuild different relationships following separation or divorce.

The mental health professional

In dealing with family law cases it is important for the professionals and the separating parties themselves to understand the emotional process involved. Berger[106] explains that there are five stages in relationship transformation following separation:

> Stage 1: The parties decide to separate. They move from being a couple to being individuals; from 'we' to 'I'. This 'disintegration' is difficult after many years of thinking as a couple. In most cases, one party may be the instigator of the separation and reconciled with the separation; the other may experience periods of 'deep hurt or anger'.
>
> Stage 2: 'Rebuilding separate selves'; each party tries to re-establish themselves as individuals and regain their own 'sense of self and independence'. During this time it is essential that the parties give each other space; any interference can trigger a disproportionate response.
>
> Stage 3: After a period of time, they reconnect again 'on a different level without the same emotional reactivity'.
>
> Stage 4: 'Team-up as parents'; putting their children's needs first and being able to co-parent effectively.
>
> Stage 5: Finally, over a longer period of time, the parties may become friends again.[107]

Mayer also commented that '[e]motions are the energy that fuel conflict. If people could always stay perfectly rational and focused on how best to meet their needs and accommodate those of others, and if they could calmly work to establish effective communications, then many conflicts would either never arise or would quickly deescalate.'[108] Whether it is anger, hurt, or sadness that the parties are feeling, it is important that the emotions are understood. Professionals dealing with the resolution of conflict should be aware of the importance of emotions in relation to parties' abilities to make decisions at crucial points in the discussions and the impact of these factors on capacity to negotiate.[109]

The collaborative model provides a structure within which clients can avail of 'coaching' to deal with the emotional issues surrounding relationship breakdown. This coaching has been described as 'brief, goal-orientated, systemic therapy'.[110] It is brief in that it involves active assistance by the coach while the party is going through the actual separation/divorce. It does not extend to therapy after the divorce has been finalised. It is goal-orientated for the same reasons, in that it is specific to the goals that the parties wish to achieve during the divorce process and, it is systemic in that the 'therapist sees the client as one member of an interconnected family system'.[111]

The coaches used during the collaborative process are licensed mental health professionals, trained in the dynamics of the collaborative process. They assist the parties to articulate their feelings, to understand how they react to their ex-spouse and to develop new ways to communicate in a constructive rather than a confrontational way; they are helping the parties to make the transition, as described earlier by Berger, from 'we' to 'I'.

Lawyers who have used the team model believe that it is better for the clients and for the process to have the coaches available from the outset rather than employing them as 'fire fighters' when an issue arises.[112] The advantage is that they see first-hand the interaction between the couple and advise the parties how to deal with the acrimony and how to communicate. One collaborative lawyer interviewed for this research commented that 'a client cannot design the model because they haven't been here before and they aren't emotionally placed to be able to deal with it.'[113] Having such a structure already in place makes the transition easier for separating parties.

The financial specialist

The financial specialist in a collaborative matter may be retained by both parties as an independent expert to assist them in assessing their financial position. He or she will examine the parties' financial position and will assist them to look at different options for their future. The financial specialist 'bring(s) an unbiased, educational and facilitative role to the process.'[114] This role involves assisting the parties to focus on how to budget for two households and how to plan their finances into the future. S/he will normally be an accountant who has undergone training in interdisciplinary collaborative practice so that s/he can 'equip clients to make their own decisions and achieve independence'.[115]

The financial specialist has been described as the one 'true neutral'[116] in the process. Jointly instructing one financial expert can save the parties considerable time and money rather than seeking to obtain this information through protracted discovery and arms-length negotiations. A collaborative lawyer interviewed for this research noted that the financial professional removes some of the distrust that arises when one party discovers that the other has not been forthcoming during the course of formal discovery within the court process.[117] The report prepared by the financial consultant adds an element of realism to the process; parties may not be fully aware how they stand financially. This realism assists the parties to negotiate the best possible outcome to ensure that they take advantage of any tax breaks, structure investments and confront, rather than seek to avoid, existing liabilities. Research carried out by the IACP[118] has also pointed to the advantages for children when their parents have reliable and accurate financial advice. Divorce or separation generally causes financial strain and it can be difficult for children to suddenly realise that the lifestyle to which they were accustomed may change.[119]

The child specialist

Gamache, a leading child specialist, notes that:

> [r]esearch indicates that the fact that a child has parents who are divorced tells us very little about the well-being of the child. In sharp contrast, knowing that a child has been exposed to prolonged conflict and/or parental depression tells us a lot.[120]

The child specialist is a licensed mental health professional with training and experience in family systems, child development, and the needs of children during and after a divorce.[121] Their role within the collaborative process is very different from that of a psychologist/social worker employed as part of the court process. In a court situation these professionals gather evidence and prepare a report that will assist a judge in making a decision based on 'the interests of the children'. In contrast, the child specialist as part of the collaborative process is 'a neutral advocate for the children who gives a voice to the children's interests'; he or she does not assist the court with determining best interests, nor provide a forum for the parents to convince a judge that they are the most worthy parent.[122] They talk to the children in an age-appropriate manner, ascertain their views and, with their consent, bring any issues that the children would like addressed to the attention of their parents in a neutral way at a joint meeting. This also avoids the delays and costs normally incurred when written reports have to be prepared and, as already noted, '[h]aving only one conversation minimizes the likelihood of misunderstanding.'[123] The input from the child specialist is short-term and focused with a view to 'scaffolding' the child through the separation/divorce process. Wolke comments that '[t]he child specialist can provide a safe place for the children to share their story, ask questions and discuss their concerns.'[124]

Child specialists may only be brought into the process when the coaches or lawyers become aware of issues that are of concern or where the parties are, perhaps, at an impasse in relation to the children. At this point the lawyers and/or the coaches will speak to the parents about the role of the child specialist and, if both parents agree, the child specialist is brought on board. The collaborative process is ideally positioned to provide children with an avenue to have their voices heard in an age-appropriate, non-adversarial way. The difficulty for children, once again, however, is that there has to be an awareness by the parents of the children's needs during the separation or divorce; parents remain the gatekeepers and a paternalistic, 'parents know best' approach is often evident.

Gamache says that hearing this feedback from their children can raise parents' awareness and help them to understand that:

> Families are dynamic systems of interrelated relationships. Parents can learn how they contribute to the very conflicts by which they feel victimized. When both parents become aware of their contributions to this conflict, they can begin to change the system so as to reduce it.[125]

During the research carried out by Resolution in the UK (examined in more detail in Chapter 4), one lawyer commented that engaging in collaborative practice:

> has made me think a bit harder about the voice of the child. And to what extent the parents are actually listening to what the child *isn't* saying. It's made me think a bit harder about involving a child specialist. Because often it is covered up.[126]

By hearing issues that the children have raised, the parents may then begin to assist their children during the separation process. As with any intervention on the part of children, parents need to be willing to *listen* and, where possible and appropriate, to *change* certain aspects of the way they are dealing with the conflict to improve the situation for their children.

Research into the frequency with which child specialists are engaged was undertaken by the IACP. The results revealed that, compared to what may be expected, child specialists were more likely to be engaged by clients with lower income levels. This is not supporting the common view that only wealthy clients can afford additional experts. It appears, however, that a willingness to recognise the *need* for such expert assistance may be a more useful barometer than a client's financial standing.[127]

The child specialist and adult children

Much academic commentary has focused on the impact of separation and divorce on children under the age of 18 years.[128] In practice, lawyers have a tendency to believe that children of a certain age, perhaps from 15 upwards, will decide for themselves where they want to live. However, these older children from 15 years into young adulthood (18 to 25), tend to be forgotten. Issues that may be of concern to these children include: loss of a family unit; loss of the family's role in the community; loss of the parental unit; loss of parent as parent; loss of family home and loss of a feeling of security. The breakdown in their family challenges what they believed to be reality and this in turn causes insecurity in their own intimate relationships.[129] Older children away at college may be torn between a desire to stay away, perhaps, because they are in denial, and a need to be there for younger siblings still living in the midst of the conflict in the family home.

Bell and Behram[130] referred to the boundary issues that may arise when one parent tends to rely on the older children as confidants, to overburden older children with their own emotional issues. Parents may be unaware that they are doing this. By facilitating a process whereby these older children speak to a child/family therapist, parents are giving their children an opportunity to voice their concerns. Will they be able to remain in college, will there be sufficient money to pay fees, where will they spend Christmas? The opportunity to engage a child specialist for these young adults is a means of providing support for families at a crisis point and gives parents a unique opportunity to think about the impact of their separation on their adult children. Additionally, in situations where parents are older when separating, grown up children may have concerns about how their parents are going to cope, perhaps living alone after many years of marriage. Children may also have financial worries for their parents. All of these issues can be addressed by the child specialist.

Team model

The parties to a participation agreement may agree at the outset on the additional experts they require and then proceed on a 'team' basis with the assistance of these experts at every stage of the process. Tesler describes the team model as 'the most thought out and well-structured approach to interdisciplinary professional collaboration ... which allows clients economical access to communication skills, coaches, child-development specialists, and financial professionals trained in collaborative teamwork with the lawyers who provide the collaborative law representation.'[131] The team model aims to provide the most holistic approach to dealing with the various aspects of divorce. Parties may choose to have their own coach, or they may both instruct one coach who will help them deal with communication and emotional issues. The parties meet the coach before the first meeting, giving them an opportunity to express any concerns and get appropriate advice from the coach as to how to deal with conflict during the meetings. The coaches will meet with the parties as required during the process.

Referral model

Sometimes however, parties may want some additional support but may not wish or financially be in a position to engage all the professionals from the outset. In such cases the parties may refer issues to outside professionals as required, to employ a child specialist to assist their children or a financial specialist, as the need arises. This method is known as the referral model. Factors influencing the type of model chosen can include: the level of additional help required for the couple; their ability to pay fees to the various professionals involved; and, depending on where the couples reside, the availability of such experts.

Lawyers and the multidisciplinary model

Engaging with the multidisciplinary model of collaborative practice is challenging for lawyers who are used to being in control of a case and adopt quite a single-minded approach. Including additional experts means practical issues need to be addressed. Firstly, how will confidential client information be dealt with? Clients' consent needs to be obtained at the outset. Agreements also need to be in place as to whether any reports or documentation prepared by such experts will be confidential within the process or whether the parties and the expert agree that, should the process fail, this documentation can be used in court. Secondly, lawyers may find working with other disciplines in this way unusual. Mental health experts too can find this challenging. Research on the process notes the importance of ensuring that cases are managed and that lawyers retain an element of control in ensuring the prospective parties and the many additional experts engaged work together to seek a more holistic solution (see Chapters 4 and 5).

An important element in the development of collaborative practice has been the formation of 'practice groups'. The role of the 'practice group' is to provide a forum in which collaborative lawyers[132] and other professionals in a particular locality meet on a regular basis to discuss and promote the process, but more importantly, to share experiences, foster relationships and build trust to enable them to collaborate effectively as part of a team for separating parties.[133] Building this trust and learning how best to negotiate with colleagues can help encourage co-operation and make negotiating across a table less alien. The importance of the 'practice group' will become evident through the results of the research, and, in particular, the need for on-going reflection and addressing issues of concern that may arise within the group.

Conclusion

Collaborative practice was developed to fulfil what was a perceived need for a more settlement-focused, less adversarial approach to family law matters with an aim being to build trust and relationships, rather than to be divisive. As a 'bottom up' process, it has been challenged on a number of levels. Those within the established Bar have questioned whether practising in this way is in accordance with a lawyer's role as 'zealous advocate' for their clients, and whether ethical considerations arise. It is evident that care needs to be taken when drafting participation agreements, that lawyers need to ensure that the client is fully informed about the unique features of the process and that clients who may not be suitable, nor have the capacity to negotiate, are screened out. Lawyers too need to be aware of their commitment to dealing with a case in this way, in particular, the agreement to higher standards of legal ethics.

Engaging in the process is thus a new challenge for lawyers, a move away from the structure and reassurance of the courts' system; they are instead bargaining in a different landscape where there is a commitment to honesty and disclosure, without the crutch of strategic negotiation. Working with other disciplines in a collaborative manner is also a challenge. Much of the lessons that need to be learned can only be achieved through using the process and refining elements that need to be addressed. The next chapter, Chapter 3, examines these issues further as they were debated and discussed during the enactment of the Uniform Collaborative Law Rules/Act in 2010.

Notes

1 Webb, S., and Ousky, R., *The Collaborative Way to Divorce: The Revolutionary Method that Results in Less Stress, Lower Costs, and Happier Kids – Without Going to Court* (Penguin, 2007) at xv.

2 Ibid. at 6.

3 Bederman, D.J., *Customs as a Source of Law* (Cambridge University Press, 2010) at 179.

4 Prefatory Note to the Uniform Collaborative Law Act, at 1. Available at http://www.uniformlaws.org/shared/docs/collaborative_law/uclranducla_finalact_jul10.pdfLast accessed 12 July 2016.

5 Webb, S., and Ousky, R., *The Collaborative Way to Divorce: The Revolutionary Method that Results in Less Stress, Lower Costs, and Happier Kids – Without Going to Court* (Penguin, 2007) at 7.

6 Tesler, P., *Collaborative Law: Achieving Effective Resolution in Divorce without Litigation* (2nd edn, American Bar Association, 2008) at 26.

7 Daicoff, S., 'The Comprehensive Law Movement' (2002–2004) 19 *Touro Law Review* 825–846, 835.

8 Dr. Peggy Thompson, Psychologist. Co-founder of the IACP.

9 Cameron, N. *Collaborative Practice: Deepening the Dialogue* (The Continuing Legal Education Society of British Columbia, 2004) at 9.

10 Daicoff, S., 'Law as a healing profession: The comprehensive law movement' (2005, Fall) *Pepperdine Dispute Resolution Law Journal.* NYLS Clinical Research Institute Paper No. 05/06–12, 3–4.

11 Douzinas, C., *Law and Justice in Postmodernity* (Cambridge University Press, 2015) at 213.

12 Webb, S., 'Collaborative Law: A Practitioner's Perspective on its History and Current Practice' (2008) 21 *Journal of the American Academy of Matrimonial Lawyers* 155–169, 160. In his earlier book co-written with Ron Ousky, *The Collaborative Way to Divorce: The Revolutionary Method that Results in Less Stress, Lower Costs, and Happier Kids – Without Going to Court* (Penguin, 2006) Stuart Webb refers to the importance of the disqualification agreement as part of the participation agreement. In the above article, published two years later, he appears to have refined the process further by acknowledging the need for a limited-scope retainer agreement to comply with ethical obligations and to provide for the disqualification provision. The disqualification agreement is not mentioned in the context of the participation agreement.

13 Webb, S., 'Collaborative Law: A Practitioner's Perspective on its History and Current Practice' (2008) 21 *Journal of the American Academy of Matrimonial Lawyers* 155–169, 160.

14 Ibid. at 169.

15 The ABA Model Rules of Professional Responsibility EC 7–1 (1969) referred to a lawyer's duty to zealously represent their client. Although this has now been amended by the ABA Model Rules of Professional Conduct R. 1.3 (2007) which provides that a lawyer shall act with reasonable diligence in representing a client – the term 'zealous advocate' is still frequently used when discussing lawyers' duties.

16 Webb, S., 'Collaborative Law: A Practitioner's Perspective on its History and Current Practice' (2008) 21 *Journal of the American Academy of Matrimonial Lawyers* 155–169, 168

17 Webb, S., 'Collaborative Law: A Practitioner's Perspective on its History and Current Practice' (2008) 21 *Journal of the American Academy of Matrimonial Lawyers* 155–169, 160.

18 Tesler, P., *Collaborative Law: Achieving Effective Resolution in Divorce without Litigation* (2nd edn, American Bar Association, 2008) at 227–228.

19 Ibid. at 227.

20 Cameron, N., *Collaborative Practice, Deepening the Dialogue* (The Continuing Legal Education Society of British Columbia, 2004) at 145–147.

21 Tesler, P., *Collaborative Law: Achieving Effective Resolution in Divorce without Litigation* (2nd edn, American Bar Association 2008) at 54.

22 Ibid. The issue of informed consent will be discussed further in the context of the requirements under the ABA's Model Rules of Professional conduct 1.2 in the USA

and the requirements of the Uniform Collaborative Law Act. For countries and States not falling within these jurisdictions, ensuring that the client is fully informed is still an important element of the process and is recommended in the guidelines laid down by the International Academy of Collaborative Professionals.

23 Cameron, N., *Collaborative Practice, Deepening the Dialogue* (The Continuing Legal Education Society of British Columbia, 2004) at 157.

24 Webb, S., 'Collaborative Law: A Practitioner's Perspective on its History and Current Practice' (2008) 21 *Journal of the American Academy of Matrimonial Lawyers* 155–169, 159.

25 Mayer, Bernard, *The Dynamics of Conflict Resolution: A Practitioner's Guide* (Jossey-Bass, 2000) at 31–33.

26 The issue of screening was discussed at length during the enactment of the Uniform Collaborative Law Act. See Chapter 3 for further analysis.

27 Cameron, N., *Collaborative Practice, Deepening the Dialogue* (The Continuing Legal Education Society of British Columbia, 2004) at 156.

28 See Ver Steegh, N., 'The Uniform Collaborative Law Act and Intimate Partner Violence: A Roadmap for Collaborative (and Non Collaborative) Lawyers' (2009) 38 *Hofstra Law Review* 699–755.

29 Tesler, P., *Collaborative Law: Achieving Effective Resolution in Divorce without Litigation* (2nd edn, American Bar Association, 2008) at 59–60.

30 Ibid.

31 Ibid. at 60

32 Shields, R.W., 'On Becoming a Collaborative Professional: From Paradigm Shifting to Transformative Learning Through Critical Reflection and Dialogue' (2008) *Journal of Dispute Resolution* 427–463. Shields notes that many lawyers do not move from an adversarial paradigm but more from a lawyer-centred interests-based approach – directed by lawyers but taking clients' interests into account. The bigger change is ceding control of the case and accepting an outcome in accordance with clients' interests rather than the law, 450.

33 Tesler, P., *Collaborative Law: Achieving Effective Resolution in Divorce without Litigation* (2nd edn, American Bar Association, 2008) at 68.

34 Ibid. at 70.

35 Tesler, P., *Collaborative Law: Achieving Effective Resolution in Divorce without Litigation* (2nd edn, American Bar Association 2008); Webb, S., and Ousky, R., *The Collaborative Way to Divorce: The Revolutionary Method that Results in Less Stress, Lower Costs, and Happier Kids – Without Going to Court* (Penguin, 2007); Cameron, N., *Collaborative Practice, Deepening the Dialogue* (The Continuing Legal Education Society of British Columbia, 2004).

36 See sample participation agreement for jurisdictions that have not enacted the Uniform Collaborative Law Act in IACP (2010) 11(2) *The Collaborative Review* 42–51, 50.

37 Peppet, S., 'The Ethics of Collaborative Law' (2008) *Journal of Dispute Resolution* 131–161.

38 Ibid. at 136.

39 Prefatory Note to the Uniform Collaborative Law Act, at 15. Available at http://www.uniformlaws.org/shared/docs/collaborative_law/uclranducla_finalact_jul10.pdf Last accessed 12 July 2016.

40 Ethics Comm. of the Colorado Bar Association Ethics Op. 115 (2007). Available at http://www.cobar.org/index.cfm/ID/386/subID/10159/CETH/Ethics-Opinion-115:-Ethical-Considerations-in-the-Collaborative-and-Cooperative-Law-Contexts,-02/24//. Last accessed 12 July 2016.

41 Comment no. 8 to Rule 1.7a (2).

42 Ibid.

43 ABA Model Rules of Professional Conduct 1.2(c) (2003) (emphasis added).

44 Formal Opinion 07–477. Available at <http://collaborativelaw.us/articles/Ethics_Opinion_ABA.pdf> Last accessed 12 July 2016

45 If the lawyers are in contractual privity, then one lawyer could sue to enforce the disqualification of the other lawyer, even if their client did not wish to do so.

46 Peppet, S., 'The Ethics of Collaborative Law' (2008) *Journal of Dispute Resolution* 131–161, 143.

47 He identified several different formats: retention agreements only with no four-way agreement; limited retention agreements and four-way agreements but no disqualification clause in the four-way; limited retention agreements plus four-way with disqualification clause; disqualification as part of a four-way and limited representation agreements (most common for CP), process four-way and client-client agreement scenario. See Peppet, S., 'The Ethics of Collaborative Law' (2008) *Journal of Dispute Resolution* 131–161.

48 Prefatory Note to the Uniform Collaborative Law Act, at 1. Available at http://www.uniformlaws.org/shared/docs/collaborative_law/uclranducla_finalact_jul10.pdf Last accessed 12 July 2016 (emphasis added).

49 Professor Byron Sher, Retired Contracts Professor, Stanford University.

50 Prefatory Note to the Uniform Collaborative Law Act, at 1. Available at http://www.uniformlaws.org/shared/docs/collaborative_law/uclranducla_finalact_jul10.pdfat 50. Last accessed 12 July 2016

51 Section 13 provides that lawyers are still bound by all of their professional and ethical requirements.

52 Section 14 of the Uniform Collaborative Law Rules/Act 2010 – applicable in jurisdictions where the Act has been adopted.

53 Many states across the US will already have requirements in place to ensure that client retainer agreements are signed e.g. Maryland Lawyers' Rules of Professional Conduct, Rule 1.2(c)(3); Missouri Rule of Professional Conduct 1.2(c); Montana Rule of Professional Conduct 1.2(c)(2); and New Hampshire Rule of Professional Conduct 1.2(c) and 1.2(g). In November 2015 the ABA Standing Committee on Ethics and Professional Responsibility issued a formal opinion (American Bar Association Standing Committee on Ethics and Professional Responsibility Formal Opinion 472 November 30, 2015 Communication with Person Receiving Limited-Scope Legal Services. Available at http://www.americanbar.org/content/dam/aba/administrative/professional_responsibility/aba_formal_opinion_472.authcheckdam.pdf. Last accessed 12 July 2016) regarding lawyers' communication with persons receiving limited scope legal services. In this, the Committee recognised that some States already require the nature and scope of the representation to be set out in writing and recommended that this should be the normal practice. It defined informed consent as: the agreement by a person to a proposed course of conduct after the lawyer has communicated adequate information and explanation about the material risks of and reasonably available alternatives to the proposed course of conduct. ABA Model Rules of Professional Conduct R. 1.0 (e). Therefore, although not required by Rule 1.2(c), the Committee, nevertheless, recommends that when lawyers provide limited-scope representation to a client, this agreement should be in writing so that the client may refer to it later.

54 ABA Model Rules of Professional Conduct R. 1.10(a) (2009).

55 Macfarlane, J., *The Emerging Phenomenon of Collaborative Family Law (CFL): A Qualitative Case Study* (Department of Justice Canada, 2005) at 39.

56 Tesler, P., *Collaborative Law: Achieving Effective Resolution in Divorce without Litigation* (2nd edn, American Bar Association, 2008) at 227.

57 Ibid. at 253.

58 Ibid. at 55.

59 Healy, C., 'American and Irish Perspectives on Collaborative Practice' (2011) 4 *Irish Journal of Family Law* 98–108.

60 Schwab, W., 'Collaborative Lawyering: A Closer Look at an Emerging Practice' (2004) 4 *Pepperdine Dispute Resolution Law Journal* 351–399. Schwab notes that lawyers will have to meet each again on other cases, 361.

61 Felsteiner, W., Abel, R., and Sarat, A.,'The Emergence and Transformation of Disputes: Naming, Blaming, Claiming…' (1980–1981) 15 (3–4) *Law and Society* at 631–654.

62 Tesler, P., and Thompson, P., *Collaborative Divorce: The Revolutionary New Way to Restructure your Family, Resolve Legal Issues, and Move on with Your Life* (Harper Collins, 2007) at 91.

63 King, M., 'Should problem-solving courts be solution-focused courts?' (2011) Monash University Research Paper, Victoria quoted in Babb, B., and Wexler, D. 'Therapeutic Jurisprudence', University of Baltimore Legal Studies Research Paper – Paper No 2014–13 at 3.

64 Ver Steegh, N., 'The Uniform Collaborative Law Act and Intimate Partner Violence: A Roadmap for Collaborative (and Non Collaborative) Lawyers' (2009) 38 *Hofstra Law Review* 699–755, 704.

65 Lande, J., 'The Promise and Perils of Collaborative Law' (2005–2006) 12 *Dispute Resolution Magazine* 30.

66 Schwab, W., 'Collaborative Lawyering: A Closer Look at an Emerging Practice' (2004) 4 *Pepperdine Dispute Resolution Law Journal* 351–399, 359. When settlement negotiations reach an impasse in positional negotiation, clients consider their best alternative to a negotiated settlement. If this is not settled, are they happy to proceed to court or is there any other credible option for settlement? Schwab argues that removing court as an option reduces clients' best alternatives when an impasse is reached.

67 Issacs, J., 'A New Way to Avoid the Courtroom: The Ethical Implications Surrounding Collaborative Law' (2004–2005) 18 *Georgetown Journal of Legal Ethics* 833–842, 838.

68 Schwab, W., 'Collaborative Lawyering: A Closer Look at an Emerging Practice' (2004) 4 *Pepperdine Dispute Resolution Law Journal* 351–399. Schwab's research indicated that while 35% of practitioners said it was 'very significant', 54.5% of the clients surveyed during the same research said that it had not kept them at the table.

69 Macfarlane, J., *The Emerging Phenomenon of Collaborative Family Law (CFL): A Qualitative Case Study* (Department of Justice Canada, 2005) at 39.

70 Gillers, S., 'How to Make Rules for Lawyers: The Professional Responsibility of the Legal Profession' (2013) 40 *Pepperdine Law Review* 365–422, 377.

71 Article 6 of the European Convention on Human Rights.

72 Prefatory Note to the Uniform Collaborative Law Act at 23. Available at http://www.uniformlaws.org/shared/docs/collaborative_law/uclranducla_amendments_jul10.pdf. Last accessed 12 July 2016.

73 Greco, A., 'Professional Fees Associated with Collaborative Divorce Resolution: The Evidence to Date' (2006) 12 (3) *Journal of Legal Economics* 75–88, 81.

74 Greco, A., 'Professional Fees Associated with Collaborative Divorce Resolution: The Evidence to Date' (2006) 12 (3) *Journal of Legal Economics* 75–88. See also Chapters 4 and 5 – findings from international research.

75 Tesler, P., *Collaborative Law: Achieving Effective Resolution in Divorce without Litigation* (2nd edn, American Bar Association, 2008) at 252 (emphasis added).

76 Spain, L.R., 'Collaborative Law: A Critical Reflection on Whether a Collaborative Orientation can be Ethically Incorporated into the Practice of Law' (2004) 56 (1) *Baylor Law Review* 141–173, 153.

77 Tesler, P., *Collaborative Law: Achieving Effective Resolution in Divorce without Litigation* (2nd edn, American Bar Association, 2008) at 136.

78 Tesler, P., *Collaborative Law: Achieving Effective Resolution in Divorce without Litigation* (2nd edn, American Bar Association, 2008) at 228.

79 Lande, J., 'Principles for Policymaking About Collaborative Law and Other ADR Processes' (2006–2007) 22 *Ohio State Journal on Dispute Resolution* 619–706, 646.
80 Also known as 'contact' in some jurisdictions.
81 Cameron, N., *Collaborative Practice, Deepening the Dialogue* (The Continuing Legal Education Society of British Columbia, 2004) at 152.
82 Hazard, G., 'Rules of Ethics: The Drafting Task' (1981) 36 *Record of the Association of the Bar of the City of New York* 77–97, 93.
83 See Chapters 4 and 5.
84 Tesler, P., *Collaborative Law: Achieving Effective Resolution in Divorce without Litigation* (2nd edn, American Bar Association, 2008) at 249 (emphasis added).
85 Menkel-Meadow, C., 'Ethics in Alternative Dispute Resolution: New Issues, No Answers from the Adversary Conception of Lawyers' Responsibilities,' (1997) 38 *South Texas Law Review* 407–454, 423.
86 Simon, W., *The Practice of Justice* (Harvard University Press, 1988).
87 Peppet, S., 'Lawyers' Bargaining Ethics, Contract, and Collaboration: The End of the Legal Profession and the Beginning of Professional Pluralism' (2004–2005) 90 *Iowa Law Review* 475–538, 479.
88 Simon, W., *The Practice of Justice* (Harvard University Press, 1988) at 8.
89 Lande, J., 'Principles for Policymaking About Collaborative Law and Other ADR Processes' (2006–2007) 22 *Ohio State Journal of Dispute Resolution* 619–706, 646.
90 Wetlaufer, G., 'The Ethics of Lying in Negotiations' (1990) 75 *Iowa Law Review* 1219–1273, 1234–35.
91 Peppet, S., 'The Ethics of Collaborative Law' (2008) *Journal of Dispute Resolution* 131–161, 157.
92 Tesler, P., *Collaborative Law: Achieving Effective Resolution in Divorce without Litigation* (2nd edn, American Bar Association 2008) at 250.
93 Schneyer, T., 'The Organized Bar and the Collaborative Law Movement: A Study in Professional Change' (2008) 50 *Arizona Law Review* 289–336, 297.
94 Peppet, S., 'Lawyers' Bargaining Ethics, Contract, and Collaboration: The End of the Legal Profession and the Beginning of Professional Pluralism' (2004–2005) 90 *Iowa Law Review* 475–538, 479.
95 Tesler, P., *Collaborative Law: Achieving Effective Resolution in Divorce without Litigation* (2nd edn, American Bar Association, 2008) at 24.
96 Ibid. at 5.
97 Ibid.
98 Macfarlane, J., *The Emerging Phenomenon of Collaborative Family Law (CFL): A Qualitative Case Study* (Department of Justice Canada, 2005) at 39.
99 Tesler, P., *Collaborative Law: Achieving Effective Resolution in Divorce without Litigation* (2nd edn, American Bar Association, 2008) at 24.
100 Ibid.
101 These issues will be addressed again in Chapter 5, in presenting the results of the research undertaken internationally. See also Shields, R.W., 'On Becoming a Collaborative Professional: From Paradigm Shifting to Transformative Learning through Critical Reflection and Dialogue' (2008) *Journal of Dispute Resolution* 427–463. Shields too notes that many lawyers are cautious and 'remain in their post-leaming contexts, unable or unwilling to move along the transformative learning cycle' 459.
102 Cameron, N., *Collaborative Practice, Deepening the Dialogue* (The Continuing Legal Education Society of British Columbia, 2004) at 51.
103 See Chapters 4 and 5 detailing the results of international research.
104 *Roche v Roche* [2010] 2 ILRM 1 24. This case involved an application to the court by a mother who sought the court's approval to allow her to use frozen embryos against her ex-husband's wishes.
105 Ibid. at 24.
106 Yuval Berger, Psychotherapist, Divorce Coach.

107 Berger, Y., 'Relationship Transformation, in Search of a "Roadmap" for Separating Couples', Workshop given at the Third European Conference on Collaboration entitled 'Challenging Conflict', Bad Aibling, 11 June 2010.
108 Mayer, B., *The Dynamics of Conflict Resolution* (Jossey-Bass, 2000) at 10.
109 Tesler refers to this as the 'shadow client'. A client consumed with the emotion of divorce may not be in a position to give proper instructions and must be given time to return to themselves.
110 Roussos, P., 'It is Therapy' (2002) *The Collaborative Review, Journal of the International Academy of Collaborative Professionals* 5.
111 Gamache, S., 'The Role of the Child Specialist' in Cameron, N., (ed.), *Collaborative Practice, Deepening the Dialogue* (The Continuing Legal Education Society of British Columbia, 2004) 189–213, 190.
112 Interview with CL 5, May 2011.
113 Interview with CL 6, May 2011.
114 Daigle, C., 'The Neutral Financial Professional: A Unique Opportunity, a Singular Responsibility' (2005) 7 (1) *The Collaborative Review* 11–15, 12.
115 Gardner Brown, D., 'The Role of the Financial Specialist' in Cameron, N., (ed.), *Collaborative Practice, Deepening the Dialogue* (The Continuing Legal Education Society of British Columbia, 2004) 223–232, 224.
116 Ibid. at 223.
117 Interview with CL3, April 2011.
118 'Research Regarding Client Experience' by The International Academy of Collaborative Professionals. Available at www.collaborativepractice.com. Last accessed 12 July 2016.
119 This was evident in the analysis of interviews carried out with young adults, as part of a wider research project. The young adults recalled being drawn into the financial battles that took place between their parents and have clear memories of being worried about whether they were going to have enough money to survive.
120 Gamache, S., 'The Role of the Child Specialist', in Cameron, N., (ed.), *Collaborative Practice, Deepening the Dialogue* (The Continuing Legal Education Society of British Columbia, 2004) 189–212 at 194.
121 Tesler, P., and Thompson, P., *Collaborative Divorce: The Revolutionary New Way to Restructure your Family, Resolve Legal Issues and Move on with your Life* (Harper Collins, 2007) at 48.
122 Gamache, S.,'The Role of the Child Specialist' in Cameron, N., (ed.), *Collaborative Practice, Deepening the Dialogue* (The Continuing Legal Education Society of British Columbia, 2004) at 213.
123 Ibid. at 218.
124 Professor Wolke, Child Specialist Workshop given at the Third European Conference on Collaboration entitled 'Challenging Conflict', Bad Aibling, 11 June 2010.
125 Gamache, S., 'Collaborative Practice: A New Opportunity to Address Children's Best Interest in Divorce' (2005) 65 (4) *Louisiana Law Review* 1455–1485, 1484.
126 Sefton, M., *Collaborative Family Law: A Report for Resolution*, Association of Family Lawyers in the UK at 49 (emphasis added).
127 Healy, C., 'The Child Specialist' (2012) *The Collaborative Review* 22–24, 23.
128 See, for example, Kelly, J.B., 'The Determination of Child Custody, The Future of Children' (1994) 4 (1) *Children and Divorce* 130.
129 The difficulties for these 'adult children' were addressed by child specialists Bell and Behram at a workshop held during the IACP annual forum in Washington, D.C., October 2010.
130 Ibid.
131 Tesler, P., and Thompson, P., *Collaborative Divorce: The Revolutionary New Way to Restructure your Family, Resolve Legal Issues, and Move on with Your Life* (Harper Collins, 2007) at 8.

132 Some practice groups also include mental health, financial and child specialists.

133 Shields, R.W., 'On Becoming a Collaborative Professional: From Paradigm Shifting to Transformative Learning Through Critical Reflection and Dialogue' (2008) *Journal of Dispute Resolution* 427–463. Shields carried out a study on training as a collaborative lawyer. He notes that for a full transformation, practitioners need both reflection and dialogue. Being part of a practice group gives this focus.

3 The advent of the Uniform Collaborative Law Rules/Act 2010 and the ripple effect

Introduction

The Uniform Collaborative Law Act was adopted by the Uniform Law Commission in 2009. It was amended in 2010 such that the final Act is now referred to as The Uniform Collaborative Law Rules/Act 2010 (UCLA). To date the Act has been adopted in 14 States across the US.[1] In addition, it has been used as a model of best practice internationally. This chapter will chart the issues that arose in bringing the Act to fruition. It will outline the key provisions of the Act, specifying the requirements it imposes on clients and lawyers wishing to engage in the collaborative law process. It will then examine the core procedural requirements and explore how the Act addresses: obtaining informed consent; screening; the disqualification provision and safeguards for low-income clients. In addition, it will consider issues surrounding: discovery, ethical concerns and the extent to which confidentiality and privilege apply to matters discussed during the process or documents arising therefrom. Finally, this chapter will explore the impact of the Act on the recommendations made by the Irish Law Reform Commission (LRC) when considering the development of collaborative practice in Ireland.

The impetus for an Act

Arguments have been made for and against the idea of regulating or imposing rules on ADR processes. Fairman, for example, has argued for a new ethical rule for collaborative practice.[2] Others, such as Menkel-Meadow believe that regulation is contrary to the purpose of these processes, namely 'to release us from some if not all of the limitations and rigidities of law as a formal legal institution'.[3] She argues against developing what she terms a 'common law' or 'jurisprudence' of ADR.[4] As the collaborative process developed, however, the International Academy of Collaborative Professionals (IACP)[5] was aware (as noted in Chapter 2) that participation agreements varied 'substantially in depth and detail'.[6] Clarity was required in respect of the essential requirements of the process, to ensure protection both for the clients and their lawyers.

The Uniform Law Commission, consisting of legislators, academics, lawyers and judges from across the US, was established over a century ago.[7] Its aim is to identify and address areas of law that would benefit from a unified approach across the United States. The IACP decided to take a proposal for a Uniform Collaborative Law Act to the Commission. The members of the IACP who were directly involved have described the drafting of the Act both as a 'teaching' and 'learning' process.[8] Teaching, in that they were presenting the concept of collaborative practice to a board of Uniform Law Commissioners, most of whom had never heard of the process before and therefore had to be educated as to how the process operated. Learning, in that by doing this, members of the IACP gained valuable insight as to how lawyers outside of the somewhat close-knit collaborative community viewed the process. Addressing the views and concerns raised by the Commissioners, and their critique of the process, enabled an objective examination of both the process itself and the draft legislation.

A number of fundamental issues arose for consideration. In drafting a Uniform Act, the role of the Commission is to provide a framework of rules and procedures that is consistent across states while remaining cognizant of the need for flexibility to reflect the diverse approaches and legislative requirements in individual states. The Act, therefore, has been drafted in a manner which allows states to adopt the provisions either as an Act or alternatively as a system of 'Rules'. In addition, states also have the option of enacting the legislation or rules under:

- *Option A* – which restricts the use of the process to family law matters, or,
- *Option B* – which permits the use of the collaborative process in any type of dispute.

The decision to include these two options arose mainly because, to date, collaborative practice has been most commonly used to resolve family law issues. It has not been embraced by the wider civil law community, arguably due to the implications of the disqualification provision. For lawyers, dealing with a specific family law matter is often, by its nature, a once-off event. Therefore if the lawyer is disqualified, he or she loses one client, one case. In the wider civil law field where a lawyer may act for a client in a number of related commercial issues, failing to reach settlement within the process may impact on the lawyer's or his or her law firm's authority to act in a number of cases. Although one of the issues addressed under the Act is the importance of clearly identifying the subject matter of the dispute,[9] it was decided that states also be given the additional safeguard of being able to choose whether to restrict the use of collaborative practice to family law matters or to take a more wide-ranging approach.

The Uniform Collaborative Law Act

The philosophy of the Uniform Collaborative Law Rules/Act (hereinafter referred to as the Act), as set out in the Prefatory Note is:

> to set a standard minimum floor for collaborative law participation agreements to inform and protect prospective parties and make a collaborative law process easier to administer. Beyond minimum requirements, however, the

> act leaves the collaborative law process to agreement between parties and collaborative lawyers.[10]

Therefore, the Act strives to strike a balance between protecting the parties involved through ensuring a degree of uniformity of practice and incorporating safeguards within the process, and, at the same time, allowing separating parties freedom to structure the process as they feel meets their needs in each particular case.

This chapter will begin by examining the key provisions of the Act that are of relevance *prior* to engaging in the process, namely, informed consent and screening. It will then address the *procedural aspects* of the process: the participation agreement, discovery, confidentiality and privilege and the disqualification clause. Finally, the chapter will examine the wider implications of the Act – using Ireland as a case study, as this will inform and complement the results of the research presented in Chapter 5.

Prior to engaging in the process

Informed consent

The issue of informed consent and what it entails for clients considering the process has already been discussed in Chapter 2. Ensuring that clients are fully informed of the risks and benefits of the collaborative process and, indeed, all other methods of resolving the issues at dispute forms the basis of Section 14 of the Act. The Prefatory Note to the Act states that:

> [t]he act thus envisions the lawyer as an educator of a prospective party about the appropriate factors to consider *in deciding whether to participate in a collaborative law process.* It also contemplates a process of discussion between lawyer and prospective party that asks that the lawyer do more than lecture a prospective party or provide written information about collaborative law *and other options.*[11]

Section 14, entitled 'Appropriateness of Collaborative Law Process' imposes a statutory obligation on lawyers to 'assess with the prospective party factors the *lawyer reasonably* believes relate to whether the collaborative law process is appropriate for the prospective party's matter'[12] and to provide them with information setting out the risks and benefits of this process and all other methods of dispute resolution.[13] Lawyers are also required to advise clients that the process is voluntary; prospective parties cannot be compelled by a court to enter the process and may leave at any point 'with or without cause'.[14] Although the duty to ensure informed consent is subjective in that the lawyers must address factors that *they reasonably believe* are important, many members of the IACP's UCLA committee objected to this provision, arguing that there was no need for the issue of informed consent to be imposed upon lawyers by statute; this was already part of their ethical obligations in representing a client in every case. However, the Uniform Law Commissioners remained steadfast in their view that the limited nature of the representation required a statutory provision on informed consent. The Act therefore seeks to address the perceived dangers associated with clients entering into the process unwittingly and without giving due consideration to its suitability for their particular case. Making informed consent a statutory requirement also, arguably, heightens lawyers' awareness of the importance of their role in the transformation of disputes, as discussed in Chapter 1.

In jurisdictions where divorce is granted on a 'no-fault' basis, the issue of informed consent is relatively straightforward. However, where clients may elect between opting for 'fault divorce' or 'no-fault' divorce, collaborative lawyers' duty with regard to informed consent becomes more onerous. It is imperative that clients understand that by engaging in the collaborative process they are choosing not to pursue 'fault based'[15] claims. Tesler notes that disclosures made during the process 'could affect the viability of such claims should the collaborative process terminate'.[16] The risks associated with advising clients in these types of cases may deter some lawyers from recommending the process. An additional factor that may cause difficulty, is the issue of the applicable law in the event that the separating parties live in different jurisdictions. Certain jurisdictions tend to provide better outcomes for women at a time of divorce, and this can lead to proceedings being issued as matter of urgency in order to gain priority. Arguably, however, if these issues cannot be agreed, then the parties may not be suitable candidates for the process in any event. Encouraging clients to engage in less adversarial means is laudable in many cases but not if the parties do not have the capacity to negotiate or are not committed to finding the best settlement outside of the courts' process. The next important issue therefore is assessing capacity through screening.

Screening

Screening for capacity under the UCLA focuses mainly on establishing whether there is any history of violence or of an abusive relationship which would lead to potential inequality of bargaining power within the process or the fear of intimidation. Section 15 of the Act places a statutory obligation on lawyers to make 'reasonable inquiry' into whether the prospective party has a history of a 'coercive or violent relationship'. The lawyer must continuously assess this throughout the case. In discussing what constitutes domestic violence, it was decided that the term 'coercive or violent relationship' would 'encapsulate the core characteristics of a relationship characterized by domestic violence' as defined by the American Bar Association's Committee on Domestic Violence namely:

> [p]hysical abuse, alone or in combination with sexual, economic or emotional abuse, stalking or other forms of coercive control, by an intimate partner or household member, often for the purpose of establishing and maintaining power and control over the victim.[17]

The approach taken to defining a coercive relationship in the Act is therefore much broader than physical violence alone, focusing also on the actions of the perpetrator and their pattern or practice of intimidation.[18]

In assisting collaborative practitioners with their screening obligations, the IACP has also developed a 'Relationship Questionnaire' which it recommends completing with prospective clients. If issues arise during the initial assessment or the questionnaire, the IACP recommends that a prospective party should be referred to a mental health professional for further assessment before proceeding with the case. Under Section 15 (c) (1) and (2) of the Act, if the lawyer believes that the parties *have* a history of a 'coercive or violent relationship' then the process may only begin if two further conditions are satisfied. Firstly, the prospective party,[19] having been fully informed about the process, requests it; and secondly, the collaborative lawyer believes that the safety of the party can be protected during the process.

It is also important for the lawyer to feel competent to deal with what may be a high-conflict case.[20] The danger of collaborative lawyers opening an issue for discussion and not having the tools or training to deal with what may be revealed has been highlighted as one of the possible dangers for separating parties engaging in the process.[21] The comprehensive law movement or taking an approach that encourages a therapeutic approach to justice, necessitates lawyers developing new skills.[22] Ver Steegh, for example, has commented that '[t]he lack of required intimate partner violence training for collaborative lawyers presents a major roadblock for implementation of the Act'.[23] Lawyers need to be aware when they are out of their depth and should engage appropriately qualified professionals to assist.[24]

The Act is silent on the issue of training for lawyers with regard to screening for domestic violence. The Prefatory Note indicates that no requirements were set 'for fear of inflexibility, of regulating a still-developing dispute resolution process.'[25] Concerns were also raised that imposing training requirements by statute would result in an interference with the separation of powers in some States. Specific training for lawyers should, at a minimum, encompass an understanding of power imbalance and the ability to recognise what may often be attempts by either party to deny the existence of domestic violence. It is notable, however, that there are also no training requirements imposed on trial lawyers dealing with issues of domestic violence, in what may conceivably be a much more volatile court setting. In this regard, Ver Steegh concedes that the UCLA 'breaks new ground by creating statutory obligations with respect to intimate partner violence'[26] and by 'offering a thoughtful guide for practice, … is likely to serve as a model for future legislation in other areas of family law.'[27]

An order from the court is the most frequently sought remedy when instances of domestic violence occur. This necessitates being involved in the criminal justice system, which may be difficult for the victim to cope with. Such an order, in any event, while it may solve the immediate problem, will not generally be effective in addressing the underlying issues. A holistic approach, which focuses not only on the needs of the victim but also on the root cause of this violence for the perpetrator, would be the 'ideal' model. While such an approach is admirable, it may not always be feasible. The parties themselves may not wish to engage. Additionally, the costs involved in a multidisciplinary approach may be a deterrent or, in some locations, the availability of appropriate expertise may cause difficulties.

The Act does not deal with issues of capacity other than as set out in Section 15. The legislators were of the view that assessing capacity in general terms is something that lawyers do in every case. Factors like the client's ability to understand the process and the commitment required to engage are of key importance both for the clients in making informed decisions and for the lawyers in deciding whether cases are suitable for the collaborative process. Considering whether a limited representation scope agreement is 'reasonable' may dictate the need for these issues to be considered in the context of ensuring 'informed consent'. However, as with issues of domestic violence, capacity may not always be easy to determine at the outset.

Screening is equally important from a lawyer's perspective. Effective screening can be the key to assessing whether settlement will be reached within the process. This highlights the importance of lawyers being able to rely on their colleagues to screen clients appropriately; it is not in lawyers' interests to take a case in which they may be disqualified.[28] The corollary of this, of course, is that prospective parties should also be discerning in their choice of lawyers. Regardless of the statutory obligations imposed, each lawyer will have a slightly different approach. Certain personalities may not work well together. In a situation in which a client is working closely with the lawyer in negotiating settlement, it is imperative that a relationship of trust exists. The research confirms that many prospective parties are meeting with several collaborative lawyers before choosing one they feel they can work best with.[29]

Engaging in the process – core procedural provisions under the Act

The Act, as finally enacted, is quite short. It sets out the core requirements for the process and clearly defines issues such as what is meant by a collaborative law communication (relevant when examining what is covered under privilege and confidentiality); the parties; non-party participants; collaborative lawyers; and what constitutes a law firm. The 'Collaborative Law Process' is defined as:

> (3) … a procedure intended to resolve a collaborative matter without intervention by a tribunal in which persons:
>
> (A) sign a collaborative law participation agreement; and
> (B) are represented by collaborative lawyers.

Section 4 (a) sets out the requirements for a valid collaborative law participation agreement under the Act, specifying that it must:

1 be in a record;
2 be signed by the parties;

3 state the parties' intention to resolve a collaborative matter through a collaborative law process under this [act];
4 describe the nature and scope of the matter;
5 identify the collaborative lawyer who represents each party in the process; and
6 contain a statement by each collaborative lawyer confirming the lawyer's representation of a party in the collaborative law process.

Setting out the requirements for a collaborative case sought to put an end to lawyers describing the process that they were providing to their clients as 'collaborative law', yet, failing to adhere to the spirit of the process by not signing a participation agreement, leaving the door open to resort to the courts' system if negotiations within the process were not successful.

Of particular note is the requirement for collaborative lawyers to be 'identified' and to 'confirm their representation'. This change of approach from early versions of the process in which collaborative lawyers signed the participation agreement as parties to the agreement arose for two main reasons. As noted in Chapter 2, the recommendation of Professor Sher[30] that '"best practice" [dictates] … that lawyers not sign the PA [participation agreement] as parties to the Agreement but rather to confirm their representation of the parties in the PA.'[31] This, the Prefatory Note to the Act, explains is to avoid situations where:

> the language and structure of a participation agreement may cause a lawyer who signs it to assume duties to another party to the agreement – a person with conflicting interests other than his or her client – a result that could raise ethics concerns.[32]

Secondly, 'identifying' the lawyers addresses the concerns raised by the Colorado Bar Association Ethics Opinion.[33] Debating this issue and exploring the consequences of lawyers becoming subject to contractual and ethical obligations to clients within the process was a valuable learning process for collaborative lawyers and highlights the importance of the Act as a model of best practice. Collaborative lawyers worldwide would be prudent to review the terms of their participation agreements in the light of this provision.

The voluntary nature of the collaborative process is provided for in the Act;[34] a court may not order parties to participate in a collaborative process and any party may terminate the process at any time 'with or without cause'.[35] The flexibility of the process is again highlighted. Section 4 (b) acknowledges that the participation agreement may include such additional provisions considered to be of particular importance to the parties, provided these matters are not inconsistent with the Act.

Setting out what signifies the beginning and the end of the process, though arguably self-evident in most cases, ensures that parameters are in place for cases in which there is any uncertainty.[36] This is particularly important in the context of the limited nature of the representation. Uncertainty has also been addressed by the definition of what constitutes a collaborative law communication, namely a 'statement whether oral, or in a record, or verbal or non-verbal.'[37] The Act in providing statutory privilege for such communications, under Section 17,[38] gives parties an assurance that, subject to specific limitations,[39] issues discussed or documents created during the process will not be admissible in court proceedings, nor will they be discoverable.

If, during the process, either party unilaterally decides to serve proceedings or to take any action that would bring the matter before the court, the process is considered terminated.[40] In addition, Section 5 (e) provides that the process shall also terminate if a party discharges a collaborative law practitioner or the practitioner withdraws from representation of the party. This may occur if differences have arisen between the party and his or her lawyer. Collaborative lawyers must also withdraw if the client is not complying with the 'good faith' ethos of the process by, for example, failing to provide voluntary discovery or seeking to subvert the process in some way.[41] Leeway is provided, however, in that, notwithstanding the discharge or withdrawal of a collaborative lawyer, the process itself may continue if the party or parties engage a successive collaborative lawyer or lawyers within a period of 30 days.[42] The parties may simply amend the participation agreement to reflect the appointment of the new lawyer and the process continues. Therefore, difficulties encountered within the process do not necessarily mean that court proceedings must follow. Arguably, changing a lawyer or lawyers could possibly change the dynamics of the process. This may also serve to heighten the parties' awareness of the implications of failure to settle; leading them to be more focused. This is a matter for consideration by the parties, one which they should be advised of at the outset as part of ensuring informed consent. As will be demonstrated in Chapters 4 and 5, research indicates that there have been occasions in which clients felt that their lawyer's attitude or lack of management within the process may have, at a minimum, contributed to, or possibly caused, the process to conclude. The option to change lawyers is therefore an important safeguard.

In cases in which parties have issued proceedings and then decide that they wish to resolve issues in a more conciliatory way, Section 6 provides that the parties may file a notice with the court indicating their agreement to engage in the collaborative process, and 'the filing operates as a stay of the proceedings'. The court may request periodic status reports during the collaborative process. These reports will only advise as to the stage of the process and not the details of what has taken place. Some states may implement the Act in such a way that this stay is mandatory; others may leave the matter to the discretion of the court.

Discovery of documents and the duty to act in good faith

Section 12 of the Act addresses the issue of discovery.[43] As the collaborative process focuses on the issues of good faith and honesty, the Act unsurprisingly provides that parties shall make:

> timely, full, candid, and informal disclosure of information related to the collaborative matter without formal discovery.[44]

Importantly, it also includes a provision that parties shall 'update promptly previously disclosed information that has materially changed'. The Act, however, permits the parties to 'define the scope of disclosure during the collaborative law process.' For example, it does not specify the position with regard to non-party participants or their reports.[45] This is something that is often agreed by the parties at the outset. They may agree to the continued use of independent reports (with the consent of the expert in question) in any subsequent litigation, thus saving costs.

As noted in Chapter 2, concerns have arisen, however, about how certain one can be that the *ethos* of the process will be adhered to. This effectively comes back to the issue of screening. Some reassurance may be gleaned from Macfarlane's conclusion that there was no evidence that vulnerable parties did less well in the process.[46] If a party is determined to hide assets, he or she will find a way to do this, even when court orders may be in place. Prospective parties will possibly be the best judge of whether their ex-partner can be trusted.

Again, as noted in Chapter 2, another issue is the extent to which information needs to be provided that would not normally be discoverable in a court setting. This may include matters such as an ex-partner's future work plans, or, something perhaps more difficult for parties to appreciate, the expectation that they will also be forthcoming about new relationships or other issues of a more private nature that would not normally be discussed. Questions arise also as to how much of this information is 'necessary' and how much may be an invasion of privacy. Care must be taken to ensure that this provision is not abused by one party perhaps refusing to progress without information that may not relevant. This again raises the importance of ensuring that the client understands this when giving their informed consent to engage in the process at the outset and that lawyers continue to manage the process throughout.

The disqualification clause

Section 4, as noted above, sets out the requirements for a participation agreement. While it mentions the issue of withdrawal, the Act does not include the disqualification provision as one of the key statutory requirements of a participation agreement. Instead, the disqualification provision is provided for under Section 9 of the Act, as is 'imputed disqualification'.[47] The disqualification provision itself and the additional restriction on lawyers within a particular firm from taking over a case that has not been resolved through the process, were, in Webb's view, essential to ensure that lawyers remained committed to attempting to reach settlement. The Act, however, provides some safeguards in relation to 'imputed disqualification'.

Firstly, it specifies the importance of defining what was meant by a related collaborative matter as including the:

> same parties, transaction or occurrence, nucleus of operative fact, dispute, claim, or issue as the collaborative matter.[48]

This addresses any concerns that lawyers may have had about matters being viewed too broadly and restricting their ability to act for a client. Nothing prevents lawyers within a firm acting for that client in future provided it is not acting on the same legal issue. Section 8 of the Act, further confirms that taking a settlement before the court, with the consent of all parties, to seek approval of the settlement does not terminate the process.[49] A collaborative lawyer is also permitted to attend court, in an emergency situation, to bring or defend any application that may be necessary, should, for example, there be any issues of domestic abuse or if one of the parties tries to dissipate assets and no other lawyer is available to deal with this matter. Action may also be taken where there is a risk of reputational damage.[50]

Further safeguards in relation to the 'imputed disqualification' of lawyers were enacted for two particular categories of cases: the first, in respect of low-income clients[51] and the second, in a situation where one of the parties is a government entity.[52] In both of these situations another lawyer within the law firm or government department may act for that party in that matter or a related matter provided the original collaborative lawyer is isolated from the case. These exceptions were included to ease the financial burden for a low income client who may not, perhaps, be able to obtain representation other than through that particular firm and should not be left without representation. With regard to government departments, it was felt that the tax payers should not have to pay for outside representation if there were other lawyers available within the organisation who could take the case over. In both cases, it must be clearly identified in the participation agreement, that this is a case to which such exception will apply.

Ethics

The issue of ethics during the collaborative law process has been much written about, with as noted earlier, quite diverse views being expressed; some commentators believe that a new ethical rule is required[53] while others, including nine State Bar Associations and the ABA, are of the view that collaborative practice does not violate the model rules of professional conduct. Section 13 simply provides that nothing in the Act alters the professional obligations and responsibilities that lawyers would already be subject to by reason of being licensed to practise law. This section also confirms that both the lawyers and any other professionals involved in the collaborative process are still under obligation to report any issues of 'abuse or neglect, abandonment, or exploitation of a child or adult under the law of this state'.[54]

A concern, somewhat ignored in the literature and Bar ethics opinions is the potential of one party to use the disqualification provision to effectively 'fire' the other party's lawyer and the cost implications that may arise as result. This was referred to in the opinion issued by the New Jersey Bar.[55] It noted that 'the client's continuing relationship with the lawyer is at the discretion of the opposing spouse' and that this could bring 'considerable hardship upon a client, who would then be required to retain new counsel to take up the case from scratch.' The New Jersey Bar took the view, however, that 'it is more accurate to analyze this condition as a limitation on the scope of representation, rather than as a withdrawal under RPC 1.16.'[56] Although the opinion refers to the parties being held 'captives' to a process that does not fulfil their needs, they concluded that this was a limited scope representation and did not violate the rules of professional conduct provided the lawyer felt the process was 'reasonable' for the parties and they had given their 'informed consent'. The risk of abuse of the process in this way cannot be denied. Clients may have expended significant time and money and have built up a relationship with their lawyer such that the lawyer, being disqualified by the actions of the *other* party, is a notable concern. Within the adversarial system similar issues have arisen with separating parties seeking consultations with family lawyers *prior* to issuing proceedings, simply to ensure that, should their ex-partner seek to instruct this lawyer, they will be unable to do so because of the conflict of interest. The difference is, however, that termination of the collaborative process by one party may result in the other party's lawyer being disqualified *at any point*, right up to the conclusion of the case. From examining the research on the collaborative process which has been undertaken internationally to date, there does not appear to be any documented evidence that this has occurred in practice. Nevertheless, it remains a real concern. Parties who are considering the collaborative process need to be aware of this risk. There needs to be a certain level of trust between the separating parties and they need to be in a financial position to be able to litigate, if settlement cannot be achieved.

Confidentiality and privilege

Confidentiality is dealt with under Section 16 of the Act. It provides that all communications made during the collaborative process are confidential, save as otherwise agreed between the parties. Section 17 of the Act, deals with the issue of privilege, prohibiting the disclosure of collaborative communications in any subsequent proceedings. This is a very important section of the Act as privilege needs to be provided for by statute. Lawyers and clients will also maintain their lawyer-client privilege. This privilege is for the benefit of the client; if the client decides to waive the privilege, he or she may do so even over a lawyer's objection. Non-party participants, e.g. experts employed as part of the process, however, retain their rights to privilege over their expert reports under the Act. Any party wishing to use the experts' reports in subsequent litigation will need to have all-party approval and the approval of the experts as well.

Exceptions to Section 17 are set out in Sections 18 and 19 of the Act. Section 18 provides that privilege does not extend to evidence or information that would otherwise have been discoverable outside of the collaborative case, for example, tax returns that were in existence prior to the collaborative process taking place. Additional protection is provided under Section 17 (c), which provides that if a court, after a hearing held *in camera* finds that the 'need for the evidence substantially outweighs the interests in protecting confidentiality',[57] then information may be disclosed. Under Section 19, privilege will not apply where there are any threats made to commit a crime or to engage in any criminal activity, abuse or abandonment of children or in cases whereby information is being used to prove or disprove claims of professional negligence.[58]

To date, the only significant case law on the issue of whether notes taken during the collaborative process can be used in court is that of *Banerjee v Bisset*.[59] The parties signed a participation agreement and attended one four-way meeting at which certain issues were discussed. Ms. Bisset terminated the process after the first four-way meeting. The plaintiff brought an action seeking a declaration that the agreement entered into at the four-way meeting was a binding agreement. In his action he sought to use notes taken, including his lawyer's notes, from the four-way meeting.

The court, having considered the matter, held that in signing the participation agreements:

> the parties agreed to have a confidential process; they agreed to forgo access to the court unless either or both of them withdrew from the collaborative law process; and they agreed that no agreements would be enforceable unless they were agreements in writing. They also, necessarily, agreed to forgo disclosing negotiations which stopped short of a written agreement for the purpose of trying to prove that an oral agreement was made and should be enforced. In other words, they agreed to a different set of rules than apply to normal litigation.[60]

It remains to be seen if courts in other jurisdictions will take the same approach.

The impact of the Uniform Collaborative Law Act – Ireland as a case study

In 2010, the Irish Law Reform Commission published a report on *Alternative Dispute Resolution: Conciliation and Mediation*.[61] The report provided a comprehensive overview of mediation, and conciliation and also examined collaborative practice and early neutral evaluation. The LRC noted the development of collaborative practice and described it as 'an emerging method of advisory dispute resolution', where 'the negotiation becomes client centred.'[62]

Collaborative practice has been available in Ireland since 2004. As has been the pattern in other jurisdictions, the development of the process has been led by lawyers who have undertaken collaborative training and who see it as a 'better way' of resolving conflict. Again, local practice groups play an important role in this development. The Association of Collaborative Practitioners (ACP) is the umbrella group for collaborative professionals in Ireland. Membership consists of approximately 450 trained collaborative lawyers, mental health professionals, referred to in Ireland as Personal and Family Consultants,[63] and financial experts. The ACP describes its aims as being to:

- promote Collaborative Practice as a mechanism for settling disputes
- support practitioners by providing documentation and ethical guidelines for the practice of collaboration.
- provide training and peer review structures for collaborative practitioners.[64]

Divorce within the Irish legal system

Ireland has a written Constitution that was enshrined in 1937 and an adversarial courts' system. The common law system inherited from England has meant that a two-stream legal system exists, comprised of solicitors, who meet directly with clients and are akin to attorneys in the US, and barristers who advocate in the higher courts.[65] Family law cases are heard *in camera*.[66] Webb has commented that the collaborative process is 'loosely analogous'[67] to the solicitor-barrister system in England (and Ireland); if agreement is not reached during the process, the case is handed over to trial attorneys. However, unlike the 'settlement attorneys' that Webb envisaged, solicitors within the adversarial process are not disqualified; they continue to act alongside the barristers until the completion of the case, thereby providing continuity for their clients. Although, this may prove equally, or arguably more expensive, it avoids the need for clients to begin again with new representation. Under this system, barristers normally draft the court proceedings. In many cases, this occurs before any settlement negotiations may have taken place. Solicitors, having ultimate control over the management of a case, tend to wait until they have exchanged Affidavits of Means[68] and/or have sought and obtained discovery before attempts are made to resolve issues.

Until 1996 under the Irish Constitution, marriage was for life. A limited form of legal separation was available was under the Judicial Separation and Family Law Reform Act 1989 (Judicial Separation Act). This released married couples from the obligation to live together but they remained spouses and could not remarry. The first referendum to amend the Constitution, in 1986, failed by a majority of two to one; divorce was introduced ten years later by the passing of a second referendum. The enabling legislation, the Family Law (Divorce) Act 1996 (the Divorce Act), came into force in February 1997.

The Divorce Act 1996 provides that couples have to have lived separate and apart for a period of four out of the previous five years to be eligible to apply for a divorce; thereafter a degree of divorce can be granted by the courts on a 'no-fault' basis, provided there is no 'reasonable prospect of reconciliation' and 'proper provision' has been made for the dependent spouse and any dependent children. This period of four years was to allow the couple sufficient time to attempt reconciliation.

Both the Judicial Separation Act and the Divorce Act include provisions that oblige lawyers to advise parties of the availability and benefits of reconciliation and mediation, and of the possibilities of negotiating settlement through a separation agreement or deed of separation.[69] A certificate must be filed with court proceedings to confirm that the client has been so advised.[70] This information is generally given to separating parties at their first consultation with a lawyer and may be the only information that many separating parties get on the possibility of using alternative methods of dispute resolution. Generally, something will have occurred that has brought the relationship breakdown to a head. As noted in Chapter 1, tensions may have been mounting over a period of time and it is arguable that the point at which separating parties decide to begin the dispute transformation process,[71] by 'naming' issues to a third party (lawyer), is not the best time for information on ADR. Additionally, research indicates that many solicitors give this advice merely to fulfil their statutory requirements. They may not do so with any sense of belief in the potential benefits of mediation. Separating parties may not get any further information on ADR processes. If no response is received to an initial letter sent to the ex-partner or their lawyer, proceedings may be issued as a matter of course. Unsurprisingly, therefore, statistics indicate that the numbers of separating parties opting for ADR has been low.[72] There is, at present, no statutory obligation on lawyers in Ireland to notify clients in relation to the availability of the collaborative process.

In seeking to address this issue, the LRC has recommended that:

> attendance at an information session on family dispute resolution processes including mediation, conciliation, and collaborative practice should, in general, be a statutory mandatory requirement in family law cases.[73]

The Commission proposes that parties should attend these information sessions either before or after an application has been made to court '*but not later than 28 days before the date on which the proceedings are first listed for hearing.*' Such mandatory information sessions would have the potential to educate clients about the role of mediation and collaborative practice, as well as the courts' process. The LRC is envisaging a system in which lawyers will be able to offer all methods of resolution as part of a 'menu of choices for clients'.[74] Exceptions would, of course, be in place for cases for which immediate court orders were required to protect the safety of parties. Alternative arrangements could be made to ensure that such parties would also attend separate mandatory information sessions. An anomaly arises, however, when one examines the LRC's view that:

> it is not appropriate to include the option of adjourning proceedings to allow parties to consider collaborative practice in primary legislation, or in the statutory Rules of Court, as it is a process which must occur *prior* to the commencement of proceedings …[75]

In permitting the parties leeway to attend the information meetings up until 'at least 28 days before the hearing' but not permitting court proceedings to be stayed to facilitate the use of the collaborative process, it is clear that if this recommendation is followed, many separating parties may not be provided with the option of using collaborative practice. This recommendation is also at odds with Section 6 of the UCLA. Section 6[76], as noted earlier, permits this flexibility and provides that the parties may indicate to the court their wish to try to resolve matters through the collaborative process and the courts will allow such application. While, as in every case, trust issues will have to be addressed in these situations, parties who realise the potential benefits of resolving their conflict in an amicable way should not be prevented from doing so, merely because court proceedings may have already been issued.

Training of collaborative lawyers in Ireland

As collaborative practice is a new and developing process in Ireland, the LRC notes the importance of training for lawyers; the importance of 'the paradigm shift'[77] required in thinking and that lawyers are aware of the ethical standards set down by the International Academy of Collaborative Professionals.[78] Critics of the process in Ireland, similarly to those in the US, argue that they settle most of their cases anyway. Lawyers in Ireland have also raised concerns about the 'efficiency' of the collaborative process. Davy, for example, comments that:

> [c]ollaborative practice cases are likely to be far more expensive and far more time consuming (*and also less profitable for solicitors*) than those cases which can be settled amicably and at an early stage in the context of the traditional approach.[79]

Taking a traditional positional approach to negotiations, as commented by Fisher and Ury, is easy.[80] The facts can be summarised quite quickly and a settlement reached once a case is listed for hearing. This does not generally involve a big time commitment from lawyers or structured, client-centred negotiations such as are necessary within the collaborative process.

The Commission, in examining the need for a Code of Practice for Collaborative Practitioners, acknowledged that lawyers practising in Ireland are already subject to the provisions of the Solicitors Acts 1954 to 2008[81] and to the Law Society of Ireland's *Guide to Professional Conduct of Solicitors in Ireland*.[82] This is in line with Section 13 of the Uniform Collaborative Law Act.[83] The Commission recommended a voluntary 'Code of Practice and Ethics',[84] referring to the 'Principles and Guidelines for Collaborative Law' as laid down by the Association of Collaborative Practitioners in the US as a 'useful template'.[85] The IACP has always been pro-active in developing and reviewing guidelines and ethical standards for collaborative practitioners.[86] These 'principles' address many of the issues legislated for under the Uniform Collaborative Law Act to include: issues of competence and the need, on occasion, for collaborative practitioners to seek assistance for their clients from other professionals; confidentiality; conflict of interest; the scope of the advocacy provided within the process and the importance of enabling clients to make an informed decision having been advised of all methods available to resolve their dispute. The standards provide that a collaborative practitioner:

> shall assist the client in establishing realistic expectations in the Collaborative process and shall respect the client's self-determination; understanding that ultimately the client(s) is/are responsible for making decisions that resolve their issues.[87]

Requirements in relation to disclosure are also addressed under the Code, as are the minimum elements of a participation agreement; the specific obligation to obtain consent to share information with other professionals if, and as, required, and the terms upon which the process may terminate or under which the parties may choose to withdraw. In addition, it specifies the ethical standards to apply to neutrals within the process, to the coaches and to the child specialists. While the Commission did not recommend that a Collaborative Law Act be enacted in Ireland, it refers extensively to the provisions of the Uniform Collaborative Law Act and urges that practitioners in Ireland use that as a guide.

The participation agreement

Examining the standard participation agreement recommended by the ACP in Ireland it is notable, firstly, that solicitors continue to sign as parties to the agreement. The agreement states that each solicitor represents his or her own client and that their 'legal duty of care extends only to their client.' All parties agree to be open and honest and to provide full disclosure, referring specifically to financial disclosure only. However, in noting the grounds upon which the process terminates, the agreement states that the solicitors shall withdraw in the event that either party has 'acted so as to undermine or take unfair advantage of the Collaborative Family Process,' and it lists failing to participate in the 'spirit' of the process as one of those grounds. Again, questions remain as to what is considered appropriate with regard to the 'spirit' of the process. Some guidance on this would be of benefit to the lawyers and to the clients. In view of the recommendations of Professor Sher, Irish collaborative lawyers may also be wise to consider signing the agreement merely to confirm their representation of their client rather than as actual parties to the agreement.

Disqualification

The Commission referred in the first instance to Section 9 of the Act, the disqualification provision, as set out earlier. The LRC also noted the position with regard to 'imputed disqualification'[88] but did not address the issue of exceptions to this rule as is the case under the Act.[89] Developing a code for collaborative practice in Ireland would necessitate addressing these issues. A collaborative lawyer should be permitted to attend court in an emergency situation, to bring or defend any application that may be necessary where there are issues of domestic abuse or the dissipation of assets. At present, the option to use collaborative practice is available to low-income parties through the Legal Aid system.[90] However, there does not appear to be a set policy as to what happens if the disqualification provision is invoked. Should another lawyer in that law centre be allowed to take over a case, provided the original lawyer is isolated from the matter, as is the position under the Act in the US? Exceptions such as these will have to be considered in developing a code for collaborative practice in Ireland, to ensure that all parties are adequately protected and where possible, to avoid any unnecessary costs.

Informed consent and screening

The Commission also stresses the importance of informed consent. The LRC considers Section 14 of the Act to be 'of extreme importance as it ensures that the fundamental principles of self-determination and voluntariness are protected'[91] and asserts that this should also form part of any voluntary code for collaborative practitioners in Ireland. Again, in accordance with the Act, the LRC notes that lawyers should inform prospective parties of the advantages and disadvantages of all the methods available for the resolution of the issues at dispute.

With regard to the issue of screening for suitability, the Commission has recommended that collaborative practitioners in Ireland address the issue of domestic violence in line with Section 15 of the Act; collaborative practitioners should ensure that 'screening takes place at intake and throughout the collaborative process'. The Commission, however, goes further than the Act by recommending that collaborative practitioners 'must be trained in this skill.'[92] Women's Aid, which deals with domestic violence issues in Ireland, has stated in this regard that it is:

> convinced that neither mediation nor collaborative law are appropriate in cases where domestic violence is present and that their use in these situations could put women at risk and further disadvantage them. This is due to the power imbalance between the parties and the fear and intimidation experienced by women subjected to domestic violence … Mediation and collaborative law are predicated on the parties having an equal relationship and being able and willing to cooperate with each other. However it is unrealistic to think that a perpetrator of violence would cooperate with his victim in an honest and open way, or that this process would be able to reverse what may have been years of dominance and control.[93]

While, at first glance, collaborative practice may seem like a safer model, in that the parties have their lawyers present during the process, the ramifications for the parties after they leave the meeting may be the same. Collaborative practitioners in the US envisage a model whereby both the victim and the perpetrator of domestic violence would have the assistance and guidance of mental health professionals throughout the process. As noted earlier, this would assist the parties to deal more constructively with the underlying issues between them, assisting both the victim and the perpetrator in a more complete way. It has to be acknowledged that taking these cases before the court is not always the best approach. In many cases it may serve to inflame the situation further, leading to higher risks for the parties involved, meanwhile not in any way attempting to 'reverse what may have been years of dominance and control'.[94]

This is contrary to the view taken in the US. The Act does not completely rule out the use of collaborative practice in situations in which there has been a history of domestic violence, but it takes the approach that 'reasonable inquiry' should be made and if, after discussions, the client, wishes to proceed, a collaborative practitioner may take the case, provided that practitioner believes that he or she can ensure the safety of the client.

Discovery

Examining the issue of disclosure or discovery, the practice recommended by the Association of Collaborative Practitioners (ACP) in Ireland is that an Affidavit of Means, setting out the parties' assets and liabilities, income and expenditure should be exchanged at the outset. These affidavits are exchanged on an 'open basis', which means that they may be used in any subsequent court proceedings. The parties are therefore aware that they may be questioned by the court in relation to the information provided. Should this be necessary if the parties were complying fully with the 'good faith' ethos of collaborative practice? Probably not. However, collaborative practitioners in Ireland have been proactive in ensuring that there are safeguards such that all parties' rights are protected. The option to engage a neutral financial specialist may override the need for long and arduous discovery documents, which are often produced during the course of a trial, many times with nothing to be gained other than increased legal costs.

Privilege

Without the benefit of a Collaborative Law Act, the ACP has sought to deal with the issue of privilege during the collaborative process through reliance on Section 9 of the Family Law (Divorce) Act 1996, which forms part of its approved participation agreement. Section 9 states:

> An oral or written communication between either of the spouses concerned and a third party for the purpose of seeking assistance to effect a reconciliation or to reach agreement between them on some or all of the terms of a separation or a divorce (whether or not made in the presence or with the knowledge of the other spouse), and any record of such a communication, made or caused to be made by either of the spouses concerned or such a third party, shall not be admissible as evidence in any court.[95]

This is less than satisfactory and is one of the key reasons why a Collaborative Law Act would have been an important development. Many of the issues that have arisen in the context of raising public confidence in ADR is the lack of regulation. While as noted earlier, regulation in ADR processes is a double-edged sword, in a jurisdiction like Ireland where the take-up on alternative processes has been low, having adequate regulation and safeguards in place may help to build public confidence in these processes.

The agreement also provides that the solicitor's representation of the client is limited to 'services within the Collaborative Law process' and that the parties agree not to call the lawyers 'to give evidence in Court, nor will they seek to have any of their notes brought into evidence'. To date, there has been no case to challenge this issue before the courts in Ireland. Therefore, it remains to be seen if the Irish courts would take the same view as that of the Supreme Court of British Columbia in *Banerjee v Bisset*[96] that the parties, by agreeing to engage in collaborative practice, had agreed to a different set of rules.

Ethical issues

The core values of the solicitors' profession in Ireland as set out in the *Guide to Good Professional Conduct for Solicitors* are 'honesty, integrity, independence, confidentiality and the avoidance of situations of conflict of interest.'[97] Lawyers, therefore, should 'advise their clients fearlessly and objectively' and should not 'allow themselves to be restricted in their actions on behalf of clients or restricted by clients in relation to their other professional duties.'[98] Does collaborative practice then allow clients to restrict their solicitors in the performance of their professional duties? Arguably it does, in that the solicitors are restricted from taking the case before the court. Is it likely to be interpreted that way? This has not been addressed in Ireland.

The *Guide to Good Professional Conduct for Solicitors* in Ireland also states that a solicitor must:

> 5.1. (a) promote and protect fearlessly by all proper means the client's best interests and to do so without regard to his or her interests or to any consequences to himself or any other person.[99]

However, it also states that:

> A solicitor is under no duty to undo the consequences of the court being misled by the prosecution or by the opposing party, otherwise than on a point of law ...[100]

Noting the fact that there is 'no duty to undo the consequences of the court being misled', lawyers, by engaging in the collaborative process, are as Peppet commented, agreeing to a higher code of ethics. The Law Society has a separate Family Law in Ireland Code of Practice. This code refers to the fact that solicitors should 'deal with matters in a way designed to preserve people's dignity and to encourage them to reach settlement.'[101] It states that:

> As a representative of clients, the solicitor performs various functions. As an adviser, the solicitor provides a client with an informed understanding of the client's legal rights and obligations and explains their practical implications. As an advocate, the solicitor forthrightly asserts the client's position under the rules of the adversarial system. As a negotiator, the solicitor seeks a result advantageous to the client but consistent with the requirement of honest dealings with others.[102]

Does collaborative practice interfere with these functions as the solicitor remains an adviser, an advocate and a negotiator? Or what is required for the lawyer to 'forthrightly assert the client's position under the rules of the adversarial system'? If this is to be interpreted as proceeding before the court, then difficulties may arise. It is expected that the answer to the question will lie in the limited representation agreement entered into between the client and his or her solicitor. The parties will have agreed to a different set of rules.[103]

The *Guide to Good Professional Conduct* also notes that: 'A solicitor must not disclose the contents of a family law file which is subject to this rule (the *in camera* rule) to any third party even if he has his own client's consent.'[104] Solicitors therefore will need to be careful as to how such experts are briefed and how the team model is managed. This will be a concern in an Irish context where family law hearings are heard in private and strict rules apply as to how such sensitive information is to be addressed.

The Family Law Code notes the importance of taking a less adversarial approach to family law matters and of stressing to clients the importance of the 'best interests' of their children. It provides that solicitors should advise clients about alternative methods of dispute resolution such as mediation and collaborative law. What is interesting though is that the guidelines go so far as to state that '[k]eeping the code is not a sign of weakness and will not expose the client to disadvantage.'[105] The fact that the Law Society felt it necessary to say this perhaps indicates the difficulty that lawyers have with taking a less traditional adversarial approach.

Significantly, however, the LRC recommends that it is appropriate for 'those in professional legal training at the Law Society of Ireland (Solicitors) and the Honourable Society of King's Inns (Barristers) to be introduced to the skills of collaborative practice as part of their educational training.'[106] This recommendation is to be welcomed. It is important for lawyers to gain an understanding and appreciation of alternative methods of dispute resolution from the outset so that they, in turn, can fully inform their clients. Interestingly, the main opposition to the Act when it was being discussed with the ABA was from the young members of the profession.[107] Perhaps this is because at this point, fresh from law school, lawyers have an ideology that justice can only be served through the adversarial system. It is to be hoped that the LRC's recommendations will address this, and thereby enable a more balanced approach for lawyers in Ireland. International research has shown that training in less adversarial methods of dispute resolution has an impact of the approach lawyers take to cases, encouraging them to reflect more carefully on their role as agents in the dispute resolution process.

Conclusion

Many of the concerns raised about collaborative practice by the Bar in the US have been addressed during the enactment of the UCLA. Clients of the process now have the assurance that lawyers are statutorily obliged to ensure that they will be fully informed as to all of the options available before they decide which process best fits their needs in the resolution of their conflict. They have the assurance that collaborative practitioners will screen to establish if, having chosen to use the process, the process itself fits their needs; that they have the capacity to engage fully; and that they understand the implications of the limited nature of the representation and the disqualification clause. Clients are assured that their decision to use the process is a voluntary one and that they can withdraw from the process at any time. They will have the benefit of a short, clearly drafted participation agreement based on the provisions of the Act. Under the Act, low-income clients will have the reassurance that they will not be left unrepresented if the process breaks down. Having a model of best practice available through the Act in the US has benefited the development of the process worldwide; it has prompted collaborative practitioners to learn from the experiences of their colleagues in the US. It is clear that the LRC in Ireland was influenced in its recommendations by the provisions of the Act and that the Commission envisages the Act as being a reference point for collaborative lawyers in Ireland.

Mosten notes that the passing of a uniform law in 'itself, provides legitimacy for new forms of legal practice.'[108] As noted in the introduction, however, the Act has only been adopted in 14 States across the US to date. Lawyers in states that have not adopted the Act and in other jurisdictions may continue to expose themselves and their clients to the difficulties of perhaps not giving due consideration to the issue of informed consent, screening or of signing the agreement as parties to the contract and to the implications of this from a professional and ethical point of view. The process will need to be reviewed and monitored continuously to address any new issues that may arise. It is hoped, however, that the 'teaching' and 'learning' process that began with the initial impetus for the Act will continue and may, as Ver Steegh noted, also serve to highlight areas in which similar reforms may be needed within the adversarial system.

Notes

1 For example, Alabama, Arizona, Florida, Hawaii, Maryland, Michigan, Montana, Nevada, New Jersey, North Dakota, Ohio, Texas, Utah, Washington. Alabama, Arizona, Michigan, Ohio, and Texas enacted version A – specifically for family law matters. North Dakota have adopted it as a court rule. The Act has also been introduced in Illinois and Massachusetts. See http://www.uniformlaws.org/LegislativeFactSheet.aspx?title=CollaborativeLaw Act. Last accessed 12 July 2016.

2 See Fairman, C.M., 'A Proposed Model Rule for Collaborative Law,' (2005) 21 *Ohio State Journal on Dispute Resolution* 73–122.

3 Menkel-Meadow, C., 'Pursuing Settlement in an Adversary Culture: A Tale of Innovation Co-Opted or "The Law of ADR"' (1991) *Florida State University Law Review* 1–46, 1.

4 Ibid. at 2.

5 The umbrella organisation for collaborative practice in the US and worldwide. The Academy describes its role as a non-profit, international community of legal, mental health, and financial professionals working to transform the way in which conflict is resolved worldwide through collaborative practice. The IACP provides training for collaborative lawyers, mental health professionals and financial specialists and through its Standards Committee sets Ethical Guidelines and training standards.

6 Uniform Collaborative Law Rules and Uniform Collaborative Law Act (Last Revised or Amended in 2010). Drafted by the National Conference of Commissioners on Uniform State Laws and Approved and Recommended for Enactment in All the States (Santa Fe, New Mexico, July 2009) hereinafter referred to as the Prefatory Note Available at http://www.uniformlaws.org/shared/docs/collaborative_law/uclranducla_amendments_jul10.pdf Last accessed 12th July 2016.

7 The Uniform Law Commission (ULC) formerly known as the National Conference of Commissioners on Uniform State Laws was established in 1892 and works towards developing the uniformity of State laws in the US.

8 Stansbury, C., Wray, L., and Pence, M., 'Lessons Learned from Drafting the UCLA', Paper delivered at the IACP 11th International Networking and Educational Forum, Washington D.C. 2010. See also Tindall, H., and Smith, J., 'The Uniform Collaborative Law Act as a Teaching Tool' (2009–2010) 38 *Hofstra Law Review* 685–698.

9 Section 4 (4): 'describe the nature and scope of the matter'.

10 Prefatory Note to the Uniform Collaborative Law Act page 19. Available at http://www.uniformlaws.org/shared/docs/collaborative_law/uclranducla_amendments_jul10.pdf. Last accessed 12 July 2016.

11 Prefatory Note to the Uniform Collaborative Law Act Available at http://www.uniformlaws.org/shared/docs/collaborative_law/uclranducla_amendments_jul10.pdf. Last accessed 12 July 2016 (emphasis added).

12 Section 14 (1) (emphasis added).

13 See *Conklin v. Hannoch Weisman*, 678 A.2d 1060, 1069 (N.J. 1996) – 'An attorney in a counseling situation must advise a client of the risks of the transaction in terms sufficiently clear to enable the client to assess the client's risks. The care must be commensurate with the risks of the undertaking and tailored to the needs and sophistication of the client.'

14 Section 5(f). A party may terminate a collaborative law process with or without cause.

15 Tesler, P., *Collaborative Law: Achieving Effective Resolution in Divorce without Litigation* (2nd edn, American Bar Association, 2008) at 141.

16 Ibid.

17 When drafting the Act the question arose as to whether collaborative practice should be used at all when there were issues of domestic violence. Rather than rule the use of the process out – in particular because of the potential benefits of the multidisciplinary model – the ABA Commission on Domestic Violence was consulted and the definition used complies with its Standards of Practice for Lawyers Representing Victims of Domestic Violence, Sexual Assault and Stalking in Civil Protection Order Cases (2007). See Boyarin, Y., 'Generating "Win-Win" Results: Negotiating Conflicts in the Drafting of Process if the Uniform Collaborative Law Act' (2009–2010) 38 *Hofstra Law Review* 495–536.

18 Prefatory Note at 34. Available at http://www.uniformlaws.org/shared/docs/collaborative_law/uclranducla_amendments_jul10.pdf. Last accessed 12 July 2016.

19 The victim of domestic violence.

20 Drew, M., 'Lawyer Malpractice and Domestic Violence: Are We Revictimizing Our Clients?' 2005 *39* (1) *Family Law Quarterly* 7–25, 8.

21 Macfarlane, J., *The Emerging Phenomenon of Collaborative Family Law (CFL): A Qualitative Case Study* (Department of Justice Canada, 2005) at 83.

22 Daicoff, S., 'The Comprehensive Law Movement' (2002–2004) 19 *Touro Law Review* 825–846, 835.

23 Ver Steegh, N., 'The Uniform Collaborative Law Act and Intimate Partner Violence: A Roadmap for Collaborative (and Non-Collaborative) Lawyers' (2009) 38 *Hofstra law Review* 699–755, 702.

24 Macfarlane, J., *The Emerging Phenomenon of Collaborative Family Law (CFL): A Qualitative Case Study* (Department of Justice Canada, 2005) at 83.

25 Prefatory Note to the Uniform Collaborative Law Act at 34. Available at http://www.uniformlaws.org/shared/docs/collaborative_law/uclranducla_amendments_jul10.pdf. Last accessed 12 July 2016.

26 Ver Steegh, N., 'The Uniform Collaborative Law Act and Intimate Partner Violence: A Roadmap for Collaborative (and Non-Collaborative) Lawyers' (2009) 38 *Hofstra law Review* 699–755, 701.

27 Ibid. at 755.

28 Boyarin, Y., 'Generating "Win-Win" Results: Negotiating Conflicts in the Drafting of Process if the Uniform Collaborative Law Act' (2009–2010) 38 *Hofstra Law Review* 495–536, 535.

29 See Chapters 4 and 5.
30 Professor Byron Sher, Retired Contracts Professor, Stanford University.
31 Sloin, S.G., 'Message from the President' 2010 11 (2) *The Collaborative Review* 5.
32 Prefatory Note to the Uniform Collaborative Law Act at 21.http://www.uniformlaws.org/shared/docs/collaborative_law/uclranducla_amendments_jul10.pdf. Last accessed 12 July 2016.
33 Ethics Comm. of the Colorado Bar Association Ethics Op. 115 (2007), available at http://www.cobar.org/index.cfm/ID/386/subID/10159/CETH/Ethics-Opinion-115:-Ethical-Considerations-in-the-Collaborative-and-Cooperative-Law-Contexts,-02/24//. Last accessed 12 July 2016. See Chapter 2.
34 Section 5 (b) of the Uniform Collaborative Law Act available at http://www.uniformlaws.org/shared/docs/collaborative_law/uclranducla_amendments_jul10.pdf. Last accessed 12 July 2016. This also seeks to avoid the possibility of court-ordered collaborative practice or mandatory collaborative practice, as occurred with mediation.
35 Section 5 (f) of the Uniform Collaborative Law Act available at http://www.uniformlaws.org/shared/docs/collaborative_law/uclranducla_amendments_jul10.pdf. Last accessed 12 July 2016.
36 Section 4 of the Act available at http://www.uniformlaws.org/shared/docs/collaborative_law/uclranducla_amendments_jul10.pdf. Last accessed 12 July 2016. There have been many books written by practitioners that set out, in detail, the steps that are to be taken in serving notices to signify the end of the process. See Tesler, P., *Collaborative Law: Achieving Effective Resolution in Divorce without Litigation* (2nd edn, American Bar Association, 2008).
37 See the Prefatory note to the Uniform Collaborative Law Act for a full discussion on what distinguishes between verbal and non-verbal communications at 43–45. Non-verbal includes actions such as nodding one's head in agreement. Communications prepared specifically for the process are considered collaborative communications but documents like, for example, pre-existing tax returns are not, as they were already in existence and not prepared specifically for this purpose. Available at http://www.uniformlaws.org/shared/docs/collaborative_law/uclranducla_finalact_jul10.pdf. Last accessed 1 July 2016.
38 Section 17 (a) Subject to Sections 18 and 19, a collaborative law communication is privileged under subsection (b), is not subject to discovery, and is not admissible in evidence.

(b) In a proceeding, the following privileges apply:

(1) A party may refuse to disclose, and may prevent any other person from disclosing, a collaborative law communication.
(2) A non-party participant may refuse to disclose, and may prevent any other person from disclosing, a collaborative law communication of the non-party participant.

(c) Evidence or information that is otherwise admissible or subject to discovery does not become inadmissible or protected from discovery solely because of its disclosure or use in a collaborative law process.

39 Ibid. Section 18 (a) A privilege under Section 17 may be waived in a record or orally during a proceeding if it is expressly waived by all parties and, in the case of the privilege of a non-party participant, it is also expressly waived by the non-party participant.

(b) A person that makes a disclosure or representation about a collaborative law communication which prejudices another person in a proceeding may not assert a privilege under Section 17, but this preclusion applies only to the extent necessary for the person prejudiced to respond to the disclosure or representation.

Section 19 (a) There is no privilege under Section 17 for a collaborative law communication that is:

(1) available to the public under [state open records act] or made during a session of a collaborative law process that is open, or is required by law to be open, to the public;
(2) a threat or statement of a plan to inflict bodily injury or commit a crime of violence;
(3) intentionally used to plan a crime, commit or attempt to commit a crime, or conceal an ongoing crime or ongoing criminal activity; or
(4) in an agreement resulting from the collaborative law process, evidenced by a record signed by all parties to the agreement.

(b) The privileges under Section 17 for a collaborative law communication do not apply to the extent that a communication is:

(1) sought or offered to prove or disprove a claim or complaint of professional misconduct or malpractice arising from or related to a collaborative law process; or
(2) sought or offered to prove or disprove abuse, neglect, abandonment, or exploitation of a child or adult, unless the [child protective services agency or adult protective services agency] is a party to or otherwise participates in the process.

(c) There is no privilege under Section 17 if a tribunal finds, after a hearing *in camera*, that the party seeking discovery or the proponent of the evidence has shown the evidence is not otherwise available, the need for the evidence substantially outweighs the interest in protecting confidentiality, and the collaborative law communication is sought or offered in:

(1) a court proceeding involving a felony [or misdemeanor]; or
(2) a proceeding seeking rescission or reformation of a contract arising out of the collaborative law process or in which a defense to avoid liability on the contract is asserted.

(d) If a collaborative law communication is subject to an exception under subsection (b) or (c), only the part of the communication necessary for the application of the exception may be disclosed or admitted.
(e) Disclosure or admission of evidence excepted from the privilege under subsection (b) or (c) does not make the evidence or any other collaborative law communication discoverable or admissible for any other purpose.
(f) The privileges under Section 17 do not apply if the parties agree in advance in a 99 signed record, or if a record of a proceeding reflects agreement by the parties, that all or part of a collaborative law process is not privileged. This subsection does not apply to a collaborative law communication made by a person that did not receive actual notice of the agreement before the communication was made.

40 Section 9.

41 In signing a participation agreement, the parties agree to negotiate in good faith and to provide voluntary disclosure. If a collaborative lawyer becomes aware that his or her client is not complying with these provisions, he or she has a duty to inform the client that failure to comply will result in the lawyer having to disqualify himself/herself as the party's representative. If having been given this information, the client persists, the lawyer will disqualify himself/herself from acting on the client's behalf. See Tesler, P., *Collaborative Law: Achieving Effective Resolution in Divorce without Litigation* (2nd edn, American Bar Association, 2008) at 227.

42 Section 5 (g) of the Act available at http://www.uniformlaws.org/shared/docs/collaborative_law/uclranducla_amendments_jul10.pdf. Last accessed 12 July 2016.

43 The Federal Rule of Civil Procedure in the US already requires disclosure 'without awaiting a discovery request' to include: names of witnesses, relevant documents etc. Each State/jurisdiction may have different rules in relation to disclosure.

44 Prefatory Note at 60. Available at http://www.uniformlaws.org/shared/docs/collaborative_law/uclranducla_amendments_jul10.pdf. Last accessed 12 July 2016.

45 See footnote 39 above regarding Section 18 (a).

46 Macfarlane, J., *The Emerging Phenomenon of Collaborative Family Law (CFL): A Qualitative Case Study* (Department of Justice Canada, 2005) at 78.

47 As a limited scope representation, disqualification is part of the process and provided for under Section 9 of the Act.

48 Definition no. 13 Uniform Collaborative Law Act. http://www.uniformlaws.org/shared/docs/collaborative_law/uclranducla_amendments_jul10.pdf. Last accessed 12 July 2016.

49 Ibid. Section 8 of the UCLA.

50 Ibid. Section 9 of the UCLA.

51 Ibid. Section 10 of the UCLA.

52 Ibid. Section 11 of the UCLA.

53 See Fairman, C.M., 'A Proposed Model Rule for Collaborative Law,' (2005) 21 *Ohio State Journal on Dispute Resolution* 73–122.

54 Section 13 (2) of the UCLA.

55 Opinion 699 Advisory Committee on Professional Ethics
New Jersey Bar Opinion available at http://njlaw.rutgers.edu/collections/ethics/acpe/acp699_1.html

56 RPC 1.16(b) (1) (withdrawal by lawyer permitted if 'withdrawal can be accomplished without material adverse effect on the interests of the client').

57 Section 17 (c) of UCLA http://www.uniformlaws.org/shared/docs/collaborative_law/uclranducla_amendments_jul10.pdf. Last accessed 12 July 2016.

58 See footnotes 38 and 39.

59 2009 B.C.L.R. 2d. 1808.

60 Ibid. Paragraph 19.

61 (LRC 98–2010) (Dublin, 16 November 2010).

62 Law Reform Commission of Ireland – Report *Alternative Dispute Resolution: Conciliation and Mediation* (LRC 98–2010) (Dublin, 2010) Paragraph 6.60 at 117.

63 Mental Health Experts are called Personal and Family Consultants in Ireland. It was believed that this term is more fitting and may encourage prospective parties to engage with such experts.

64 The Association of Collaborative Practitioners. See www.acp.ie. Last accessed 1 August 2016.

65 Berger, M.J., 'A Comparative Study of British Barristers and American Legal Practice and Education' (1983–1984) 5 *Northwestern Journal of International Law and Business* 540–584.

66 In private.

67 Webb, S., 'Collaborative Law: A Practitioner's Perspective on its History and Current Practice' (2008) 21 *Journal of the American Academy of Matrimonial Lawyers* 155–169, 156.

68 Setting out details of assets and liabilities, income and expenditure.

69 Sections 5 and 6 of the Judicial Separation and Family Law Reform Act 1989; Sections 6 and 7 of the Family Law (Divorce) Act 1996.

70 Ibid.

71 Felsteiner, W., Abel, R., and Sarat, A., 'The Emergence and Transformation of Disputes: Naming, Blaming, Claiming…' (1980–1981) 15 (3–4) *Law and Society* 631–654.

72 Coulter, C., *Family Law Reporting Pilot Project; Report to the Board of the Court Service* (Courts Service, 2007) at 40 – only 3% of separating couples availed of mediation.

73 Law Reform Commission of Ireland. Report *Alternative Dispute Resolution: Conciliation and Mediation* (LRC 98–2010) (Dublin, 2010) Paragraph 6.17 at 109.

74 Ibid. Paragraph 6.75 at 121.

75 Ibid. (emphasis added).

76 (a) Persons in a proceeding pending before a tribunal may sign a collaborative law participation agreement to seek to resolve a collaborative matter related to the proceeding. Parties shall file promptly with the tribunal a notice of the agreement after it is signed. Subject to subsection (c) and Sections 7 and 8, the filing operates as a stay of the proceeding.

77 Change from thinking in an adversarial way to thinking in a more facilitative way.

78 As noted in the Introduction, this work does not go into detail on the training received as this is dealt with in other works. Suffice to say that collaborative lawyers are trained in interest-based negotiation, active listening, brainstorming ideas for settlement, engagement with other disciplines through role play and breaking down barriers as to each profession's perceptions of the other. Many practitioners interviewed stressed the need for on-going training and training in specific aspects of the process, particularly screening and understanding the implications of domestic violence and how to detect it.

79 Davy, E., 'Problems Associated with Collaborative Practice' 1 (2009) *Judicial Studies Institute Journal* 14–18, 16 (emphasis added).

80 Fisher, R., and Ury, W., *Getting to Yes* (2nd edn, Random House, 1992) at 157.

81 Solicitors Act 1954 available at www.irishstatutebook.ie/1954/en/act/pub/0036/index.html, Solicitors (Amendment) Act, 1994 www.irishstatutebook.ie/1994/en/act/pub/0027/index.html. Last accessed 1 August 2016.

82 *Guide to Professional Conduct*, 3rd edition (Dublin, 2013) available at https://www.lawsociety.ie/Documents/committees/conduct-guide.pdf. Last accessed 1 August 2016.

83 Section 13 of the UCLA http://www.uniformlaws.org/shared/docs/collaborative_law/uclranducla_amendments_jul10.pdf. Last accessed 12 July 2016.

84 Law Reform Commission of Ireland. Report *Alternative Dispute Resolution: Conciliation and Mediation* (LRC 98–2010) (Dublin, 2010) Paragraph 6.68 at 119.

85 Ibid. Paragraph 6.69 at 119.

86 Ibid.

87 Section 5. Scope of Advocacy. The most updated version of the Ethical Standards set down for collaborative practitioners in available on their website www.collaborativepractice.com. Last accessed 12 July 2016.

88 In addition to the particular collaborative lawyer dealing with the case, all the lawyers on his or her firm are also disqualified from acting for that client in 'that matter or any related matter'.

89 See Sections 10 and 11 of the UCLA Act 2010 available at http://www.uniformlaws.org/shared/docs/collaborative_law/uclranducla_amendments_jul10.pdf. Last accessed 12 July 2016.

90 The Legal Aid Board Corporate Plan for 2015–2017 places more of an emphasis on mediation as the Legal Aid Board has taken over the state-run Family Mediation Service. However, prospective parties may still avail of collaborative law. To qualify parties need to have an income of less than €18,000 p.a. and capital assets of less than €100,000. See Civil Legal Aid Act, 1995. http://www.legalaidboard.ie/lab/publishing.nsf/650f3eec0dfb990fca25692100069854/65e313863a2a5b0e80257df10056ce54/$FILE/Corporate%20Plan%202015.pdf. Last accessed 1 August 2016.

91 Law Reform Commission of Ireland. Report *Alternative Dispute Resolution: Conciliation and Mediation* (LRC 98–2010) (Dublin, 2010) Paragraph 6.71 at 120.

92 Ibid. Paragraph 6.73 at 120.
93 Women's Aid, *Submission to the Family Law Reporting Committee* (January 2009). Available at: www.womensaid.ie. Last accessed 1 August 2016.
94 Ibid.
95 Family Law (Divorce) Act 1996. No. 33 of 1996 available at www.irishstatutebook.ie/1996/en/act/pub/0033/index.html. Last accessed 12 July 2016.
96 2009 B.C.L.R. 2d. 1808.
97 Law Society of Ireland, *A Guide to Good Professional Conduct for Solicitors* (3rd edn, Law Society of Ireland, 2013) https://www.lawsociety.ie/Documents/committees/conduct-guide.pdf at 105–106.
98 Ibid. at 3.
99 Law Society of Ireland, *A Guide to Good Professional Conduct for Solicitors* (3rd edn, Law Society of Ireland 2013) Appendix 4 'Family Law in Ireland Code of Practice' 2008 at 37, https://www.lawsociety.ie/Documents/committees/conduct-guide.pdf.
100 Ibid.
101 Law Society of Ireland, *A Guide to Good Professional Conduct for Solicitors* (3rd edn, Law Society of Ireland 2013) Appendix 4 'Family Law in Ireland Code of Practice' 2008 149, https://www.lawsociety.ie/Documents/committees/conduct-guide.pdf.
102 Ibid. at 149.
103 *Banerjee v Bisset* 2009 B.C.L.R. 2d. 1808.
104 Ibid. at 35.
105 Ibid. at 110.
106 Law Reform Commission of Ireland. Report *Alternative Dispute Resolution: Conciliation and Mediation* (LRC 98–2010) Dublin, 2010, Paragraph 6.65 at 119.
107 Shephard, A., and Hoffman D., 'Regulating Collaborative Law: The Uniform Collaborative Law Act Takes Shape' (2010) 17 (1) *Dispute Resolution* 26–29, 28.
108 Mosten, F.S., 'The Future of Collaborative Practice: A Vision for 2030' (2011) 49 (2) *Family Court Review* 282–291.

4 What has the research revealed?

Introduction

This chapter provides an insight into the research undertaken on collaborative practice internationally. Four main studies will be examined. Two that were undertaken in the US/Canada: *The Emerging Phenomenon of Collaborative Family Law (CFL): A Qualitative Case Study* by Macfarlane[1] and *Research Regarding Client Experience* by the International Academy of Collaborative Professionals (IACP);[2] and two undertaken in England and Wales: *Collaborative Family Law: A report for Resolution*[3] and *Mapping Paths to Family Justice*[4] by Barlow and her team. Additional, less extensive, studies will also be referred to, as appropriate.[5] In synthesising the research, this chapter compares and contrasts clients' and lawyers' opinions on the effectiveness of the process in reaching settlement, and clients' satisfaction with the process and the outcomes achieved.[6] It will examine the impact, if any, of the disqualification provision; does it affect prospective parties' decisions to use the process, and is it viewed as a positive or negative by clients and lawyers? Finally, it will outline any concerns expressed by clients and recommendations made for improving the collaborative process, and will assess whether, in their view and in the view of the lawyers interviewed, using the process is an 'easier' or more difficult option than positional negotiation. The results of the research undertaken in Ireland are detailed in Chapter 5.

International research – methodology

Macfarlane's research, undertaken between 2001 and 2004, was the first substantial study of collaborative law and was 'practice based'. A case study approach was used, interviewing clients and lawyers at various stages of the process. In considering the findings presented it is important to bear in mind that many of the concerns raised in relation to informed consent, screening and consideration of the ethical issues have since been discussed and debated at length during the enactment of the UCLA (as detailed in Chapter 3), the IACP arguably having embraced Macfarlane's challenge to be 'unafraid to reflect … and humble about how much there still is to learn'.[7]

The IACP's research was quantitative in nature. From October 2006 to March 2008, a collaborative practice survey was conducted through the IACP website. Information was gathered on: client demographics; type of proceedings; models used; length of case; and fees. In August 2006, a Client Experience Survey was launched. This ran until 31 August 2007. Thirty-seven clients responded.

Resolution's study, the first to have taken place in England and Wales, took a mixed-method approach using questionnaires to obtain an overall perspective: focus groups with collaborative lawyers; and semi-structured interviews with twelve persons who had used the process for a more in-depth analysis. The study took place in 2008.

Most recently, the project entitled 'Mapping the Paths to Family Justice' was undertaken by the Universities of Exeter and Kent between 2011 and 2013.[8] This is the most wide-ranging study of family dispute resolution processes in England and Wales, encompassing a national survey on public awareness and views on the different processes (namely mediation, collaborative practice and solicitor negotiation), and qualitative analysis through interviews with separating parties and solicitors. A small sample of each process was also recorded for analysis. The aim of the study was to provide an understanding of the various pathways of dispute resolution and their suitability depending on the facts of the case. It is not within the remit of this book to explore all the findings, only those that are directly relevant to collaborative practice.

Who is using the process?

Comparing the demographics of participants across the various studies, those opting to use collaborative practice are, on average, in the 40–59 age group and have been in marriages of at least ten years' duration.[9] Over 60% of the US respondents had at least a four-year college degree. The income level of clients taking part in the process in the US was quite high, with 41% of respondents having a personal annual income of $100,000 or more and over 80% of respondents with a household income of $100,000 or more. The average age-group of the study participants in England and Wales was slightly younger than those in the US, with the typical client being in the 35–54 age bracket. Again, most clients were educated to a first degree level and were described as 'economically active'.[10] Collaborative practice is used mainly in the resolution of separation or divorce.[11]

The research therefore confirms the widely held view that those using the process are generally well educated and have some level of financial security.[12] However, collaborative practice is also available through legal aid services in certain jurisdictions.[13] Sefton, researching on behalf of Resolution, noted that there was evidence of cases in which participants were not necessarily wealthy or well educated.[14] On occasion, private solicitors have facilitated low-income clients' use of the process by agreeing a payment schedule over a period of time or, when the process was unsuccessful[15] have helped secure legal aid funding to enable clients to proceed before the courts.

Barlow *et al.*'s national survey noted that public awareness of collaborative practice was low; only 14% of those who took part in the national survey had heard about the process.[16] Significantly, those in the 45–54 age group were more likely to have heard of mediation or solicitor negotiation. This is a concern for collaborative practitioners as international research indicates that the majority of clients that use this process are from this particular age cohort.

Clients' motivations for using collaborative practice

Macfarlane concluded that clients had more pragmatic reasons for choosing collaborative practice than did their lawyers.[17] A number of clients in her study had chosen the process believing that it would be faster and cheaper; this was not always the case. Others chose it because they wanted to take responsibility for role modelling, so that their children would be able to look back and see them as having dealt with divorce in a responsible way. For some it was a means of achieving personal growth leading to closure.[18]

The research undertaken by the IACP produced similar results. The key factors in decisions to use the process were the hope of a better outcome and the framework the process provides to focus on issues that were of importance to clients. Other important motivations were: the promise of being less adversarial; that meetings could be scheduled at convenient times; and that the process was 'respectful'.[19] For participants in Resolution's research in England and Wales and those who were interviewed in Ireland, it was less about the issue of costs or time and more about the belief that the collaborative process could facilitate a better outcome, causing less damage to their children and helping to maintain future parenting and family relationships.[20]

Although Sefton's report for Resolution notes that by 2007 collaborative practice had entered the 'mainstream' and that 'there was real potential for the process to become a primary method of dispute resolution rather than an "alternative"',[21] Barlow's study published in 2014 revealed the process was 'not well known and not necessarily well understood' by the general public.[22] Those who had heard about it, however, again often the more affluent and well-educated clients, were well informed. She describes parties' willingness to use one process or another as being determined by 'the steer' that they are given by solicitors.[23] Of concern was that many participants commented that 'feeling they had a real choice of options was a relatively rare experience', and that lawyers tended to promote what was within their own 'comfort zone'.[24] Barlow noted the factors that influenced whether clients used the process were: 'awareness, access to two collaboratively trained solicitors and costs'.[25]

Collaborative practice *v.* mediation

Macfarlane, in noting that participants frequently chose collaborative practice over mediation, questioned whether this was because collaborative lawyers were promoting their process over mediation. She spoke about the 'sibling rivalry' between mediation and collaborative practice and the need for transparency from lawyers. Clients, she opined, would be better served if they received information on all of the available processes.[26] Mediation has been in existence for much longer than collaborative practice and is more widely known, however, there is a perception that it is not a complete process.[27]

While some clients were positive about mediation: ‘It worked really well because if either one of us started getting into an argument or too aggressive in our manner or anything like that, the mediator was really good at calming it down’,[28] many ‘were frustrated by the fact that a mediated agreement, unless approved by the court as a Consent Order was not enforceable’.[29] Most chose collaborative practice over mediation because they felt that they needed the support of their lawyers.[30] Separating parties expressed the view that they ‘[n]eeded legal representation’,[31] and:

> [t]he benefit [of collaborative] is that it is less costly, faster, and definitely more fair in that you have the professional support (financially, legally and mental health-wise) not provided in mediation. I felt my needs and concerns were heard and fought for, and that I came out of the process feeling more whole and positive than a typical adversarial divorce would have been.[32]

Similar views were expressed in Sefton’s research:

> I didn’t fancy it [mediation] at all because I felt as though I needed someone on my side. If it had just been one person who was like mediating between us, I knew that … I wouldn’t stand a chance[33]

Barlow’s participants likewise spoke about the need to have ‘someone in my corner’[34] and ‘someone on my side’.[35] Although the collaborative process is client-led, the evidence suggests that the lawyers help the separating parties at the outset until they get over the initial fear of discussing matters directly; as client confidence increases, lawyers play a lesser role in the negotiations. Having this support appears to be the main determinant in the decision to use collaborative practice over mediation.

The IACP has recommended that all collaborative lawyers undertake 60 hours mediation training to supplement the collaborative training. Many collaborative lawyers have noted that doing so has increased their understanding of the concept of ‘interest-based’ processes, thereby strengthening their beliefs as to the benefits of such an approach. Indeed, the research shows that lawyers who have been most successful in using the collaborative process are those who have undergone mediation training.[36]

Lawyers’ motivations for engaging in the process

Macfarlane’s view was that lawyers in the US and Canada appeared to have idealistic views of the Collaborative Family Law (CFL) process. They cited motivations such as ‘value re-alignment, seeing CFL as a process of uncovering and embracing a new professional identity’.[37] Significantly, similar to the views expressed by clients, they saw collaborative law as less damaging than the court process, but more complete than mediation because each party is separately represented.[38] She cautioned that there is a risk that collaborative practitioners, holding the conviction that this is a better way, 'may sometimes be imposing their own motivations onto clients who are simply trying to get their divorce completed quickly and inexpensively'.[39] Additionally, she highlighted the dangers of lawyers imposing their value systems on clients, arguably the 'good lives' model, as referred to in Chapter 1. Macfarlane cautioned that clients need to be aware that even though collaborative law may be better than court, it will still take time and will 'hurt – both emotionally and financially'.[40]

Lawyers in England and Wales also saw collaborative practice as a better way for clients to deal with separation or divorce, referring to experiences of cases that were settled with reduced costs and less acrimony compared to the litigation process. They commented that negotiation through solicitors is often 'fiercely positional', with much 'inefficient, ritualised to-ing and fro-ing'.[41] They also spoke of the benefits for themselves in 'feeling better about myself, and my job as a lawyer'.[42] Barlow, however, cautioned against solicitors within the collaborative process or mediation portraying a court hearing as the 'worst option'.[43] She noted that there has to be an acceptance that many cases may require the formality and finality of a court hearing to resolve matters.[44] Setting processes up in competition with each other achieves little for the client. The overall aim should be to learn lessons from each process with a view to improving the system for family law clients; contributing to what Wright refers to as the 'evolutionary process already apparent in family practice'.[45]

Legal advice

Macfarlane identified three different approaches amongst collaborative lawyers: the traditional lawyer who commits to cooperation; the lawyer as friend and healer and the lawyer as team player.[46] The 'traditional lawyer' approach focuses on clients being given full information about their legal rights and then helped to collaborate. The 'lawyer as friend' model generally involves the lawyer giving less rights-based information to clients and more general advice. Rather than acting as advocate, they see their position as more of a supporting role. The final category is lawyer as team player. Such lawyers' emphasis is on the purity and integrity of the process and seeking to find a solution within the process. Lawyers' views varied significantly depending on the approach they took. For the more traditional lawyers committing to co-operation, their view was:

- I think, to be honest, it's natural for an attorney … that my best friend in the room is always going to be my client.[47]
- I absolutely think I have a special responsibility to my client. I mean, I am their attorney. I am her attorney or his attorney and there is no question in my mind that that is my primary duty. I mean, that's what my job is, that's what I'm being retained for, and if that's not the case, there can be a mediation with two mediators who are neutrals.[48]

Whereas at the other extreme, lawyers as team players commented that they were more concerned with the integrity of the process rather than the outcome.

- I don't really care about whether the outcome is optimal in terms of dollars and cents, but that [my client] and I live up to our collaborative principles.[49]

Arguably, by taking this justice as per the 'process' or system approach, lawyers are reverting to their tendency to slavishly follow a set of rules or procedures, as they do within the courts' system, without considering the wider issues involved for the clients.

The results from the IACP research indicate that lawyers viewed their greatest responsibility to their own client, followed by responsibility to the process itself and then to the wider family.[50] Lawyers in Ireland and England and Wales take the more traditional but collaborative approach;[51] clients are advised of their rights and are then free to make decisions having had adequate legal advice. Resolution found that, in England and Wales, 'legal norms were still important in providing a framework for clients in negotiations',[52] and that few lawyers had difficulty in acknowledging that their 'primary responsibility'[53] was to the client. However, collaborative lawyers strive against giving clients information in a way that encourages parties to take a positional stance. Resolution's research noted that the information given to clients at the initial meeting was key in determining clients' expectations for the process, and that it was better not to be too specific or to give information that sets the parties up as adversaries.[54] Sefton, for Resolution, notes in particular that lawyers were conscious of not giving advice as to 'what should happen,'[55] but insisted that it was important for the clients to have a 'frame of reference' so that they could 'reality check' offers against what they might be likely to receive from the courts.[56]

Clients, on the other hand, were more specific in relation to their needs for legal advice. As Sefton notes they felt 'they had gone to a lawyer because they wanted legal advice, and they expected to get it'.[57] This varied from some clients wanting to know 'everything' to others being happy with general guidance. Most clients in Resolution's research were of the view that they got the legal advice they needed during the process. However, two participants said that they were unsure of where they stood legally.[58] This corresponds with the experience of Irish clients, as will be detailed in Chapter 5.

Macfarlane concluded that as there are 'probably as many variations within CFL as there are within a traditional divorce practice [as such] there is a need to provide clients with greater clarity about what they should expect at the outset'.[59] Lawyers should clarify whether legal advice will be given in private meetings or in general terms during the course of the joint meetings. This is an important element of ensuring informed consent.

Models used

Only two of the 16 cases studied in Macfarlane's research used the team approach, with seven other cases using the referral model, i.e. instructing neutral experts as required.[60] In contrast, the team model was used in 40% of cases reported in the research undertaken by the IACP. More than half the cases surveyed by the IACP used an interdisciplinary model. Of these, 59% engaged a financial consultant; 48% engaged at least one mental health professional, with 27% of cases involving two mental health professionals and 13% engaging three.[61]

By contrast, there is a resistance to the notion of counselling or mental health experts evident in the results of the research undertaken in England and Wales, from a costs perspective and also from of a sense of reluctance to seek assistance. Clients needed to be convinced that there would be some value to engaging experts. Lawyers interviewed by Resolution noted that '*family consultants* had been useful in helping to re-establish negotiation between the parties before embarking on the process and in negotiating parenting agreements'.[62] It is interesting to note the difference in terminology from that of the model in the US. This change has also been made in Ireland, with a view to making such assistance more palatable for clients.[63] However, there was a sense that work needed to be done to 'normalise' these types of intervention,[64] and there was still a common perception that: 'We don't need that. We can manage. Stiff upper lip.'[65]

Another barrier to the multidisciplinary model is that therapists and lawyers find it difficult to discuss clients' cases with each other, each having being used to maintaining high standards of confidentiality in matters discussed with their own clients. Issues also mentioned by clients in the context of the team model was the fact that, in some cases, they felt that the family consultants took over or led the process. Clients emphasised the importance of lawyers managing the process and ensuring that progress is made at each meeting. There was, in some cases, evidence of what Macfarlane described as 'a blurring of boundaries',[66] where lawyers took on the role of counsellor and imposed what were perceived as their own values. A frustrating element for clients can be the illusion that they will be given more control, yet they may still have little or no actual control over the pace of the processes, timing of meetings, etc. Keet, quoting Mayer, refers to the need for 'effective engagement', encompassing: 'authenticity' of the client's voice; 'meaningful engagement'; and that clients feel 'safe and protected by a clear set of rules, procedures and positive role of advocates'.[67] Lawyers need to keep the process under control, know the role of each of the experts engaged, and provide a safe space for clients to speak in the knowledge that these negotiations are confidential and that they will not be facing the same lawyers in court at a future date.

It is clear, particularly in England, Wales and Ireland, that work needs to be done to promote the benefits of the multidisciplinary approach to clients and, indeed, to members of the legal profession.[68] In concluding her research, Macfarlane was of the view that:

> [t]he team model can offer a depth and range of client services that traditional legal practice cannot match, and for those clients who can afford it and who see the value of a comprehensive transition plan for their family in its new form, the team model offers enormous potential.[69]

Clients too expressed satisfaction with the team model:

> I had had lots of counselling before but on my own. I had not expected to get so much from the coaching but [have] found this to be invaluable. I have now been able to change the pattern of my interaction with my husband – and my coach has really helped. She can mirror back to me what I did that was different and ... point out to me when I am returning to my old patterns.[70]

For some, the realisation that additional assistance would have been of benefit, only came after the legal process had concluded. Admitting that they would probably have resisted this model had it been offered to them at the time, in hindsight they felt that assistance with the emotional issues would have been valuable.

Settlement rates

Settlement rates within the process are quite high, and this is consistent across all the empirical studies. On occasion, parties have reconciled through the process. At the conclusion of Macfarlane's study, 19% of the cases were ongoing; 69% had settled (in one of these cases proceedings were issued subsequent to settlement); 6% had reconciled and 6% had terminated. Examining the research undertaken by the IACP (a much larger quantitative study), 90% of cases settled and 10% terminated prior to settlement of all issues. No clients reconciled with their spouse during the collaborative process in the US. Similarly, in the UK 83% of cases settled, with 2% reconciling.[71] In Ireland, the picture was much the same, with 86% of cases having settled by agreement and the parties having reconciled in 2% of the cases.[72]

Of the eight cases examined in Barlow's research, seven settled the financial issues through the process. Less success was evident in negotiating issues surrounding 'children's matters', with only one out of three cases resolving; however, two cases resulted in partially agreed settlements. Settlements reached during the process were considered 'fair'.[73] The most common reasons for failure to settle were issues surrounding 'entrenchment' and 'clashing ideological principles'.[74]

Outcomes

Do outcomes in the cases vary much from outcomes in court? This can be quite a subjective issue. In terms of financial outcomes, it was found that the substance of the outcomes was no different overall than what would be achieved in the traditional litigation/lawyer negotiation process. The difference seems to be in the way the parties got to this settlement. Macfarlane noted that in some cases, using the collaborative process resulted in what she termed 'value added',[75] additional flexibility and creativity in the way outcomes were reached and in the substance of the agreements. This creativity facilitated tailor-made solutions that in certain circumstances were more far-reaching and appropriate than those likely to have been achieved through traditional processes.[76] Importantly, Macfarlane found no evidence that weaker parties do less well in terms of outcome, or that wealthy parties succeeded in using the process to hide assets.[77]

Clients' satisfaction with outcomes was high across all studies. In Resolution's research only one client indicated unhappiness with the outcome. Sefton noted that:

> [i]t is quite common in family law to measure satisfaction with outcomes in terms of whether they are ones which the parties are comfortable with, or at least feel they can live with. It appeared that such outcomes, and sometimes much more, had been achieved via the collaborative process – or were imminent – for eleven clients (out of the twelve clients interviewed).[78]

Comments made by participants included:

- Both my ex [spouse] and I feel that the outcome was reasonably fair. And that there was no one individual who was damaged by it. And that it was reasonably – as sort of amicable as it could be expected to be, as you could possibly hope it could be. Under the circumstances. And that was in large measure down to the process.
- ... I was very happy ... I'm sure it was a damn sight easier than – I've seen people go through long drawn out divorces, and it's horrible ... We're both very pleased that the process existed, because it kind of, it was a kind of embodiment of the kind of divorce that we wanted.
- I genuinely in my heart of hearts haven't found anything negative ... For me it has been a positive and helpful way, of resolving something that I didn't want in the first place.[79]

Improved communication

Macfarlane, as noted previously spoke about a sense of 'value added' in having engaged in the process. This is displayed in two main themes that emerged. Firstly, a sense of improved communication between the parties. Second, a sense of empowerment. As the process develops it will be interesting to assess whether this 'effective engagement'[80] has long-term benefits for their own relationship post-separation and for any children they co-parent. Comments made by those who referred to improved communication included:

- ... think we're both quite proud of ourselves and of each other about the way that we behaved. And I would say that the collaborative process has given us a sort of avenue, a sort of guideline in that respect. So it has had a value.
- I certainly feel that it's much better to be around the table discussing things rather than letters backwards and forwards between the solicitors. Because you're able to keep a lot of goodwill between you by doing that ... So I feel like it was definitely the way to go.[81]

Macfarlane concluded that the outcomes achieved in the cases that had settled, 'matched or exceeded the legal standard in most respects'.[82] She pointed to the benefits of what she termed 'trial outcomes': outcomes that can be tried and re-visited if not suitable for the parties, something that would not be available during a typical court case. She cautioned, however, that safeguards should be in place to protect any perceived 'weaker parties'.

A sense of empowerment

Protection for weaker parties is an issue in all dispute resolution processes. In Keet's study of collaborative practice, for example, six out of eight of the participants noted that there were underlying power imbalances between them and their ex-spouse. Four of these had experienced some form of violence. For one of the participants, the process helped her reach a settlement that she was happy with and that she felt improved her relationship with her ex-spouse. For the other three participants who had experienced violence and emotional abuse, they felt that it was not adequately dealt with. These participants felt that there was a 'lack of process management' and they found the team atmosphere in the four-way meetings 'isolating' and that they lacked emotional support and back-up. Keet highlighted the need for proper screening prior to signing the participation agreement and that screening should continue throughout the process, especially as agreements reached with the benefit of legal advice are, as she noted, difficult to challenge.[83] Those who took part in her research used the lawyer-only model. It is clear however that the extent of the underlying difficulties in these cases may have required appropriate expertise from suitably qualified mental health experts. As noted earlier, lawyers need to be aware of when they are out of their depth.

Lawyers need to be cognizant that power imbalances between couples can be complicated and deep seated; the one who may appear the weaker party may not always be the most vulnerable. There can often be a reluctance on behalf of some participants to admit or acknowledge this,[84] emphasising the need for lawyers to understand the theoretical frameworks and psychology behind how a dispute develops and how people view, approach and deal with conflict.[85] It is notable, however, that Keet *et al.* found that even in a case in which there were issues of power imbalance, the process was still 'affirming, empowering and indeed transformative'.[86] This sense or theme of empowerment was evident across many of the studies. One of Keet *et al.*'s participants said that she felt that the process gave some weight to: 'my history and the contributions that I had made to the marriage … I felt I had my voice … I felt stronger'.[87]

Similarly, speaking in the aftermath of using the process, one of Barlow's participants also spoke about empowerment:

> it gave me a lot of confidence that actually I wasn't … that I was a reasonable person and an intelligent person and someone who could find things out and act on them and … I suppose for the lawyers to be able to … for your ex's lawyer to be able to almost give that kind of vibe too, obviously it was a very positive thing … an on-going positive outcome.[88]

This theme of empowerment was also evident in the Irish research; a sense that the process had enabled a realisation that this participant had value in their own right and was no longer in the shadow of their spouse:

> [I had] … started feeling all these inferior things, oh my God, X is so much better than I am, he has a better job, he has been doing this and that and I suppose the breakdown of a marriage does reduce you to nothing. Whereas when we went into the collaboration and as long as the counselling went on and when I listened to x talking and I was hearing the same things I heard 10 years ago, I thought, you know I am not the person that he made me feel I was, … and I am a, b, c, d and e … and I was able to see.

Disqualification provision

Do clients understand the significance of the disqualification provision or does it put extra pressure on them to settle within the process? What was evident across the studies was that clients did not engage in the process lightly. The majority of clients had researched the process independently of what they had been told by their own, or ex-partner's, lawyers. Having made the decision to engage in the process, both clients and their lawyers were committed to the process and therefore felt that this provision has no real impact.

In the research carried out by Resolution, all but two of the twelve clients interviewed understood the implications of this provision. For those that did not understand, one confused the disqualification provision with the issue of privilege while another understood it to mean that if settlement could not be achieved that you had to go to court. For the remainder, comments made included:

- … I think I'd understood that, this was something that if you embarked on, you committed to it.
- … made me all the more determined to make sure that it worked … it's a good discipline to have behind you.[89]

This view was also expressed by Irish participants.[90] Again, Irish participants confirmed their commitment to the process, and two referred to the fact that the disqualification provision was a positive aspect to the process as it focused them on what needed to be resolved in order to move on.[91]

There was a general sense that the disqualification posed more of an issue for the lawyers. As noted by Macfarlane and referred to earlier, clients are often surprised that lawyers need to go to these lengths to remove the possibility of the case being taken before the courts.[92] This view had also been evident in Schwab's research, where he noted that: '[o]f the answers received 35% of practitioners said it was "very significant", 43% said it was "somewhat significant", and 22% said it was "not at all significant"'.[93] Of the clients surveyed during the same research, '54.5% said that it had not kept them at the table while 45.5% said it had'.[94] One of Keet's participants commented that they felt it was more about the lawyers 'wanting to keep their boundaries clear as opposed to helping families'.[95] While critics suggest that the disqualification clause puts pressure on the clients to settle, this would not seem to be strongly borne out in the research.[96]

The research undertaken by Resolution and the Irish research both indicate that none of those who considered the collaborative process were discouraged from using the process as a result of the disqualification provision. The separating parties viewed it as of no importance because they were committed to the process. Others viewed it as more of an impediment on the solicitors.[97] The same view was evident from Barlow's research:

> None of the parties we interviewed, however, chose not to enter collaborative law because of the disqualification clause. And for most who undertook the collaborative process the presence of the disqualification clause was viewed as either inconsequential, a means of ensuring that the parties remained at the negotiation table or a financial incentive to the solicitors to find a solution. In two cases the collaborative process broke down and the parties had to instruct new lawyers, but both were happy with their new representatives and did not appear to have resented the change.[98]

In cases in which settlement was not reached within the process, participants expressed disappointment rather than anger. Nobody felt that engaging in the process was a waste of time. In general participants commented that even though the process did not work for them, they would like to think that it is a process that 'could work' for others.

> I'm very disappointed that – I had expectations, and I would still *like* to think, that it's a process that could work. But it didn't for me.[99]

On concluding her research Macfarlane questioned the need for the disqualification provision. However, she commented that:

> data gathered by this study, where every case had a DA [disqualification agreement] suggest the collaborative process fosters a spirit of openness, cooperation and commitment to finding a solution that is qualitatively different, at least in many cases, from the atmosphere created by conventional lawyer-to-lawyer negotiations – even those undertaken with a cooperative spirit.[100]

Satisfaction with the process

Of the participants who took part in the IACP research, 79% indicated that they were satisfied with the process, of whom 37% were extremely satisfied and 42% were somewhat satisfied. As that research was quantitative in nature, reasons were not given for these views. However, in response to some open-ended questions, particular aspects of the process that the participants found helpful were that meetings could be scheduled to accommodate client needs; that the process gave them an opportunity to address concerns directly and freely with the other participant; and that the process was respectful.[101]

Comments made in Macfarlane's research included:

- I don't want this [the divorce] to change me. I don't want this to make me bitter. So I think this is the best process so that you don't become bitter. I don't want to be an angry person and I think this will be helpful.
- I like the idea of no fighting. Bypass the fighting and let's get to it. It's going to happen anyway, you know. It's not a nice process but it's happened, so let's get to the other side where I can heal.

Resolution's research showed that most participants were satisfied with the process and outcome. Of the 12 clients who were interviewed for Resolution, 11 expressed satisfaction with the process. The overall result of the research was that clients felt that their divorce had been as amicable as they had hoped it would be and that as a result, it had been less damaging to their children. Most, also, felt that their level of participation in the process was appropriate.[102] Comments made included:

- We're both very pleased that the process existed ... it was a kind of embodiment of the kind of divorce that we wanted. I would certainly recommend it. But on the other hand, hopefully it's something I will only do once. So I wouldn't know what the alternatives are like!
- Both my ex [spouse] and I feel that the outcome was reasonably fair. And that there was no one individual who was damaged by it. And that it was reasonably – as sort of amicable as it could be expected to be, as you could possibly hope it could be. Under the circumstances. And that was in large measure down to the process ...[103]

The response from those interviewed by Barlow's team was much the same. Positive factors mentioned included: the ability to resolve issues in a less adversarial way while still being supported by their solicitors; the fact that settlement was reached more quickly; and that misunderstandings could be dealt with immediately rather than by engaging in protracted correspondence.[104] Specific comments made included:

- I couldn't fault it. It was just so, without having to wait for letters or worrying ... [T]here was no uncertainty and ... it was all quick and it was all sorted out together and explained together ...[105]

Disclosure

Heavin and Keet note, the 'open release of information between the parties is the apparent antithesis of litigation'.[106] This imposes obligations on litigators to ensure that they have asked the right questions. Understandably, therefore, lawyers caution clients that discovery is for their benefit:

> I think we have to explain to the clients that actually, *you* might be happy with this. But in order for the agreement to be binding, and in order for us to give you proper advice, we have to have that information. It's there to protect you rather than me.[107]

As noted earlier, however, there are occasions when the time delays and costs associated with the discovery process can outweigh the benefits of the documentation received. Ethically, and for fear of suit, this is not a risk that many lawyers are prepared to take and one that they struggle with during the collaborative process and in other alternative methods of dispute resolution. Increasingly, however, lawyers have begun to question whether 'we're doing it for the client's benefit or, to cover our own backs'.[108] Collaborative lawyers have also commented:

> when you do cases in the traditional way there is a presumption on behalf of your client, that he or she knows *nothing* about the financial situation of his or her husband or wife. What I'm finding in collaborative is, they *know* an awful lot about each other and the family finances … if you prepare your client in the right way for the first four-way, they come along very often with a lot of the financial information … So you can actually deal with a whole tranche of things very quickly, and get down to talking about the *real* issues …[109]

Engaging in the collaborative process requires separating parties to be open and upfront in relation to disclosure. They agree to provide 'relevant information' in a timely manner. Clients need to know that disclosure is a rigorous process, and no less so because they have chosen collaborative practice. On the contrary, the process requires parties to go beyond what would normally be considered discoverable within the courts' process.[110] There has been, as noted by Macfarlane, no consistent standard of relevancy and many differing practices.[111] Situations have arisen where one party will seek information that may not be strictly necessary and questions arise as to whether this should be accommodated in the 'spirit' of the process or refused as an invasion of privacy.[112] Ethical dilemmas have also arisen for lawyers when their clients refuse to provide requested information within the process.

Has the enactment of the UCLA clarified the situation regarding discovery? Arguably it has, in that S.12 specifies that:

> Except as provided by law other than this [act], during the collaborative law process, on the request of another party, a party shall make timely, full, candid, and informal disclosure of information *related to the collaborative matter* [emphasis added] without formal discovery. A party also shall update promptly previously disclosed information that has materially changed. The parties may define the scope of disclosure during the collaborative law process …

However, while important, what is related to the collaborative matter may still be a matter of debate. Also, this will apply only in States across the US in which the Act has been adopted. In other States and jurisdictions, without the benefit of a statutory provision or court order, the process continues to rely on the good will of the parties.

Clients' concerns and recommendations

The issue of informed consent was raised as a concern in that some clients felt that they could have been given 'a more thorough explanation of what to expect and how much it would cost'.[113] Additionally, parties who are not suitable should be identified or screened out of engaging in the process at an earlier stage.[114] Indeed, all of the research undertaken to date has pointed to the importance of screening. Two main issues emerged. Firstly, the vulnerable need to be protected. Secondly, clients' ability to, as noted by Coser, set parameters for the end of the conflict[115] determines to a large extent whether a case settles or not. Those who do not have the capacity to engage should be screened out of the process.

Clients expressed the view that the process should not be used in cases where there were issues of domestic violence[116] or personality disorders, and where parties were just not willing to be honest in their negotiations or unwilling to move from entrenched positions. Where there were instances of bullying or unequal bargaining power, it was found that mental health professionals were better at assessing cases than were the lawyers.[117] However, as noted earlier, mental health professionals are not routinely used in all cases and this points to the need for lawyers engaging in this process to undergo additional training with regard to screening. The findings were similar in Resolution's research. That research also highlighted the importance of establishing the extent to which the parties were willing and able to negotiate, to communicate and to understand the importance of the best interests of their children.[118] Trust between the clients was also an important factor.

Concerns were also expressed in relation to timing, indicating that in some cases lawyers could have done more to move the process forward and to improve the scheduling of meetings. For the participants in Barlow's study, issues of concern included: the difficulty of discussing matters face to face; the fact that some solicitors were perceived as too impartial; and the lack of a mechanism to ensure disclosure of information.[119] The issue of costs was cited as a negative aspect of collaborative practice by Barlow's participants; this was in contrast to the findings in the Irish research and that of Resolution.[120]

Aside from their own ability to participate and negotiate, clients rated the ability of their lawyers as a key factor in the success or failure of the process. This was evident across all studies.

- I very much think that the whole process depends on how skilled your solicitor is at the process really. I think I would be telling you a different story if [my solicitor] hadn't been as good at it.[121]

A number of clients commented that their lawyers seemed to underestimate the level of emotionality that would inevitably colour the negotiation process between separating/divorcing spouses.[122] Sometimes clients experienced this as a denial of their feelings and an attempt to impose a false 'harmony' on the situation. Comments made included:

- Emotionally, it is very difficult. The real danger is that they deal with people in an emotionally dangerous time … The lawyers are encouraging the expression of emotions. So we both do. But they are not psychologists! They encourage the expression of emotion but they don't know how to deal with it.[123]
- I think anybody contemplating it would have to be aware of just how traumatic it is, to actually sit down, and discuss something in very dispassionate terms, when you're not actually feeling that way.[124]

Is it only for low conflict cases?

In assessing the suitability of different processes for different types of cases, it has been asserted that collaborative practice is really only suitable where there is low conflict.[125] However, the research has shown that in many cases there were considerable issues and tension between the parties, varying between the relationship being described as 'delicate' through to 'a great deal of animosity', and that engaging in the process, though difficult, helped the parties to work through the separation.[126] In analysing the research undertaken by the IACP, it is clear that what it terms 'difficult' and 'very difficult cases' are more likely to terminate. Factors that were recorded as being the most significant indications that a case may terminate included:

> one or both clients invaded the privacy of the other, verbal abuse, cooperation between clients was always or almost always impossible, one or both clients was reluctant to disclose everything right away or refused to disclose some information at all, one or both clients threatened to go to court, one or more clients stopped attending meetings, and one or both clients acted unilaterally.[127]

Clients' comments also indicate that many cases were challenging:

- The first four-way was a huge fight. The lawyers just sat back and looked amazed … they should have done a better job of screening us at the outset so this would be expected. Have lawyers not been trained to manage the process?[128]
- [T]he lawyers seemed shocked that the clients had emotional baggage – but this was a 24-year marriage. What did they expect?[129]

For about half of the clients who took part in Resolution's research, they considered important issues to be 'contentious'.[130] In some of the cases presented in that research, however, the atmosphere was described as difficult – either at times or throughout, and a small number of clients found the four-way meetings very difficult to cope with: 'It felt very tense for me, I felt very tense, all the way through' and '... it remained difficult. And to be honest, I wouldn't have been able to do it without [my solicitor]'.[131]

Barlow has noted that collaborative practice can be suitable for cases in which there is significant psychological disparity between the clients, a power imbalance, or complex financial issues, as the parties will have their lawyers present to assist them in dealing with these issues or indeed they may choose a team approach.[132] This would seem to accord with the research findings in that many cases, though difficult and challenging, were settled through the process.

Costs

Logic would suggest that using the collaborative process should be more cost effective. Achieving settlement within the lawyer-only model, costs of protracted litigation and a court hearing are avoided. Engaging in the multidisciplinary model, experts are engaged by the parties jointly, saving the costs of two sets of experts. Collaborative lawyers, however, have been cautious about presenting the model as a cheaper option. Members of the Bar have argued to the contrary, speaking of the additional costs involved when cases do not settle and another lawyer is engaged. However, could this be more expensive than the current model in England and Ireland, in which clients will often have both solicitors and barristers by the time a case is finalised through a negotiated settlement or trial?

Macfarlane noted that some of the participants she interviewed were enticed into the process by what she describes as the 'pitch' that it would be a faster and cheaper process.[133] In 2006, Greco carried out an analysis of 'an extensive survey' on collaborative cases collected over a six month period in 2004. Of 160 cases reported, 127 or 79.4% settled. Eight cases or 5% reconciled. Greco reports that the survey 'produced results strongly suggestive of the cost effectiveness or efficiency of the collaborative divorce process, at least with regard to the level of professionals fees involved'.[134] He noted that costs are lower for collaborative divorces than for contested divorces, and he attributes this to the 'long accepted notion in economic theory that specialised use of resources increased the efficiency of the production of goods and services'.[135]

In the US, 81% of the parties surveyed considered the attorney's fees that were charged for their own lawyer very reasonable or somewhat reasonable.[136] Resolution's research indicated that in 29% of the cases examined, clients saved both time and money. For 34% of cases the timescale was quicker and the costs were about the same. However 13% of respondents thought there was no difference in timescales or costs, and 13% thought that the process was more expensive than the traditional courts' process.[137] One client was of the view that the collaborative process was more expensive:

> It was *bloody* expensive, but, actually I – well, quite expensive ... And I – it had crossed my mind, earlier, to try and do a cheap and cheerful or whatever,

but I think, the final outcome was worth the amount of money. Because I think, if I'd tried to do a cheap one I felt, I think I would have left loose ends … at the end of the day …[138]

As noted earlier, the issue of costs was raised as a negative aspect of the process in the research undertaken by Barlow *et al.* Expectedly, where cases did not settle within the process, costs were higher. In general, where there were high levels of acrimony costs tend to increase accordingly.

The best interests of the child

Across all of the studies, separating parties cited that one of their main reasons for choosing the collaborative process was that it would be better for their children. The expectation was that it would help with reducing the conflict, learning to communicate effectively so as to co-parent more effectively in the future, and allaying concerns about 'role-modelling', so that their children could look back on how their parents dealt with the separation and how respectful they had been towards each other and the family.

- For me, with all the benefits of CFL, the issue of the children is the one that's still foremost in my mind, because … almost every client I have who has children will tell me in one form or the other that's what matters most to them. And when they're looking back on this 20 years later, it will [be] how their kids emerged from this that's really going to matter to them the most. That's where the greatest benefits can come – if they can find something even as simple as an access schedule that never would have occurred to them, that isn't measured of percentages of hours and days, but measured in terms of real quality [time] with their children, and if they can just get [to] that point of trust where they know that they will voluntarily help each other.[139]
- My mind-set for this process was, I never want to have any circumstance happen in the future where … my children would come to me and say, 'You know, Dad, you really weren't fair with Mom'.[140]

Despite this motivation, it was interesting to note across all studies that there was a lack of willingness to engage the services of a child specialist to hear their children's views or to scaffold them through the transition. There is no research to date on the extent to which children whose parents used the process felt that it benefited them or the family as a whole. Neither is there any research on children's actual experience of engaging with a child specialist.

One issue that arose, however, was that the process enabled a wider consideration of the family as a whole. Frequently, within the adversarial system, little consideration is given to older children. One lawyer commented:

- You'd ask how old the children were, and if they're over 18 well they're just off the agenda completely. And yet as parents they're still concerned about them.[141]

As noted in Chapter 3, the collaborative process provides a forum within which the needs of all of the family members can be taken into account, regardless of their age.

Ethical issues

Macfarlane found that there was little explicit acknowledgement of ethical issues that may arise for lawyers during the collaborative process. As a method that allows for and encourages flexibility and diversity of practice; it is important that clear ethical guidelines are established as to what is considered appropriate behaviour within the process. The unique features of the process, including the contractual nature of the participation agreement, the commitment to acting in good faith and being open regarding disclosure and more complex extraneous issues of new relationships, and the consequences of the disqualification provision all heighten the need for lawyers to behave ethically in the advice that they give to their clients and in the management of the process. As noted earlier, the IACP has addressed the issue of ethics in its code of practice, and this has also been legislated for under the UCLA. However, the fact that there was little reference across the studies to ethical issues that may arise in the course of the process, points to the need for more debate.

One lawyer voiced concerns:

> So what if an outcome that my client wants is not one that is really good for the family? I can reflect this judgment back to the client ... but I do not know what is best for my client – the client does ... [T]he grey issues are difficult here.[142]

In reality, lawyers have to make difficult decisions in advising clients regardless of the process used. There are no ethical standards that apply to negotiating through lawyers or on the steps of the court. Under Section 13 of the UCLA, lawyers remain subject to their professional and ethical standards. Difficulties may arise where other experts engaged as part of the process may not be subject to such regulation. It is recommended by the IACP that all mental health experts are licensed. However, it is also important to note that the IACP is not a disciplinary body.

Is it an easier option for lawyers and clients?

As noted in Chapter 1, critics of collaborative practice and the comprehensive movement generally have commented that such processes may arise from lawyers' 'intellectual laziness, woolliness, a discomfort with conflict, or the realities of the adversarial system of justice'.[143] With the exception of one lawyer in Macfarlane's research, who cites lack of preparation as freeing him from having preconceived ideas as to how a case should be settled:

> I don't sit there and go through the three inches of information that they bring me, and I'm not going to do that. I am going to go into the meeting

> and look at it there and I always joke and say, 'Yeah, you don't want to pay me twice to look at that,' and everyone goes, 'Yeah, ha ha ha.' … [B]ecause we're going to look at it anyway … in the meeting,[144]

Most lawyers saw their role as being more onerous in the collaborative process than in positional negotiation. Indeed, as will be outlined in Chapter 5, one of the Irish collaborative lawyers interviewed highlighted lack of preparation on the part of lawyers as one of the main reasons for issues not being resolved through the collaborative process. The difference for him between positional negotiation and negotiation during the collaborative process is that lawyers have spent more time discussing the case with their own client and with the lawyer on the other side, so that by being more prepared, the negotiation can be more relevant, meaningful and effective with the clients themselves actively engaged in finding a solution.

Macfarlane has commented that 'the culture of adversarial litigation has remained remarkably impervious to change',[145] and the majority of collaborative lawyers interviewed across all studies were of the belief that rather than it being an easier process, it can be more difficult to think collaboratively:

> Sometimes we catch ourselves. It's hard not to [bargain positionally], because we have done it for a long time. We are used to it. That's what we learned at law school from day one. It's really hard work.[146]

Nevertheless, Macfarlane notes that a 'number of CFL lawyers say CFL has affected their whole approach to the practice of law'.[147] Lawyers in Sefton's research also commented on this change in practice:

- the way we litigate has probably changed, in that we talk much more, and we do potentially look outside the box more …[148]
- I think it's made us more aware, and more rounded lawyers.[149]

Clients too commented that: 'It's a lot easier to do hierarchy decision making. It's much more familiar and comforting'; they also described it as 'painful but easy'.[150] Others expressed the view that in many ways it is easier to 'write a big cheque and pull the trigger'.[151] However, the general consensus was that they would recommend the collaborative process to a friend in a similar situation:

- If anyone asked for my recommendation I would suggest if they could afford it, or if they could manage it, I would do this … If you can possibly do it this way I would recommend doing it this way.
- The whole system was, as painless as it could be … And I think it would be something that I would recommend to people. And say, at least try.

An issue that was evident in all of the research was the importance of trust between lawyers. As the process requires a fundamental change in the way lawyers approach family law cases, it is very important that each lawyer can rely on his or her colleagues to screen clients as to their suitability and to work constructively to reach the best settlement for all of the parties. Important elements of establishing this trust hinge on a lawyer's reputation for being trustworthy in the past. If this trust is broken it may be difficult or impossible to regain. Equally important is a recognition that not all lawyers are suitable for collaborative practice; Macfarlane notes that 'not every lawyer will have the necessary skills to deal with every potential collaborative case.'[152]

Macfarlane cautions that there is a tendency amongst collaborative lawyers to 'overemphasize process structure and to underemphasize the skills and techniques lawyers need to properly manage high-conflict cases, or cases that are at an impasse or stalled'.[153] As noted in chapter 1, developing additional skills is an important element of the comprehensive law movement. Key skills identified as being necessary for lawyers during the collaborative process include: active listening; allowing the clients autonomy to contribute to the settlement negotiations and have their voices heard; and also, perhaps, most significantly, challenging their own clients' perceptions of the dispute and helping them to see the issue from different perspectives.

Many of the lawyers interviewed in Resolution's research spoke about the need for ongoing training and development, as engaging in the process is 'a constant learning curve' with each case bringing up something new.[154] Central to this skill development is an appreciation and understanding of the role of emotions within the separation process. Emotions are often side-lined within the adversarial system, but they play an important role in resolution during the collaborative process. Such concerns highlight the value in the interdisciplinary model; however, as the lawyer-only model is often the one that is most frequently used, this again raises the importance of skills training for lawyers, even if merely to recognise when they are out of their depth and need to engage additional assistance rather than taking on a semi-therapeutic role without the requisite knowledge or experience.[155] Indeed, as Macfarlane commented, '[i]n some of these cases, it may be inadvisable for lawyers to proceed without a commitment from their clients to incorporate the expertise of coaches into the team.'[156]

Conclusion

Collaborative practice has been available for over twenty years. As with the courts' process, ordinary lawyer negotiation and mediation, it has been commended and criticised. The research undertaken to date, much of which was carried out before the process was scrutinised by the Uniform Law Commission, highlights that safeguards need to be in place to ensure that clients entering the process do so with informed consent, and that they have the capacity to engage. It is not in the clients' or the lawyers' interests to proceed with a case that is not suited to the structured nature and good-faith ethos of the process. Vulnerable parties need to be protected through proper screening. Lawyers need to develop the skill-set required to practice in this way, and to appreciate when they need the assistance of other professionals, rather than risk causing further trauma to a client by not being sufficiently equipped to deal with the emotional or other issues that may arise.

Although over twenty years in existence, in the context of the history and long-established traditions of the legal profession internationally, collaborative practice is in its infancy. The research across all the studies examined in this chapter demonstrates that settlement rates and client satisfaction within the process appear to be high. Many participants spoke of experiencing improved communication and empowerment, and the research would not seem to support the contention that the process is only suitable for low-conflict cases. Clients throughout all of the studies have indicated that they did not enter the process without due consideration, but once they chose this option, there was a strong sense of commitment to making the process work.

Is this influenced by the disqualification provision? In some instances it is, but this seems to be more from the perspective of not wanting to lose their lawyer rather than the issue of costs. The research does not indicate that prospective parties failed to use the process because of the implications of the disqualification provision. Many, in fact, saw it as a positive aspect to the process that encouraged them to confront issues and move on.

Despite the assertions that collaborative practice is prohibitively expensive, there was no evidence of this in the research undertaken. Many clients across the studies, with the exception of that undertaken by Barlow, were keen to highlight the fact that they saved time and money. In cases where settlement was not reached or where there was increased conflict, costs were higher. This would appear to be the case no matter what process was used.

Clients were keen to stress the importance of the skill of their lawyer in managing the process and in supporting them throughout the process. Where the process failed, this seemed in no small part to be down to a lack of management by the lawyers. In general clients felt that they got the legal advice that they needed; however, they were keen to express the view that they expected to get this legal advice from their lawyers. Indeed, one of their main reasons for choosing collaborative practice over mediation is that they would have this additional support and advice as part of the collaborative process. Only further longitudinal research will show whether the initial positive response of participants who used the process will lead to long-term benefits for these clients and their families.

Notes

1 Macfarlane, J., *The Emerging Phenomenon of Collaborative Family Law (CFL): A Qualitative Case Study* (Department of Justice Canada, 2005).This research was undertaken at nine locations across the US and Canada in the first year, with more in-depth follow-on research undertaken in four locations: Vancouver and Medicine Hat in Canada and San Francisco and Minneapolis in the US.

2 Wray, L., and Lloyd, S., *Research regarding Collaborative Practice: A Comparison of Findings from the International Academy of Collaborative Professionals and Resolution* (IACP 10th Annual Forum, October 2010).

3 Sefton, M., *Collaborative Family Law: A report for Resolution* (Resolution, 2009).

4 Barlow, A., Hunter, R., Smithson, J., and Ewing, J., *Mapping Paths to Family Justice* (Economic and Social Research Council (ESRC), June 2014) Available at http://

socialsciences.exeter.ac.uk/law/research/frs/researchprojects/mappingpathstofamilyjustice/. Last accessed 1 August 2016.

5 Schwab, W., 'Collaborative Lawyering: A Closer Look at an Emerging Practice' (2004) 4 *Pepperdine Dispute Resolution Law Journal* 351–399; Keet, M., Wiegers, W., and Morrison, M., 'Client Engagement Inside Collaborative Law' (2008) 24 *Canadian Journal of Family Law* 145–204; Shields, R.W., 'On Becoming a Collaborative Professional: From Paradigm Shifting to Transformative Learning Through Critical Reflection and Dialogue' (2008) *Journal of Dispute Resolution* 427–463; Lande, J., 'An Empirical Analysis of Collaborative Practice' (2011) 49 (2) *Family Court Review,* 257–281; Wright, K., 'The evolving role of the family lawyer: the impact of collaborative law on family law practice' (2011) 23 *Child and Family Law Quarterly* 370–92; Healy, C., 'Dispute Resolution through Collaborative Practice: A Comparative Analysis' (2015) 27 (2) *Child and Family Law Quarterly* 173–193.

6 Where possible, direct comparisons are made. This was not always feasible, however, as different studies often focus on different aspects of the process.

7 Macfarlane, J., *The Emerging Phenomenon of Collaborative Family Law (CFL): A Qualitative Case Study* (Department of Justice Canada, 2005) at 85.

8 Barlow, A., Hunter, R., Smithson, J. and Ewing, J., *Mapping Paths to Family Justice* (ESRC, June 2014).

9 Keet, M., Wiegers, W., and Morrison, M., 'Client Engagement inside Collaborative Law' (2008) 24 *Canadian Journal of Family Law* 145–204, 157.

10 Sefton, M., *Collaborative Family Law: A report for Resolution* (Resolution, 2009) at 18.

11 Percentage of cases relating to separation or divorce: US 97%, Ireland 100%, England/Wales 95%.

12 Schwab, W., 'Collaborative Lawyering: A Closer Look at an Emerging Practice' (2004) 4 *Pepperdine Dispute Resolution Law Journal* 351–399, 373.

13 The Legal Aid Board in Ireland was proactive in organising training in collaborative practice for its lawyers, and it offers low-income clients the option of availing of the service.

14 Sefton, M., *Collaborative Family Law: A report for Resolution* (Resolution, 2009) at vi.

15 This was also evident in the research carried out by Resolution, which revealed that private solicitors took cases for low-income clients at significantly lower rates. See Sefton, M., *Collaborative Family Law: A report for Resolution* (Resolution, 2009) at 31.

16 Barlow, A., Hunter, R., Smithson, J. and Ewing, J., *Mapping Paths to Family Justice* (ESRC, June 2014) at 4. This accords with findings in Wright, K., 'The evolving role of the family lawyer: the impact of collaborative law on family law practice' (2011) 23 *Child and Family Law Quarterly* 370–392, 372.

17 Macfarlane, J., *The Emerging Phenomenon of Collaborative Family Law (CFL): A Qualitative Case Study* (Department of Justice Canada, 2005) at ix.

18 Ibid. at 23.

19 Wray, L., *The International Academy of Collaborative Professionals Research Regarding Client Experience* at 7; presented by Linda Wray (IACP 11th Annual Forum, Washington D.C., October 2010).

20 70% of Irish participants expressed this view, as did the majority of participants in Resolution's study.

21 Sefton, M., *Collaborative Family Law: A report for Resolution* (Resolution, 2009) at 1.

22 Barlow, A., Hunter, R., Smithson, J., and Ewing, J., *Mapping Paths to Family Justice* (ESRC, June 2014) at 5.

23 Ibid.

24 Ibid.

25 Ibid. at 7.

26 Macfarlane, J., *The Emerging Phenomenon of Collaborative Family Law (CFL): A Qualitative Case Study* (Department of Justice Canada, 2005) at 75.

27 Ibid. at xiii.
28 Ibid. at 14.
29 Barlow, A., Hunter, R., Smithson, J., and Ewing, J., *Mapping Paths to Family Justice* (Economic and Social Research Council, June 2014) at 18. Available at http://socialsciences.exeter.ac.uk/law/research/frs/researchprojects/mappingpathstofamilyjustice/. Last accessed 1 August 2016.
30 Healy, C., 'Collaborative Practice: An Interdisciplinary Approach to the Resolution of Conflict in Family Law Matters' in *Family Law and Culture in Europe, Developments, Challenges and Opportunities*, Boele-Woelki, K., and Dethloff, N., (eds) (Intersentia, 2014) 119–134 at 130; Keet, M., Wiegers, W., and Morrison, M., 'Client Engagement inside Collaborative Law' (2008) 24 *Canadian Journal of Family Law* 145–204 at 186–187.
31 Wray, L., and Lloyd, S., *Research regarding Collaborative Practice: A Comparison of Findings from the International Academy of Collaborative Professionals and Resolution* (IACP 10th Annual Forum, October 2010) at 8.
32 Ibid. at 16.
33 Sefton, M., *Collaborative Family Law: A report for Resolution* (Resolution, 2009) at 30.
34 Barlow, A., Hunter, R., Smithson, J., and Ewing, J., *Mapping Paths to Family Justice* (ESRC, June 2014) at 7.
35 Ibid. at 13.
36 See Chapter 5.
37 Macfarlane, J., *The Emerging Phenomenon of Collaborative Family Law (CFL): A Qualitative Case Study* (Department of Justice Canada, 2005) at 18.
38 Ibid.
39 Ibid. at 26.
40 Ibid. at 27.
41 Sefton, M., *Collaborative Family Law: A report for Resolution* (Resolution, 2009) at 25.
42 Ibid.
43 Barlow, A., Hunter, R., Smithson, J., and Ewing, J., *Mapping Paths to Family Justice* (ESRC, June 2014) at 16.
44 Ibid.
45 Wright, K., 'The evolving role of the family lawyer: the impact of collaborative law on family law practice' (2011) 23 *Child and Family Law Quarterly* 370–392 at 392.
46 Macfarlane, J., *The Emerging Phenomenon of Collaborative Family Law (CFL): A Qualitative Case Study* (Department of Justice Canada, 2005) at viii.
47 Ibid. at 8.
48 Ibid.
49 Ibid. at 11.
50 Ibid. at 8.
51 Wright, K., 'The evolving role of the family lawyer: the impact of collaborative law on family law practice' (2011) 23 *Child and Family Law Quarterly* 370–392, 388.
52 Sefton, M., *Collaborative Family Law: A report for Resolution* (Resolution, 2009) at viii.
53 Ibid. at 8.
54 Ibid. at 36.
55 Ibid. at 37.
56 Sefton, M., *Collaborative Family Law: A report for Resolution* (Resolution, 2009) at viii.
57 Ibid. at 37.
58 Ibid. at 38.
59 Macfarlane, J., *The Emerging Phenomenon of Collaborative Family Law (CFL): A Qualitative Case Study* (Department of Justice Canada, 2005). at 48.

60 Ibid at xi.
61 Wray, L., *The International Academy of Collaborative Professionals Research Regarding Client Experience* (IACP 11th Annual Forum, Washington D.C, October 2010) at 2.
62 Sefton, M., *Collaborative Family Law: A report for Resolution* (Resolution, 2009) at 50 (Emphasis added).
63 In Ireland, mental health experts are called 'Personal and Family Consultants'.
64 This was also evident in the research undertaken in Ireland. See Chapter 5.
65 Sefton, M., *Collaborative Family Law: A report for Resolution* (Resolution, 2009) at 50.
66 Macfarlane, J., *The Emerging Phenomenon of Collaborative Family Law (CFL): A Qualitative Case Study* (Department of Justice Canada, 2005) at 7.
67 Mayer, B., *Beyond Neutrality: Confronting the Crisis in Conflict Resolution* (Jossey-Bass, 2004) at 6.
68 Collaborative lawyers in Ireland cited 'lethargy' amongst lawyers as one of the main barriers to the multidisciplinary approach. See Chapter 5.
69 Macfarlane, J., *The Emerging Phenomenon of Collaborative Family Law (CFL): A Qualitative Case Study* (Department of Justice Canada, 2005) at 78.
70 Ibid. at 52.
71 92% of the settled cases achieved settlement on all issues, and 4% reached partial settlement.
72 In the quantitative research undertaken in Ireland, 81% of cases settled, and in one case the parties reconciled.
73 Barlow, A., Hunter, R., Smithson, J. and Ewing, J., *Mapping Paths to Family Justice* (ESRC, June 2014) at 19.
74 Ibid.
75 Macfarlane, J., *The Emerging Phenomenon of Collaborative Family Law (CFL): A Qualitative Case Study* (Department of Justice Canada, 2005) at 58.
76 Ibid. at 2.
77 Ibid. at 57.
78 Sefton, M., *Collaborative Family Law: A report for Resolution* (Resolution, 2009) at 43.
79 Ibid.
80 Mayer, B., *Beyond Neutrality: Confronting the Crisis in Conflict Resolution* (Jossey-Bass, 2004) at 6.
81 Macfarlane, J., *The Emerging Phenomenon of Collaborative Family Law (CFL): A Qualitative Case Study* (Department of Justice Canada, 2005) at 52.
82 Ibid. at xii.
83 Keet, M., Wiegers, W., and Morrison, M., 'Client Engagement inside Collaborative Law' (2008) 24 *Canadian Journal of Family Law* 145–204, 201 referring to *Hartshorne v. Hartshorne*, 2004 SCC 22, [2004] 1 S.C.R. *550; Miglin v. Miglin*, 2003 SCC 24, [2003] 1 S.C.R. 303.
84 Keet, M., Wiegers, W., and Morrison, M., 'Client Engagement inside Collaborative Law' (2008) 24 *Canadian Journal of Family Law* 145–204, 186–189.
85 Mayer, B., *The Dynamics of Conflict Resolution: A Practitioner's Guide* (Jossey-Bass, 2000) at 31–33.
86 Keet, M., Wiegers, W., and Morrison, M., 'Client Engagement inside Collaborative Law' (2008) 24 *Canadian Journal of Family Law* 145–204 at 152.
87 Ibid. at 170.
88 Barlow, A., Hunter, R., Smithson, J., and Ewing, J., *Mapping Paths to Family Justice* (ESRC, June 2014), at 21.
89 Sefton, M., *Collaborative Family Law: A report for Resolution* (Resolution, 2009) at 33.

90 See Chapter 5.
91 See Chapter 5.
92 Macfarlane, J., *The Emerging Phenomenon of Collaborative Family Law (CFL): A Qualitative Case Study* (Department of Justice Canada, 2005) at 39.
93 Schwab, W., 'Collaborative Lawyering: A Closer Look at an Emerging Practice' (2004) 4 *Pepperdine Dispute Resolution Law Journal* 351–399, 379.
94 Ibid.
95 Keet, M., Wiegers, W., and Morrison, M., 'Client Engagement inside Collaborative Law' (2008) 24 *Canadian Journal of Family Law* 145–204 at 192.
96 Schwab, W., 'Collaborative Lawyering: A Closer Look at an Emerging Practice' (2004) 4 *Pepperdine Dispute Resolution Law Journal* 351–399 at 379.
97 This correlates with Macfarlane's research, where she notes that clients are somewhat mystified at the length that lawyers have to go to avoid court.
98 Barlow, A., Hunter, R., Smithson, J., and Ewing, J., *Mapping Paths to Family Justice* (ESRC, June 2014) at 13.
99 Ibid. at 44.
100 Macfarlane, J., *The Emerging Phenomenon of Collaborative Family Law (CFL): A Qualitative Case Study* (Department of Justice Canada, 2005) at 78.
101 Wray, L., *The International Academy of Collaborative Professionals Research Regarding Client Experience* at 14 (IACP 11th Annual Forum, Washington D.C., October 2010).
102 Sefton, M., *Collaborative Family Law: A report for Resolution* (Resolution, 2009) at 43.
103 Ibid.
104 This was also mentioned in Keet's study. See Keet, M., Wiegers, W., and Morrison, M., 'Client Engagement inside Collaborative Law' (2008) 24 *Canadian Journal of Family Law* 145–204 at 180.
105 Barlow, A., Hunter, R., Smithson, J., and Ewing, J., *Mapping Paths to Family Justice* (ESRC, June 2014) at 13.
106 Heavin, H., and Keet, M., '"Skating to Where the Puck Will Be": Exploring Settlement Counsel and Risk Analysis in the Negotiation of Business Disputes' (2013) 76 *Saskatchewan Law Review* 191–211 at 194.
107 Sefton, M., *Collaborative Family Law: A report for Resolution* (Resolution, 2009) at 39.
108 Ibid. This was also evident in the Irish research. See Chapter 5.
109 Sefton, M., *Collaborative Family Law: A report for Resolution* (Resolution, 2009) at 38 (emphasis in the original).
110 To disclose new relationships, future work plans, etc.
111 Macfarlane, J., *The Emerging Phenomenon of Collaborative Family Law (CFL): A Qualitative Case Study* (Department of Justice Canada, 2005) at x.
112 Ibid. at 68–69.
113 Wray, L., *The International Academy of Collaborative Professionals Research Regarding Client Experience* at 17 (IACP 11th Annual Forum, Washington D.C., October 2010).
114 Ibid.
115 Coser, L.A., 'The Termination of Conflict' (1961) 5 (4) *The Journal of Conflict Resolution* 347–353 at 347.
116 Keet, M., Wiegers, W., and Morrison, M., 'Client Engagement inside Collaborative Law' (2008) 24 *Canadian Journal of Family Law* 145–204 at 195, also highlighted the need for screening.
117 Sefton, M., *Collaborative Family Law: A report for Resolution* (Resolution, 2009) at 29.
118 Ibid. at vii.
119 Barlow, A., Hunter, R., Smithson, J., and Ewing, J., *Mapping Paths to Family Justice* (ESCR, June 2014).

120 Ibid. at 13.
121 Sefton, M., *Collaborative Family Law: A report for Resolution* (Resolution, 2009) at 34.
122 Barlow, A., Hunter, R., Smithson, J., and Ewing, J., *Mapping Paths to Family Justice* (ESCR, June 2014).
123 Macfarlane, J., *The Emerging Phenomenon of Collaborative Family Law (CFL): A Qualitative Case Study* (Department of Justice Canada, 2005) at 35.
124 Ibid. Similar results were recorded in Keet's research; five out of seven participants were satisfied with the process.
125 Schwab, for example, questions whether settlement rates would be the same if high-conflict, low-functioning clients were not screened out. See Schwab, W., 'Collaborative Lawyering: A Closer Look at an Emerging Practice' (2004) 4 *Pepperdine Dispute Resolution Law Journal* 351–399, 376.
126 Sefton, M., *Collaborative Family Law: A report for Resolution* (Resolution, 2009) at 39.
127 Cox, G., and Wray, L.K., 'Comparing Difficult with Very Difficult Terminated and Settled Collaborative Cases' available at https://www.collaborativepractice.com/media/2818/Comparing_Difficult_Very_Difficult_Terminated_Settled_Cases_2011_08_29.pdf. Last accessed 14 August 2016.
128 Macfarlane, J., *The Emerging Phenomenon of Collaborative Family Law (CFL): A Qualitative Case Study* (Department of Justice Canada, 2005) at 35.
129 Ibid.
130 Sefton, M., *Collaborative Family Law: A report for Resolution* (Resolution, 2009) at 40.
131 Ibid. at 41.
132 Barlow, A., Hunter, R., Smithson, J., and Ewing, J., *Mapping Paths to Family Justice* (ESCR Council, June 2014) at 25.
133 Macfarlane, J., *The Emerging Phenomenon of Collaborative Family Law (CFL): A Qualitative Case Study* (Department of Justice Canada, 2005) at 23.
134 Greco, A., 'Professional Fees Associated with Collaborative Divorce Resolution: The Evidence to Date' (2006) 13 (3) *Journal of Legal Economics* 75–88 at 84.
135 Ibid. at 78, referring to Smith, A., *The Wealth of Nations* (Dent, 1905).
136 Wray, L., and Lloyd, S., *Research regarding Collaborative Practice: A Comparison of Findings from the International Academy of Collaborative Professionals and Resolution* (IACP 10th Annual Forum, October 2009) at 24.
137 Sefton, M., *Collaborative Family Law: A report for Resolution* (Resolution, 2009) at 53.
138 Ibid. (emphasis in the original).
139 Macfarlane, J., *The Emerging Phenomenon of Collaborative Family Law (CFL): A Qualitative Case Study* (Department of Justice Canada, 2005) at 20.
140 Ibid. at 23.
141 Sefton, M., *Collaborative Family Law: A report for Resolution* (Resolution, 2009) at 23.
142 Macfarlane, J., *The Emerging Phenomenon of Collaborative Family Law (CFL): A Qualitative Case Study* (Department of Justice Canada, 2005) at 46.
143 Freckelton, I., 'Therapeutic Jurisprudence Misunderstood and Misrepresented: The Price and Risks of Influence' (2008) 30 *Thomas Jefferson Law Review*, 575–596, 593.
144 Macfarlane, J., *The Emerging Phenomenon of Collaborative Family Law (CFL): A Qualitative Case Study* (Department of Justice Canada, 2005) at 36–37.
145 Ibid. at 4.
146 Sefton, M., *Collaborative Family Law: A report for Resolution* (Resolution, 2009) at 32.
147 Macfarlane, J., *The Emerging Phenomenon of Collaborative Family Law (CFL): A Qualitative Case Study* (Department of Justice Canada, 2005) at 33.
148 Sefton, M., *Collaborative Family Law: A report for Resolution* (Resolution, 2009) at 48.
149 Ibid.
150 Macfarlane, J., *The Emerging Phenomenon of Collaborative Family Law (CFL): A Qualitative Case Study* (Department of Justice Canada, 2005) at 81.

151 Ibid. at 22.
152 Ibid. at 85.
153 Macfarlane, J., *The Emerging Phenomenon of Collaborative Family Law (CFL): A Qualitative Case Study* (Department of Justice Canada, 2005) at 80.
154 Sefton, M., *Collaborative Family Law: A report for Resolution* (Resolution, 2009) at 48.
155 Keet, M., Wiegers, W., and Morrison, M., 'Client Engagement inside Collaborative Law' (2008) 24 *Canadian Journal of Family Law* 145–204 at 201. The importance of 'informed understanding of the impact of abusive relationships' is highlighted.
156 Macfarlane, J., *The Emerging Phenomenon of Collaborative Family Law (CFL): A Qualitative Case Study* (Department of Justice Canada, 2005) at 80.

5 Exploring the development of collaborative practice in Ireland

Introduction

This chapter will provide an insight into collaborative practice in Ireland. As there was no pre-existing research into the process from an Irish family law perspective, this was an exploratory study aimed at beginning a discussion and laying the groundwork for further analysis. Through a national survey of collaborative lawyers, it provides a snapshot of the development of collaborative practice; using qualitative research methods (semi-structured interviews), it provides an in-depth and robust contextual analysis of the views expressed by a sample of clients who used the process, and also, of Irish collaborative lawyers who purport to have made the 'paradigm shift'. Unlike the research undertaken internationally, this study also provides an insight into the views of a sample of adversarial lawyers who, to date, have not embraced alternative methods of dispute resolution and who have been somewhat critical of the collaborative process in particular. It will address whether these criticisms have been borne out in the research findings. Significantly, it will also highlight what the legal profession views as the barriers to using a collaborative approach and, in particular, the multidisciplinary model, requiring as it does, not only an acceptance of a more client-inclusive process, but also of one that promotes the benefits of experts from other disciplines working with lawyers, to provide a more holistic solution to conflict resolution.

The key research questions

Following on from the research undertaken internationally, similar questions are addressed in this study, including: the extent to which the collaborative process has been used by separating couples in Ireland; their satisfaction or otherwise with the process; whether outcomes achieved through the collaborative process are different from those determined within the courts' process and if so, in what way? Is there a need for such a process or can cases be settled as effectively by solicitors/barristers negotiating for clients within the adversarial system? Is the process only suitable for wealthy clients? What impact, if any, does the disqualification provision have on clients' decisions to use the process, and, to what extent did it keep them at the negotiating table longer than they may have chosen to remain, without the existence of such a provision? Finally, in a climate in which separation and divorce are becoming more commonplace with clients seeking less adversarial and more holistic approaches, the chapter will conclude by examining the extent to which lawyers are willing to embrace new methods of dispute resolution outside the long-established, and somewhat change-resistant, adversarial legal system.

Methodology

Having examined the literature on research methodologies,[1] it was decided to use a mixed-method approach to gather data, and to analyse the findings through the lens of interpretative phenomenological analysis (IPA). IPA facilitates a 'detailed examination of human lived experience'.[2] Each party's experience of separation or divorce is unique and this research technique allows for the philosophical, and idiographic, aspects of the participants' experience to be interpreted by the researcher. Additionally, a phenomenological approach is suitable when examining a small sample within each category of participants. Typically, between five and ten participants are interviewed, as larger samples would not allow for in-depth analysis. Common themes are identified across the sample by eliciting areas of convergence and divergence.[3]

O'Leary notes that the 'product of phenomenological studies is phenomenological descriptions'. The 'process of generating such descriptions generally involves sourcing people who have experienced a particular phenomenon.'[4] Once identified, these participants are questioned (in this case, using in-depth interviews), until 'saturation' is achieved, i.e. additional interviews no longer add a new perspective.[5] This provides what Kvale describes as a 'construction site of knowledge'.[6] Taking this approach ensures that issues of interest to the researcher are addressed, while also allowing 'the participant's perspective on the phenomenon ... (to) unfold as the participant views it (the emic perspective), not as the researcher views it (the etic perspective).'[7]

A specific topic guide was designed for each category of interviewee, using social science research methods.[8] Efforts were made to avoid ambiguous or leading questions and to recognise and bracket any potential subjective opinions affecting the data. In all categories, full details of the research were given to the interviewees in advance. All participants were volunteers and were assured that they could end the interview at any time. Consent forms were signed in advance, either in person or consent was given by e-mail. All interviews were recorded and transcribed. Each interview typically took from 30 minutes to one hour.

To gain an understanding of the development of collaborative practice nationally, quantitative methods of research were also used.[9] A questionnaire, sent to collaborative lawyers registered with the Association of Collaborative Practitioners, included both closed and open-ended questions. Thus, the quantitative research was undertaken from what O'Leary describes as a 'qualitative perspective with an acceptance of quantitative data'.[10] This approach added breadth to the study by allowing for its representativeness to be tested through triangulation with similar research carried out internationally.

Sampling

Quantitative research

In constructing a sampling frame for a nationwide questionnaire, the target population was lawyers trained in the collaborative process. The only way of identifying this group was to seek permission from the Association of Collaborative Practitioners (ACP), the umbrella group for collaborative lawyers in Ireland. Permission was obtained to send the questionnaire to all collaborative lawyers registered as members of the Association. When the collaborative process first became available in Ireland, the Legal Aid Board[11] was proactive in organising training for the Board's own solicitors and also for private solicitors. In view of the volume of family law undertaken by the Board, permission was also obtained to send the questionnaire to all of the Board's solicitors.

Qualitative research

The first category of interviewees, clients who had used the process, was a purposive sample.[12] In February 2010, the author attended the Annual General Meeting (AGM) of the ACP and spoke to key experts within the Association. In addressing the meeting, the author outlined the framework of the research and sought assistance from all collaborative lawyers in attendance in an effort to secure a broad-based sample. The importance of a balanced view was explained, and thus the need to speak to clients who had resolved matters through the process and also to clients for whom the process did not work was emphasised. Subsequent to the AGM, five collaborative lawyers got in touch with the author providing names and contact details of clients who were willing to participate. These participants were contacted by telephone. Further information in relation to the research was sent to them by e-mail. Interviews were arranged with ten participants. Some of the interviews were carried out face-to-face and other participants, because of their schedules, preferred to speak over the phone.

The second category of participant, collaborative lawyers, was again a purposive sample.[13] Some of these practitioners were known to the author as experts in the field prior to attendance at the AGM, others expressed an interest in the research on the day of the AGM. Eight collaborative lawyers were interviewed. All interviews were carried out face-to-face.

The third category of participants was solicitors and barristers who typically practise within the courts' system. O'Leary notes that 'experts' or 'insiders' '(are often) … precisely the right people to help to answer your research questions'.[14] This was, therefore, a handpicked sample based on the author's knowledge of the key family law practitioners. Eight participants were interviewed. Again, face-to-face interviews were carried out.

Analysis

All interviews were recorded, transcribed and were analysed through the lens of Interpretative Phenomenological Analysis (IPA) using NVivo, Version 10. The analysis consisted of a thorough seven-step process: coding of themes, assigning labels, and re-ordering these codes into categories of codes for each participant group. These codes were broken down further into sub codes to enable better understanding of the meanings embedded therein; for example, where the participant referred to a general theme of 'participation', this was broken down further to determine what 'participation' meant to that interviewee. Does this differ from another interviewee's interpretation of 'participation'? In phase 4, the themes identified were divided between the: 'topic guide' themes, detailing issues that the participants were specifically asked about in order to address the key research questions; and, also 'emergent themes', which are themes that emerged as being of importance to the participants themselves during the course of the interviews. This was undertaken in order to minimise the risks often associated with qualitative research of, arguably, predictable findings being categorised as emergent themes. Background profiling information was compiled for each participant so that 'topic guide themes' and 'emerging themes' could be also be assessed across factors such as: gender, age, socio-economic and socio-cultural backgrounds. The findings were also examined by reference to the theoretical framework underpinning the research, for example the existing literature on 'dispute resolution' (see Chapter 1). The final phase involved validating the data once again to ensure that the findings were a true account of the participants' contribution to the research based on the hermeneutic circle, working back and forth, looking at particular comments made individually, and then examining these comments in the context of the interview as a whole.

The quantitative data was analysed through Excel. Responses to open-ended questions in the nationwide questionnaire (qualitative) were also analysed through NVivo, coding for themes as per the same seven-step process used in the qualitative analysis, outlined above. The results of the quantitative analysis were used to examine and highlight areas of convergence and divergence between this data and the information obtained through qualitative methods, for example, the impact of mediation training on the lawyers' use of the collaborative process, the importance of practice group membership, etc.

Limitations

Before examining the results, it is necessary to acknowledge the limitations of the empirical study. The findings of this research are being presented as representing the views of the particular participants interviewed and are not being held out as being representative of all clients who used the collaborative process, nor of all professionals in any particular category. Because there is no central register of parties who have separated and no record of the process used, it was not possible to select a random sample. The author had to rely on referrals from collaborative lawyers, other participants and her own personal knowledge of key family lawyers.

Clients' experiences will obviously vary depending on the lawyer used. In addition, there may have been an element of selection bias in the clients that the lawyers contacted. Of the ten clients interviewed, however, eight settled within the process. Though not being presented as being representative, the settlement rate within the sample interviewed is therefore similar to the settlement rate within the process as borne out by research internationally.[15]

Nationwide questionnaire

The results presented in this section are based on an analysis of forty-one questionnaires received from collaborative lawyers nationwide, detailing the profile of lawyers who have trained in the collaborative process and how practitioners address: screening for suitability; the disqualification clause; costs; and over-all satisfaction with the process.[16] The questionnaire was designed so that information was gathered on collaboratively trained lawyers who have been successful in encouraging clients to engage in the process and those who have not, and what distinguishes them. It also sought the views of all lawyers on what they perceived as the benefits and drawbacks of the lawyer-only and multidisciplinary models.

Profile of collaborative lawyers

Firstly, examining the profile of the respondents to the questionnaire, it is notable that the lawyers who had trained in the collaborative process are experienced family lawyers; most of those who responded had been in practice for between ten and twenty years. Three-quarters were female, with a workload which comprised of up to 40% family law. Thirty-two per cent of the respondents had undergone collaborative training in 2008.[17] As noted earlier, the International Academy of Collaborative Practitioners (IACP) also recommends that all collaborative lawyers undergo 60 hours of mediation training. Examining this from an Irish perspective, it is notable that 49% of all of those who completed the questionnaire had trained in mediation. Fifty-four per cent were also members of local collaborative practice groups. Thirty-seven per cent of the practitioners who replied had dealt with a case through the collaborative process. The replies indicate that number of cases has increased steadily over the years, with respondents recording: four cases in 2006; nine in 2007; 14 in 2008; 20 in 2009; 32 in 2010 and 30 ongoing in 2011. It is clear, however, when examining these figures as a percentage of the number of applications made to the Circuit Court[18] alone in 2012 (3,462 applications), the numbers opting for the process are very low compared to numbers that issue court proceedings. As noted by Barlow, this may be due to the fact that engaging in the courts' process is often a more passive decision for clients.[19] Other factors that were evident throughout this research included: the extent to which lawyers spoke positively about ADR as an option, and to which, by issuing proceedings, clients fully understand the implications of a court hearing. One lawyer interviewed commented that:

> I think you should actually say to them, you must give evidence, you will be cross-examined by counsel on the other side, things you say can never

be unsaid – that is actually telling them what court is all about. It is not some sort of nice, soft, woolly place.

Public awareness of the process

Respondents to the questionnaire were asked for their views as to whether the public were aware of the existence of the collaborative process when attending their first consultation. The overwhelming view of almost all collaborative lawyers who responded was that the public are not aware of the process. This contrasts with the views expressed by the sample of collaborative lawyers who were interviewed: albeit, with an acknowledgement by those interviewed that their views may be influenced by the fact that many separating parties consult them specifically because they have a reputation for being an expert in the area, or for taking a less adversarial approach in family law matters.

Settlement rates

Of the cases that were completed, 81% settled and 19% terminated. In one case the parties reconciled through the process.[20] Sixty per cent advised that they had used the interdisciplinary model.[21] The most commonly employed expert was the financial expert, with 67% of practitioners who used the interdisciplinary model employing a financial expert. Forty-four per cent had used child specialists and 22% engaged personal and family consultants. Twenty-two per cent advised that they used all three experts and two respondents, while using the interdisciplinary model, did not advise as to the experts they used.[22]

Case outcomes from the process

The average number of four-way meetings in each recorded case was four. Seven was the highest number of four-way meetings recorded, and two respondents completed cases with just two four-way meetings. There was general consensus amongst the collaborative lawyers who replied to the questionnaire that an easy case would take six months or less to complete, with a difficult case taking up to 12 months and the more difficult cases taking up to two years.[23]

When asked if the outcomes achieved within the collaborative process were different from those achieved within the adversarial process, 57% of the practitioners who used the collaborative process felt that the outcomes were different. There was general agreement that outcomes did not differ in financial terms, but that they were more structured and tailored to the clients' individual needs. Comments made included: being involved in the settlement allowed the separating parties to 'grow in to the separation as opposed to being married one day and declared separated another'; that the process allows settlements to be 'custom made' for the families involved; and that settlements are 'more considered'. One practitioner commented that: '[m]y client and spouse got back together as a result of the process. If the matter had gone to Court that could not have happened'.

Reasons for termination of cases

Lawyers who had used the process were asked to specify the reasons for termination in cases that had not been settled. Reasons given included: medical reasons; client difficulties outside the process; lack of agreement on issues; bad faith; lack of trust and honesty; emotional issues; and high levels of conflict. One lawyer indicated that 'the parties were not suited to the process'. This raises the question of how practising collaborative lawyers screen parties as to their suitability for engaging in the process.

Screening

An analysis of the questionnaires indicates that most screening is done through an in-depth interview with the client. Two lawyers also mentioned using a standard questionnaire and having a checklist of issues that they look out for when assessing clients as to their suitability. One practitioner, who uses the interdisciplinary process, advised that he would carry out the initial screening, and a more extensive screening would be undertaken by the coach/personal and family consultant.

In response to the question assessing what the most important issues in determining clients' suitability for the process were, lawyers listed: emotional maturity, which was the most frequently cited factor, followed by ability to negotiate, understanding and willingness to compromise. Additional factors mentioned were: the level of conflict in the relationship, the extent to which parties were able to prioritise their children, trust and the ability to communicate. The impact that a third-party relationship can have on the parties' ability to engage in a face-to-face process was also raised: this often makes negotiations more difficult. The presence of domestic violence was only mentioned by two lawyers, and only one mentioned the need to determine where the power lay in the relationship. This raises concerns about the extent to which lawyers screen for issues of domestic violence, and how it is managed if present. Trust was a factor to be taken into account when considering the relationship between the lawyers, with one lawyer commenting that 'who is representing the other side' is a relevant consideration.

Disqualification clause

When asked about the significance of the disqualification clause in keeping clients at the negotiation table, 50% of the practitioners said it was significant, 43% said it was very significant and one respondent did not comment. Two commented further by saying it was 'significant in bringing the parties to the table', while another noted that it was 'significant, but not overly – when parties are really upset or unreasonable, it is no deterrent'.

Two respondents to the questionnaire said that they had had clients who chose not to use the process because of the implications of the disqualification clause. This is in contrast to the views of the collaborative lawyers interviewed, who advised that no one had refused to engage in the process because of the disqualification provision.[24]

Costs

An issue frequently raised in commentary on collaborative practice is that of the costs involved. All collaborative lawyers were asked if, in their opinion, the costs in collaborative cases were higher, lower or much the same as they would be in a litigation case. Forty-three per cent who used the lawyer-only process felt that the costs in a collaborative case would be lower than those incurred in a court case, with one noting that they would be the same 'because we have kept it low, but need to be higher to compensate for the time/expertise which we commit in collaborative cases'.

With regard to the interdisciplinary model, 36% of the practitioners in the study said that the fees would be higher, with 28% being of the view that the fees would be lower and 36% indicating that they did not know or not answering.

Interdisciplinary model

For collaborative lawyers who used the interdisciplinary model, the most commonly cited benefit was that it provided clients with skills that lawyers do not have in terms of assisting with the emotional issues surrounding a divorce or separation. Two of the respondents commented that having the emotional issues dealt with by someone else frees up the lawyers to get on with the legal issues. One of these two respondents commented that 'it can allow the lawyers and clients to park certain heated emotive issues which could have otherwise hampered progress of resolution'. Other advantages noted were:

- It's essential to have relevant expertise to contain the emotional elements, which are allowed to come out in the collaborative process.
- It aids the finalisation of robust durable solutions.
- It has its advantages. However, the biggest challenge facing all separating couples at the moment is lack of financial resources. Unfortunately they do not have the money to pay for Personal and Family Consultants.
- [It is] [m]ore client centred. [It] [c]aters for emotional upheaval and enables parties to move on with their lives.
- I think the interdisciplinary model is absolutely crucial. There are huge emotions involved in the bereavement of separation and divorce.[25]

Lawyers who had trained but had *not* used the collaborative process also saw potential benefits in the interdisciplinary model. Comments made included:

- I think most of the reason that people end up in court is lack of proper communication and, also, people do not know how to confront issues in a constructive way. Often there are deeper issues. Having a trained mental health professional involved seems extremely beneficial.
- It removes the emotions from the process and helps the individuals find a satisfactory resolution that they can live with.

- From my experience on the course, I can see that assistance from Personal and Family Consultants would be very beneficial. From my practice as a solicitor in family law, I feel that some of the issues that need to be addressed by the parties (particularly regarding children) could be far better addressed by mental health professionals. However, until it is an established practice country wide (or people are forced to do it), I cannot see me being able to convince clients of its worth.
- It could be of great benefit, although it can be difficult to persuade the client in circumstances where monies are tight, that paying for a third professional is worthwhile.
- I think it would help the parties to cope with the trauma and assist them in making important decisions during a very stressful time of their life.[26]

Examining these comments, there seems to be an awareness amongst Irish lawyers of the impact of the emotional issues. Lawyers need additional training in dealing with this aspect of the process, particularly as they refer to the difficulties in *convincing* or *persuading* clients to use the multidisciplinary model.

Barriers to the interdisciplinary model

Lawyers who used the process were asked what they perceived as the barriers to the interdisciplinary model. The most commonly cited issue was the costs involved,[27] followed by the availability of trained experts. Some respondents noted that there is a social stigma attached to counselling. Other respondents felt that there was a lack of understanding on the part of the lawyers as to the potential benefits for clients of receiving help with the emotional issues involved in separation or divorce, and also a 'lethargy' on the part of lawyers to engage with the interdisciplinary model.

Similarly, almost half of the practitioners who had *not* used the collaborative process cited the issue of the costs involved in an interdisciplinary case as a barrier to its use.[28] The next most commonly cited reason amongst these practitioners was, again, lack of trained professionals,[29] with lack of interest from the profession also being rated as a significant factor.[30] Other issues raised were lack of education and knowledge. Again, the stigma involved in seeking counselling was raised, as was the fact that clients are 'hostile and unwilling to deal openly with the matter'.

Collaborative lawyers' concerns with the process overall

The most commonly expressed concern amongst both practitioners who had used the process and those who had not, was that of other lawyers' commitment. Twenty per cent said that many lawyers remain in an adversarial frame of mind and may undertake collaborative training simply to bring clients into the practice. This corresponds with the views of collaborative lawyers who were interviewed.

Two respondents raised the issue of costs should the process fail, and one was concerned about the emotional awareness of clients. Other comments made included:

- The court still tends to interfere and impose extra terms, which may imbalance the fairness and consent of the heads of settlement.
- [My] [m]ain one [concern] is level of skills: the two-day basic training is inadequate, and if solicitors do not engage in other relevant training, the outcome for the clients will be doubtful.

Other concerns raised by practitioners were wide and varied. Some respondents were concerned about clients' lack of interest and level of understanding of the process, and their ability to trust in 'its effectiveness and enforceability'. Others raised queries about disclosure. The ability of the 'Irish psyche' to engage in collaboration was also mentioned. One lawyer was of the view that it is:

> considered more efficient by solicitors to deal with settlements … by way of negotiating a separation agreement rather than trying to organise 4-way meetings based on a contract signed by parties, which seems more cumbersome in cases where there is not much really to fight over anyway and cases can usually be settled in a less cumbersome manner once the matter is listed for court.

Similarly, respondents were concerned about clients 'not wasting our time', and felt that '[c]ollaboration requires too sophisticated a participation'. One collaborative lawyer does not 'see any place for it in an Irish family law context'. This practitioner does see a place for mediation, 'but with solicitors for each side attending the mediation process'. As noted in Chapter 3, Davy also raised this issue of the efficiency of the process and suggested that some cases could be settled more effectively in a less structured way.[31]

Despite these concerns, many of the practitioners participating in this research who had not used the process remained convinced of the benefits of the collaborative approach, with 31% of the respondents noting that they thought the process had 'potential', and 12% noting its potential where there were children involved. Others thought it provided 'an excellent way of resolving family law matters', with 12% believing that it would be a less traumatic way for separating parties to deal with issues. Twelve per cent, however, felt that the potential of the process was limited to big-money cases. One practitioner, while 'initially very optimistic about the potential of collaborative practice', encountered resistance from clients who do not wish to dispense with their services if the process breaks down.

Ethical issues

The responses received to the nationwide questionnaire indicate that there is an awareness amongst Irish lawyers of ethical difficulties that may arise in using the collaborative process. One respondent feared that the disqualification clause would be abused to take a solicitor off a case. Other concerns raised included: the difficulties of advocating for one's own client while at the same time seeking a resolution that benefits all parties, and, also, in a situation where a case does not settle, whether the prospect of losing a client would 'ever cloud a practitioner's judgment'.

An important concern raised by one of the respondents was the issue of privilege within the process and if 'notwithstanding the participation agreement, if the collaborative process is unsuccessful, can we as solicitors be called to give evidence if our former clients waive privilege?'[32]

This is a concern for parties engaging in mediation and collaborative practice in Ireland. There is no Act governing either process that specifically provides for privilege, nor has this matter been tested before the Irish courts.[33] In the absence of such legislation, as noted in Chapter 3, the participation agreement recommended by the Association of Collaborative Practitioners relies on Section 9 of the Family Law (Divorce) Act 1996.

Factors identified as being of importance to the development of collaborative practice

Further analysis was carried out to assess the similarities or differences between collaborative lawyers who had been successful in assisting clients to resolve their issues through the process and those who had not, to establish the most important factors in the development of the process.

Eighty-seven per cent of those who were successful in using the process were members of local practice groups. Another important factor was having undergone mediation training. Seventy-three per cent of the respondents who had used the process had undergone mediation training. The need for more collaboratively trained lawyers was highlighted as being of importance to the development of the process. Difficulties arise when one client attends a collaborative lawyer but their ex-partner's lawyer is not trained in collaborative practice.[34] The need for training beyond the initial course was also mentioned, with many participants in the research of the view that regular training in various aspects of the process would be beneficial. Training may, however, also pose difficulties. Some lawyers may only become collaborative lawyers to 'tick a box', as it were, and proceed to negotiate as they have always done.

The main concern raised by collaborative lawyers, both those who have been successful in using the process and those who have not, was genuine commitment from lawyers. There is still a wariness about, and a suspicion attached to, any process that is described as or considered, 'alternative'. As noted in Chapter 1, some lawyers are risk-averse and feel more comfortable working within the process and structure of the courts' system. Lack of interest from clients,[35] and lack of suitable cases,[36] were also cited as being reasons why lawyers had not been successful in using the process.

Impact on approach to practice

Examining the overall picture of collaborative practice in Ireland as presented through these questionnaires, it is evident that just under 40% of those who trained in the process have dealt with collaborative cases.

A significant finding is that, regardless of whether they had used the process or not, the majority of all lawyers (96%) who participated in this research said that collaborative training had had an impact on their approach to practice. Of those who had used the process, one commented that it helps them to be a 'positive influence for the client, which was not really possible up until this', with another commenting that they were 'more creative in the solutions I suggest'.

In contrast, comments made by collaborative lawyers who had *not* used the process tended to focus less on issues such as creativity and more on the fact that their approach is now less adversarial:

- It also taught me that long letters (particularly of a negative nature) hinder rather than help the process.
- Yes, I have developed a tendency against briefing counsel and going into contentious litigation in favour of the ADR approach for family law.
- It has changed my approach to the initial consultation, in that my focus is more on where the client wants to be in say 2/5/10 years' time.
- You are more likely to see the family as a whole rather than take a positional approach.
- I am more amenable to resolution outside the court model, be it through negotiating separation agreements or through mediation.
- The approach to family cases is joint resolution of problems in as far as possible, to enable the parties to move on, but that should also seek to enable/ equip the parties to resolve future matters jointly in a non-adversarial manner.
- Made me more aware of the necessity to avoid zero-sum resolution, which merely stokes up resentment for future conflict.
- I am more frustrated with opposition who insist on 'blame game'.
- I'm very aware that misunderstandings can occur when communication is through legal representatives only and I ensure that I get very clear instructions before penning a letter.
- It has given me a more focused approach to alternative means of resolution.
- It greatly affected my practice. On the plus side I empathise more with my clients. On the negative side I empathise more with my clients! Generally it has highlighted the limitations of the adversarial process in family law cases.[37]

Only one collaborative lawyer specifically mentioned the benefits of the process for children:

- Emphasis on conciliation and putting children and parties' future at top of priority list.

This single reference to children arguably displays a lack of appreciation or understanding of the impact of separation and divorce on children, even amongst trained collaborative lawyers who purport to take a more holistic, whole family approach. This highlights the need to raise awareness of children's concerns amongst lawyers.

Two per cent of respondents said that collaborative training did not change their approach to dealing with family law cases, while a further two per cent were of the view that the collaborative training had no impact but that mediation training had been 'useful'.

The views of clients who used the collaborative process

Demographics

In examining the demographics of the clients who used the collaborative process in this particular sample, it is notable that eight of the participants were between the ages of 40 and 59.[38] The majority of the participants[39] had been married for more than ten years, with four having been married more than 21 years. All participants interviewed had children, with the majority having children who were under the age of 18.[40] Four described themselves as home-makers, with six participants working outside the home. The majority indicated that their household income was in excess of €50,000.[41] Six were women, and seven of the participants had third-level education. Of those interviewed, six were the applicants in the case and four were the respondents.

The demographics for these participants are largely consistent with those of clients who used the process in other jurisdictions and to an extent confirm that, to date, the process has been chosen most frequently by those who are educated and have a reasonably good income. With the exception of one participant, none of the participants interviewed would consider themselves as being wealthy. In situations where there was some financial difficulty, the participant worked out a payment schedule with their lawyer, under which fees were paid in instalments. In another, where the process failed, the participant's collaborative lawyer was instrumental in assisting them to secure representation through the Legal Aid Board for finalising their case before the court.[42]

How did they hear about collaborative practice?

In examining how participants heard about the process, there was no single, clear, referral source. Three heard about collaborative practice from their own solicitors, three through their spouse's solicitor, three heard about the process from friends, and one learned about the process on the internet. This is consistent with the research carried out in the US.[43] Of those who heard about the process through friends, they had also researched the process themselves before deciding to use it. One participant, having decided to use the process, interviewed three collaborative lawyers before deciding which she felt most comfortable with.[44] This is an important issue. In addition to lawyers screening clients as to their suitability for the process, clients should also consult a number of collaborative lawyers until they find one they trust and feel that they can work well with.

Why did they choose collaborative practice?

Participants were asked if they considered mediation or the courts' process as methods of resolving their issues and the reasons they decided to opt for the collaborative process.

Firstly, in relation to mediation, six of the collaborative clients interviewed had actually attended some form of mediation before engaging in the collaborative process, with the majority having done so through the state-run Family Mediation Service.[45] However, there still appears to be a misconception that mediation is akin to counselling: a means of trying to assist the parties to reconcile. One participant commented that, for mediation, there has to be 'some glimmer of hope of reviving the marriage'; another was of the view that 'going to the mediation makes you feel like you did everything you can to stay, to make it work out. This is the only reason I would say it is good'.

Collaborative practice was chosen over mediation by one participant because 'at the end of the day I would still have to do it legally anyway' (referring to the fact that a mediated agreement is not legally binding), and another participant commented that:

> I didn't find the mediation process helpful at all. I would be reluctant to go down the mediation route a second time. I think a lot depends on the skill of the mediator. They need to be prepared to be fair and have enough insight to know when to intervene. They need to have a protective role, maintain neutrality and yet be fair. Having the support of my solicitor in the collaborative process made a great difference.

The issue of timing in respect of the two processes was raised by one participant, who commented that:

> From my own point of view, the difference between the mediation and that [collaborative practice] was, it was eight years on. I suppose the hurt was gone. I had moved on and I was able to look at things from a much more practical, unemotional way. Obviously when your marriage is breaking down around you, it is an awful place to be. No matter how much you want it, your dreams are still gone out the window. So, I did find the divorce coaching or counselling in the collaboration beneficial.

As noted earlier, in Canada, Macfarlane had questioned whether clients' somewhat negative views on the mediation process were influenced by what they had been told by their collaborative lawyers.[46] This would not appear to be a concern amongst the Irish participants, as the majority of them had actually engaged in some form of mediation and were therefore speaking from personal experience rather than relying, specifically, on the views of their collaborative lawyers. The fact that six of these participants had tried mediation may indicate that they were more receptive to alternative methods of dispute resolution. Previous research undertaken by Conneely[47] and Coulter[48] in Ireland noted that the up-take on mediation in a family-law context overall was much lower, at approximately 3%. This, however, may also be due to the increased focus on alternative methods in recent times.[49]

For some participants, there was a 'fear' of the courts' process. Collaborative participants routinely referred to bad experiences that friends or colleagues had, of cases being acrimonious and expensive. Their view was that going to court 'wouldn't be fair or equal'; that 'it would be very black and white and the whole family unit would not come into it'. Another commented that:

> I have friends who got divorced through a court order and I knew I didn't want that. They have no relationship with each other. I think there are no winners in that situation. I think it is bad for the kids and the separating couple.

For one collaborative participant, however, the courts' process emerged as a more attractive option. While she had 'loved the idea of it [collaborative practice] – being part of the arrangement', she felt that 'it allows parties who don't want to negotiate to get away with murder'. With court, this participant felt that separating parties have 'a finite point and you cannot go beyond it'. Additionally, she felt 'that there was a huge burden [within the collaborative process] to do it right for the kids'. The courts' process, she felt, 'allows you detach yourself.'

As was evident throughout the research internationally, the main motivation for Irish participants in choosing the process was also that they could deal with the separation 'a little less acrimoniously'. One client commented that: 'My main goal would be that I would be able to separate without any major stress or hassle, that we would still be able to talk and that the kids wouldn't be affected.'

This participant found the fact that she had to go into court to have the consent order ruled very upsetting. She said that she and her partner had 'separated in a nice way, we separated nicely in the room, polite and everything, and having to go into court was very sterile. I cried my eyes out'. The need to maintain a working relationship for the benefit of the children was also an important consideration for many interviewees, with comments made including: 'This is not about me or you or us anymore, it has to be doing the right thing for the children'. Lower costs, better outcomes and the hope that the outcome would be 'fair' with 'no ongoing problems' were also cited as reasons to use the collaborative process. For one interviewee, the goal was simply to 'get divorced and to get away'.

Duration of case and format of the joint meetings

Based on the collaborative participants interviewed, cases were taking on average one year to complete, with more difficult cases taking up to two years. Two participants engaged Personal and Family Consultants, and two others engaged financial experts. Where Personal and Family Consultants were engaged, they sat in on, on average, four meetings. While two participants took advice from financial experts, none of these financial experts attended any of the meetings.

In relation to the format of the joint meetings, participants advised that the solicitors did most talking at the beginning of the process, with one commenting:

> [i]n the early stages it was mainly the solicitors and we sat back a little as we were quite nervous. Once we felt a bit safer in the process, then we began to speak ourselves and at the end I would say that it was 25% for each of us.

Others commented that, at the end there was a 'much warmer atmosphere', and that for them, 'it was definitely the right way of doing things … if I had to do it again, I would do the same thing'.

For those who used the multidisciplinary approach, one felt that perhaps the solicitors could have been more in control, as the counsellors seemed to take over. This issue also became important when examining the pace of the process.

Pace

Three participants were concerned about the pace of the process, with one expressing the view that there should be clearly defined goals set out in a letter of engagement at the beginning. As noted earlier, two others commented that the lawyers need to be in control – either to keep the process moving along or to call an end to it if things are not progressing. One participant felt that if something more urgent came in, their solicitor moved the collaborative case down their list of priorities, and they found this frustrating.

The pace of the process has been raised and discussed by collaborative lawyers and by the IACP. It is a difficult issue. One party may not be able, emotionally or financially, to deal with issues as quickly as another. This may also be influenced by the fact that either party may have decided some time prior to the process commencing that, for them, the marriage was over and they are now at a point where they are ready to move on, whereas for the other party the break-down of the relationship may have been unexpected. In four cases, even where participants were aware of difficulties, they were willing to continue in the relationship rather than end it.[50]

Settlement rates

Eight of the parties interviewed settled their cases through the collaborative process. Another stated that the agreement reached during the collaborative process formed the 'foundation of what we took into court two years later'. This is broadly in line with the findings of the research carried out by the IACP, which, using a larger sample, found the settlement rate in collaborative process cases to be 90%.[51]

Impact of the disqualification provision

When questioned about the disqualification provision, the interviewees were fully aware of the implications of not reaching settlement within the process. One participant commented:

> I was clear at the outset that that would happen and, at one point it looked like we weren't going to get the information we needed, but I always wanted to keep in the collaborative process. I never wanted to go away from that.

A common theme that emerged was a sense of commitment to the process. Many clients had researched collaborative practice themselves and, having chosen the process, were committed to it. Two participants said that they had concerns initially at the thought of losing their lawyers, but they did not have sufficient concerns to prevent them using the process. In both cases they forgot about this issue once the process started. Only one expressed the view that the disqualification clause was the 'biggest clincher, the biggest stumbling block' in deciding to use the process, not because of the cost implications, but again because of the possibility of losing her lawyer.

Seven of the ten participants said that it did not have any bearing on their decision to use the process. For two participants, the disqualification clause was a positive aspect to the process. One commented 'it makes you grasp the nettle and move on'. And another stated:

> the fact that the solicitors were in a position as well to walk away and not just us, you kind of have more respect for each other, if you know what I mean. You think more. It wasn't an effect of keeping me there, as in blocked me by keeping me there, it kept me there out of respect for the other three people involved in it.

Support/legal advice

Another issue often raised by critics of the collaborative process is the extent to which collaborative lawyers can advocate for their clients in a process designed to focus, in many respects, on the interests of the family as a whole. Interviewees were therefore asked if they felt that their lawyers were on their side and if they felt supported throughout the process. Without exception, all collaborative clients interviewed felt that they had the support and loyalty of their lawyers during the process. Many were keen to stress the importance of their relationship with their collaborative lawyer and, as noted earlier, the prospect of losing their collaborative lawyer in the event of non-settlement was a greater concern for them than the additional costs involved:

> definitely, as each meeting went on, it was much easier and I think my solicitor … always made it plain to me, look you can break this when you want and go out … She was very good at taking up the vibe if I was having difficulties. She would jump in and help me … (I) always felt that my solicitor had

> my best interests at heart and she always said to me, 'I won't let you agree on anything', and, beforehand, we would really have flogged out the best and worst case scenarios for everything.

Other comments made included:

- I had that understanding in my heart that she was there to support this separation and anything that would arise from it ...
- Yes. I felt that his loyalty was to me. But I have to repeat that divorce is a difficult undertaking, but certainly from what I have heard, collaborative was very good.

Though happy with the overall settlement, in that 'mentally it worked out better for me. We are still talking and the kids are happy', one participant felt, at times:

> very unsure whether I was doing the right thing as regards the house and the estate and things. I didn't know if that was the right amount. I was never really sure if I was giving too much to too little or whether [the other party] was giving nothing at all ...

Some collaborative practitioners are of the view that it is better not to focus too much on rights or entitlements, but instead to let the parties reach their own agreement. While this approach may have advantages, it is also extremely important to clients that they know where they stand, being aware of what Fisher and Ury called the 'objective criteria', namely, what they would be likely to receive in court.[52] Regarding this issue of legal advice, most participants interviewed were aware where they stood legally. Four, however, were unsure in this regard. One participant felt that:

> X or Y [the solicitors] came up with the figure and I just said that's fine if that's what you think the law says, but they never said, 'well look, the last two cases that went to court, this is how it worked out, and this is what we have decided would be the best thing'.

One of these three who was unsure commented that they 'didn't clearly know my rights – this does not mean that it wasn't explained to me, but you need things on paper'. At the end of the research, this participant had progressed to the courts' system. When asked for their view on the courts' system, this client felt that their entitlements were 'still not very clear – depends on the judge on the day'. They went on to say that this creates 'a lot of fear as you are unsure about where you are going'.

Interdisciplinary model

Only two of the ten participants interviewed had used coaches or Personal and Family Consultants as part of the process. In both cases each party had their own coach, and the separating parties, their coaches and their solicitors met approximately four times during the course of the cases. One client acknowledged that they were somewhat sceptical when the solicitor explained the model to them initially. They thought it 'sounded like a money racket'. However, when they engaged in the process they felt that it was beneficial to have the counsellors on board. They commented that:

> At the initial meeting, number one, we were back in a counselling situation for the first time in years. Probably the first time we sat down in a room together without solicitors, and, I suppose, bringing up all the old stuff again, kind of. But the coaches were good and they were really tuned into us straight away [clicks their fingers], what was happening and they were in control … I felt that it put everybody together, because I mean you have the law side of it obviously, and the coaches doing the emotional side of it, so it was it was just nice to put it all together.

The other participant who used coaches commented that 'the whole thing was kind of brilliantly done'.

Those who had not used the multidisciplinary model were asked for their views. Two clients said that they would have resisted it, had it been offered to them at the time, with another of the view that: 'looking back that I was a total maniac and … your emotions are heightened and that I was all over the shop'. Cost, however, would have been a factor for this participant, in that they would not have been able to afford it.

One client said that they are 'very cautious about counselling in general' and that they 'don't think that the standards of training are particularly high'. This client went on to say that 'from talking to other people, there was a general feeling that it could do more harm than good'. The same interviewee emphasised that in situations in which people are breaking up, counsellors 'need an awful lot of training to do it well', and expressed concerns about the standards of training in Ireland. Another interviewee was similarly sceptical about the benefits of counselling, believing that children will have problems as they grow up 'whether this is because of the separation, or whether the child would have had these problems anyway'.

Costs

Six of the interviewees said that the collaborative process was a lot cheaper than going to court. Two said that they would not consider it a cheaper option, and two said that they did not know how the costs would compare if they had used the courts' process. Three participants noted that the fact that it would be a cheaper option was a motivating factor in choosing the process:

- We were told that we could save costs and this was a factor for me … I saved a good few bob.

- I felt that the process would be less acrimonious and that it would probably cost less than going down the legal route …
- It was all fairly agreeable and I didn't want to incur mad legal bills.

The two interviewees who did not consider the collaborative process a cheaper option were, unsurprisingly, those who did not settle within the process and ended up going to court. In terms of placing these cases in context, one was a 'lawyer-only' case, in which the participant interviewed felt that they were not making progress within the process. This interviewee had tried mediation prior to engaging in collaborative practice, and the other party had also walked out of the mediation process. In the other case, the couple used the interdisciplinary model. Again, the process failed because one party was refusing to engage. In both cases, the participants felt that the collaborative lawyers could have taken more control within the process and should have been more attuned to screening parties that were not suitable for the collaborative process.

Satisfaction with the process

All of the participants were asked if they were satisfied with the process. While the majority were satisfied with the overall outcome, this did not always equate with getting the majority of the assets. Satisfaction, particularly in family law matters, as noted in Chapter 1, is subjective. The participants interviewed for this research reached a conclusion that suited their particular needs. Only one participant was sure that she would have done better financially in court, but her motivation in using and staying in the process was to maintain 'a working relationship' with the other party. Therefore, she was happy with the outcome because they have a good relationship now:

> I can ring X at any minute of the day, if I wanted to, and I can talk to him. I wouldn't rush to do it, but I know I can. If he drops the kids back, he comes in and has a cup of coffee around the table, which we wouldn't be doing if I had gone the other way.

Eight out of the ten participants have a good relationship post-separation, and this they attribute to using the collaborative process. All participants were nervous before the first joint meeting. For some, this nervousness eased as the process progressed; others found all meetings difficult.

Two of those interviewed did not settle their cases within the process and proceeded to court. Of these, one case had not been heard or settled by the time this research was concluded. The other case settled on the steps of the courthouse, and the settlement was approved by the judge without there being any further increase in maintenance than what had been agreed in the collaborative process two years earlier. The only difference in the overall settlement was that the father agreed to pay €20 per week pocket money to the eldest child, as he was a teenager by the time the case was eventually finalised.

Emotional impact

An issue that was evident in the analysis of the data was the significance of the emotional impact of relationship breakdown. This came across more strongly amongst the female participants, with only one male expressing emotional difficulties as a result of the separation. Many participants indicated that it is only in hindsight that they realised that they needed counselling. Amongst the emotions they expressed were: a sense of shattered dreams; fear and uncertainty; and, in some cases, particularly when they were the parties to instigate the separation, a sense of blame. Another issue raised, and perhaps one that is not immediately recognised by legal professionals, was a sense of shame. One participant commented:

> I remember being in the solicitor's office. I had been well brought up and I had a sense of how … did I end up here? I was sitting there with everybody else and I felt very apprehensive. I had a sense of shame and failure.

Recommend the collaborative process to a friend?

A key test, in many ways, of any new process is whether someone would recommend it to a friend. All of the interviewees said that they would recommend the process, and some participants have already recommended it; approximately half of the participants qualified this with statements such as: it would depend on 'where the parties were at' and 'how well they were able to communicate'. Another commented that:

> If you are out for everything you can get, I don't think it would work for someone. I think it is great if the two of you want to come to a conclusion, especially if you have children. They are not going to be stuck in the middle. I think it is fantastic for people with children, but I do think you would have to be very open and that you would have to get on together.

One of the parties interviewed, while recommending the process, would only recommend it for 'the long-term separated who had an arrangement that they wanted to legalise, if it is a mutual decision'.

Clients' concerns about the process

Three out of the ten clients interviewed mentioned the need for the lawyers to remain in control of the process – both in terms of ensuring that matters progressed at a reasonable pace and being aware when the process was not working or one of the parties was not suitable for it. For two of these three participants settlement was not reached within the process. This they attributed directly to either their own solicitor or the solicitor on the other side not being in control. One commented:

> I feel that there should be some way of identifying that somebody is not suitable – that they are not emotionally or intellectually prepared. That needs to be recognised sooner.

Another concern is that four of the interviewees felt that they were not clear about their legal entitlements during the process. One said that she probably was told, but that she did not take it in. As noted earlier, in one case the participant stated she felt that the solicitors had come up with the figures and she just went along with it. She felt that there should have been more flexibility in the figures negotiated. It is clear that different collaborative practitioners take different approaches. While Irish collaborative lawyers, as per the questionnaire, were of the view that their primary loyalty was to their own client, this apparent lack of transparency raised concerns for clients, particularly in view of the purported good-faith ethos of the process. Collaborative lawyers in Ireland and internationally have acknowledged that on occasions they can unintentionally revert to positional negotiation: the lawyers take control and propose settlement terms rather than assisting clients to reach their own informed decision.

The collaborative lawyer's perspective

Introduction

Building on the information gleaned from the quantitative research, further insight into the collaborative lawyer's view of the process was obtained during the course of the semi-structured interviews. Eight collaborative lawyers were interviewed: five women and three men. All were experienced family lawyers. All were members of practice groups, and seven had undergone mediation training.

Benefits of the process

The collaborative lawyers interviewed saw the benefits of the process as being two-fold. Firstly, it allowed them to provide a more focused service that was tailored to their clients' needs. Through the process, they had developed an increased awareness of the need to actually listen more carefully to their clients, and to help them to reach more creative solutions than may be available through the courts' process. Secondly, they felt that dealing with a case through the collaborative process was a more dignified way to handle separation/divorce cases. It empowered clients to learn to manage their relationships more effectively and gave them the tools required to build a new type of relationship, which would be of benefit to them and to the children they would continue to co-parent. One collaborative lawyer summed up the difference between 'ordinary lawyer' negotiation and the collaborative process by saying that even when lawyer settlement goes well and matters are agreed amicably:

> still that was us [the two solicitors] getting on constructively, the two clients were in two separate rooms both feeling anxious and unhappy and uncomfortable and reliant on their lawyer.

One experienced family law solicitor commented that they explain the difference between collaborative practice and court negotiations as follows. With court negotiations:

> you tell me and I tell the barrister and he tells the barrister on the other side and he tells your husband, your husband goes back to his – who knows what the message is! … They feel more in control [in the collaborative process] when they sort of hear what is going on, even if it is something that they don't want to hear, than hearing this sort of Chinese whispers …

An easier option for lawyers?

Addressing the issues of whether engaging in the collaborative process is an easier or more difficult option for the lawyers, there was general agreement among those interviewed that practising the collaborative way was in fact more challenging. Positional negotiation requires little preparation. It can simply be a case of making excessive demands and offering less than will settle the case, until some middle ground is reached. Easier still is allowing the case to proceed to hearing before the court, particularly within the two-stream solicitor/barrister system. One collaborative lawyer interviewed commented:

> The lazy solicitor packs it off to the barrister. The barrister drafts the papers. You wait your turn. You sit in the court. The solicitor really can take a very detached view of the thing, doesn't have to be proactive at all. It can be a very lazy approach …

Another commented that '[s]ometimes it [collaborative practice] can be [more difficult] because we know our way around the courts so well'.

Domestic violence and screening

There is a view that processes such as mediation or collaborative practice are not suitable in any situation in which domestic violence has been a factor in a relationship.[53] All collaborative lawyers interviewed acknowledged the difficulties that such a history may present within the process. They were divided on whether they would consider it a complete bar to using collaborative practice. One collaborative lawyer was of the view that the collaborative process would be more suitable than mediation because 'there is nobody at your back in the mediation process'. All noted that there would have to be an acknowledgement of what had happened and an agreed willingness to proceed before they would consider using the collaborative system. One commented that:

> Knowing the way that domestic violence is dealt with in court – with the best will in the world and I think judges try and do their best – but it's a blunt instrument and it doesn't really solve any of the bigger issues that are there

> with this family. And so, knowing that, you can't say you're better off going to court, because you know that that's not true. You have to say to them that it has to be done in a certain way and unless you're agreeable to that, then you can't do it.

This also raised the issue of screening, and the importance of being able to trust your colleague as to whether the other party is suitable for the collaborative process. All practitioners felt that, with experience, a lawyer will generally have a good feeling as to whether their own client is suitable. Clients need to 'want to do what is best' for the family. It was also accepted that the lawyer needs to be able to assist the client to choose the most suitable process for them and that there is an onus, particularly on collaborative lawyers, because of the implications of the disqualification clause, to ensure, in so far as possible, that the client understands what is expected of them within the process and the commitment that is required. Collaborative lawyers who encourage clients that are not suited to the process to engage in it are doing a disservice to their clients and to the process. One collaborative lawyer recounted that she had:

> one case where I was talking to the husband about collaboration and he was actually walking around the room saying, 'This is what I'm looking for, do I get to speak to her, and I'll tell her and I'll tell her', and I am thinking to myself, this guy would no more collaborate than the man in the moon. So if I was asked honestly by a colleague, 'Do you think Mr. X is suitable for collaboration?', I would have to say 'Well, he thinks it is wonderful, but I don't think he understands the word'.

Two collaborative lawyers acknowledged that the stress and pressure of a separation may cause parties to do something that may be out of character. In that situation, once there is an acceptance and acknowledgement of what happened, the parties may be able to engage. The consensus was that if there was a history and ongoing pattern of domestic violence, with no acknowledgement of the behaviour, the collaborative process would not be suitable.

Outcomes

Again, in accordance with the quantitative research, the majority of collaborative lawyers interviewed for this research agreed that the outcomes are not significantly different in purely monetary terms, with one practitioner indicating that:

> No, not significantly no – maybe on an issue-by-issue basis if you broke it down … Finance-wise we would have come out probably the same from court, but if you took the children and the access and custody-issue wise, we could have got anything under the sun from the court, whereas through the collaborative process the parties were able to craft their own workable agreements in relation to these issues. So I think, in general, it is a similar outcome, but it

> is much more finely crafted and the issues that are of importance are given, I suppose, are given more emphasis.

Another collaborative lawyer commented that, while the process is often used by clients with more financial resources, the process is:

> enormously more creative, and when you have limited resources you have to be creative. The courts have a very limited time to be creative. In collaboration, and particularly the team model, because you have so many people working together, ideas generate. It's just with that synchronicity, ideas will generate.

Disqualification clause

The collaborative lawyers interviewed, all of whom had used the process, believed that the disqualification provision was less of an issue in practice. This can be contrasted with the views of collaborative lawyers expressed as part of the quantitative research, whereby 50% viewed the implications of the disqualification provision as significant, with 43% viewing it as a very significant factor in the process. Perhaps, however, this discrepancy is addressed in the comment of one collaborative lawyer interviewed, who advised that:

> I have found, however, that where you explain to the client that the disqualification provision is ultimately an incentive for everybody to make sure that it works and to avoid litigating, that they do come around to that, on reflection. ... In fact, I have had no client saying 'no' to collaborative on the grounds of the disqualification clause. I think it is more a problem for solicitors who don't practise in the area.

Another experienced collaborative lawyer interviewed indicated that they had 'never, ever lost a collaboration because of the disqualification clause': 'No-one has ever said to me that they couldn't possibly do that because of the disqualification clause. No-one has ever said that.'

One collaborative lawyer noted the benefit of the disqualification clause in helping clients 'think again – that they don't, at the first little hiccup, say right we'll see you again – because they've spent too much money in it', and 'if that wasn't there a lot of cases would fall more easily'. A lawyer, who has practised for many years within the adversarial system and who continues to do so, explained the pressure of settling on the steps of the court as follows:

> They [solicitors and barristers] say knock heads together. I'm not saying a huge amount of pressure, but quite a lot of pressure of the day, the circumstances, the court building, the everything else. The judge is ready to hear your case, these are the terms it is done under and the party goes away settled. Now if counsel thinks that is a good result, I don't think it is a good result. ...

> they [the separating parties] might be relieved that is about the best that you can say, that they are relieved, but are they coming out of the court saying 'I really feel that that was very fairly done and I was so pleased with the outcome and the whole thing', no they are not. They are bruised and battered and they are just absolutely terrified of the thing and relieved it is over.

She therefore was of the view that any pressure the clients felt to stay in the collaborative process had to be compared to this and clients needed to know that this type of settlement might be their alternative to settling within the collaborative process. Explaining this, she felt was a key element in ensuring informed consent. She described it thus:

> If you go in to a doctor and you have something he will say look we can do surgery, this is what it is going to, you can take some pills or maybe you can change your lifestyle, so they're your choices and he gives you the various options. But with litigation, I think there is a huge reliance of the client on the expert. So if the expert sort of says, well I think we are going to have to issue proceedings, I mean they [separating parties] are not sort of saying, well hold your horses I want to do it collaboratively. I want you to do this this and this. The client is not, I don't think making informed choices.

Whereas another collaborative lawyer felt that clients viewed the restriction as being on the lawyers, not on them:

> They are aware, certainly, that it keeps us in the process and that we can't do anything else. They are well aware of that. They are aware that they can go and do other things. If they choose to, they can quit out of it if they want ... It is your choice. I can do this for you, if you think you can do better elsewhere off you go ... I think what happens is that they have put time effort and energy into it and the system is up and running. They have a communication process. It mightn't be working at this point in time, but that is the challenge, to make it work.

Again, it appears that, in some cases, the disqualification provision is a bigger concern for lawyers than for the clients. This may be, as one collaborative lawyer commented, because '[t]he professionals, I think, focus too much on the process whereas the clients simply want solutions'.

Interdisciplinary model

Similar to the results of the quantitative research, the most commonly employed expert amongst the collaborative lawyers interviewed was the financial expert. For those collaborative lawyers whose clients chose to use coaches, the lawyers commented that the coaches can be invaluable at explaining things to clients in a way that the client understands and appreciates rather than from a strictly legal point of view. One collaborative lawyer was of the view that:

> ignoring the other elements of what is happening for people is doing them no fairness or justice or service … there is a time for negotiation and there is a time for dialogue, and the collaborative process offers the best mechanism for the interaction between the various disciplines.

He went on to comment that 'a client cannot design the model because they haven't been here before and they aren't emotionally placed to be able to deal with it'. It was evident, however, that difficulties remain for clients in seeing beyond the additional costs involved in having other experts engaged as part of the collaborative process.

Legal advice

There was a general consensus amongst the collaborative lawyers interviewed that clients should be fully advised of their legal rights before entering the process. Comments made in this regard include:

- I think they need the background of the advice first, but to be honest, they normally look for that anyway. I think they need it because they need to be making their decisions with the knowledge as to what they're giving up or not giving up.
- They do, yeah, absolutely, they would be fully briefed on (a) what their entitlements were and (b) what their potential expectations might be if the case were litigated, i.e. what a judge would be likely to do, you know. So, they will have a good overview in relation to that on each issue as it arose.

Only one collaborative lawyer said that legal advice is often given to both parties together at the four-way meetings. When asked about the issue of support or advocacy, lawyers believed that it was important that clients felt that they were on their side. The lawyers provide such advocacy while having:

> regard for what the other players are doing … I have to be conscious of what they [the other lawyer and client] are doing, I have to try to facilitate my client in understanding what they are doing and what they are saying … to embolden them to be able to feel that they can use the process in the best way.

This built-in legal advice would appear to be the element that distinguishes negotiations within the collaborative process from those undertaken in mediation. Therefore, it is an essential element of the process. Indeed, legal advice has been referred to as 'an integral part of the process' by the Association of Collaborative Practitioners.[54]

Impact on approach to practice

In accordance with the results of the quantitative research, the collaborative lawyers interviewed also said that the training has had a positive impact on their approach to practice. It has made them question routine practices within the adversarial system and has alerted them to the impact on the family as a whole. One practitioner described it as: 'putting a definition or a system to a process that I needed, to find about how to resolve issues for people in the people's interest … substantially, it met a need.'

Another collaborative lawyer noted that using this process has taught them to give the client the freedom to tell their story as they see it, rather, as Cameron noted earlier,[55] moulding their story into a predetermined framework:

> Before, I would come to a meeting with a client and I would have a list of things that I wanted that client to answer. I'd come with a form … and I'd have my questions already set out and I wouldn't want them starting at where I would see as the end and telling me the story backwards. I would want them to start where I saw as the beginning, which is probably not what they saw at all, and so I would squish them into the peg that I wanted … I don't do that anymore so it's changed me dramatically in that regard.

Solicitors' and barristers' views on the courts' system, mediation and collaborative practice

The main focus of this study was the experiences of separating parties who used the collaborative process and on collaborative lawyers. Due to the negative response that the process has received from many litigators, and the claims that cases can be resolved as effectively within the courts' system, it was decided to interview a handpicked sample of experienced adversarial family lawyers. The aim was to test the assertion that, in effect, the concept of an adversarial family lawyer is outdated, and to gain an understanding of litigators' views on the courts' process, mediation and collaborative practice. It is important to reiterate that this research is not being presented as representative of the views of all litigators; it was undertaken simply to gain some insight, so that their views or criticism can be addressed.

Eight participants were interviewed. Fifty per cent were of the view that the courts' system as it stands serves clients well, referring only to facilities at courthouses and lack of judges as possible problems. The other half were of the view that efforts could be made to keep acrimonious letters at a minimum and to avoid 'upping the ante'. Overall, there was unanimous recognition that the attitude and personality of the lawyer on the other side of the case can determine how matters will progress.[56] One solicitor commented that the identity of the legal advisors contributes:

> greatly … to whether a case will settle or not. Some practitioners take the view that the matter goes to a full hearing no matter what, and no amount of meetings will advance settlement in those circumstances.

Others referred to the fact that 'solicitors are inclined to be adversarial in their outlook', and explained that how a case progresses 'depends on who I am dealing with completely'. There was also a sense that solicitors who did not normally specialise in family law began to take cases during the economic downturn and approached them in the same way as they would any civil litigation matter. This resulted in an increase in adversarialism and competitiveness amongst practitioners. One solicitor commented that:

> The lawyers … [are] sort of point-scoring … It is very bitter between the lawyers, which is astonishing, but they seem to take more of an evangelical role in looking after their poor client who is hard done by and just considering their client's point of view.

Another issue that was raised was that of family lawyers indulging their clients too much and not bringing any objectivity to bear when issues like access are being decided. In doing so, it was suggested, lawyers were inadvertently disempowering their clients and causing them to become over-reliant on them and on the courts' system to resolve issues. Examples of this included solicitors micro-managing access visits, resulting in clients not communicating directly themselves and therefore not building a post-separation relationship that allowed them to co-parent without intervention or supervision.

Solicitors and barristers were asked for their opinions on mediation and collaborative practice. Overall, there is some limited acceptance of mediation. Three of the adversarial lawyers interviewed recognised some benefits with mediation. Two others, however, felt that it added an additional layer of costs, and one said that they advised clients about mediation simply because they were obliged to do so under the legislation. One barrister commented that 'I don't think that mediation works in the vast majority of family law cases', while another barrister asserted that:

> I think there's a sort of general tendency to commit people to the courts. Clients will be guided, but it needs both parties to be guided. There's no point in encouraging one party [into mediation] if that encouragement doesn't come from both [solicitors] and I would see that there's an absence of that coming from within our system.

Concerns were raised about mediation being used 'inappropriately, by one party or another, perhaps one solicitor or another inappropriately to put pressure on the other side', and the fact that although discussions are 'without prejudice', things said at mediations 'come up'. This is obviously a concern and a deterrent for clients considering engaging in the mediation process.

When it comes to collaborative practice, however, only one solicitor could see any benefits in the process. The other solicitors, though dealing with family law, were not familiar with the process. Barristers, in general, were, unsurprisingly, quite negative about the process.[57] One described it as 'daft', going on to say:

> I think you either mediate with the mediator who will do a sort of a – whereas the costs of collaborative law just seem to me to be phenomenal and also our role as barristers and solicitors – it is an adversarial type of role.

Other reasons given for regarding collaborative practice negatively were the cost implications for clients and the pressure to settle. Comments made include:

> I also don't understand for the life of me. Like, of course, once they [the solicitors] have signed up to settle the case they are going to bloody well try and settle it, because they [the solicitors] are not going to want to lose the case either, so that has financial implications for them.

Litigators were also of the view that 'a good barrister and solicitor should be able to do family law in that manner in the first place'. Barristers spoke about the advantages of having a detailed conversation with the client, in advance of the case and away from the pressure of the courthouse. One raised concerns about the issue of 'duplicating and duplicating with new processes'. This barrister was of the view that rather than creating more processes, the profession needed to have a greater awareness and understanding of the importance of leaving 'both sides with dignity'.

Solicitors and barristers who resolve issues through the courts' process referred to the fact that it is the break-up of the relationship, and not the method used to resolve the issues, that causes the conflict.[58] Similarly, they argue that if separating parties have a relationship in which they can sit down and work things out, then there is no reason that they could not do this just as effectively with a mediator – saving themselves the expense and structure of the collaborative process.[59] Therefore, in an effort to test this assertion – that these parties would have settled their cases anyway – a review was undertaken of the information gleaned from the interviews with participants who took part in the collaborative process to determine the level of acrimony present at the time they entered the process, and the effectiveness or otherwise of collaborative practice as a method of dispute resolution.

It was noted that two of the participants were communicating relatively well with their ex-spouse at the time that they entered into the process.[60] For the other eight, the situation was not as straightforward. A significant amount of time had passed since the initial break-up for two of the participants.[61] This was a double-edged sword. Things that used to annoy them immediately after the break-up, now seemed less significant.[62] Against this, however, another commented that it was difficult to go into a situation in which they were back sitting in a room together many years later, particularly in view of the fact that, in this case, the parties did not speak to each other even when their children were being handed over for access. For the majority of the participants there was, in fact, quite a level of conflict and apprehension. Participants' comments included:

- It [the relationship] was just good enough to get through it. Before the collaborative process we were at each other's throats.

- I was driving it and at that point in time X didn't want it at all, so he was very angry and very negative, so the first meeting was quite nerve wracking.
- I think, you see, he was very antagonistic about the whole thing, but I think he was much more favourable to than going to a court, the pressure of lawyers, solicitors and stuff is very cold-faced.

Another said that they were 'absolutely terrified' and that the first meeting did not go particularly well. They noted that their ex-spouse was quick to lose their temper, but that 'each meeting was slightly better'. By the end of the process, they 'felt that the meetings were helping them to communicate'. One commented that they thought their solicitors saw their case as 'one of the most difficult collaborations', indicating that his ex-wife was 'spinning her wheels'. Therefore, these cases do not appear to have been low-conflict or straightforward. While the parties may have 'settled anyway', it is evident that many of the separating parties had a number of issues to work through as part of the process.

Barristers, because of the way the profession is structured, are more detached from the client. In general, once a barrister finishes a case he or she will not have any further contact with the client unless the case comes back before the court again. This, however, may not always be indicative of a robust settlement. Any on-going queries or concerns are dealt with by solicitors.

Conclusion

Clients

Comparing the Irish study to international research on the collaborative process conducted in Canada, the US and England and Wales, there was little to differentiate between the substance and findings of the studies undertaken. The Irish experience seems to fit the international norm, in that there appear to be significant benefits to be gained from attempts made to resolve family conflict in a less adversarial fashion than the traditional method.

Opinion on the process has confirmed that, in many respects, collaborative law provides a bridge between mediation and the courts' process/ordinary lawyer negotiation, whereby clients participate and have more control and yet are supported in relation to their legal rights. Clients who used the process have noted the positive effects of learning to communicate in a different way and have described achieving a sense of empowerment. They were directly involved in the decisions being made and they had input into those decisions. Again, there was no evidence that weaker parties do less well and participants stressed that their lawyers made sure that their interests were protected. Overall, high settlement rates were achieved, and clients reported having a better relationship afterwards. Only time and further research will reveal whether the post-separation relationships continued to remain amicable.

Although many clients cited the potential benefits of the process for their children as reasons to engage, there seemed to be a lack of awareness echoed throughout the international studies of the 'best interests' of the children involved or providing them with any support or assistance to deal with the family transition. There remains a paternalistic attitude to deciding what is best for children and although collaborative practice provides an admirable framework through the role of the child specialist, there does not appear to be evidence that parents were willing to engage. The option to discuss concerns about the breakdown of the family unit should not be left to the authors of the breakdown to decide, or only be available with their permission. This should be available as a coping mechanism to all children should they wish to avail of the support.

Critics of collaborative practice point to the implications of the disqualification provision. Tested in an Irish setting, the research findings accord with those of international research. Overall, clients were not dissuaded from using the process because of this requirement and expressed a sense of commitment to making sure the process worked. They valued the fact that the lawyers had also made a commitment to negotiating settlement and felt supported by their legal advisors. Many saw it as a positive aspect to the process, one that encouraged them to address issues and move on. Two clients expressed concern about the level of legal advice that they received. This is a concern as the built-in legal advice is one of the main elements that differentiates between mediation and collaborative practice.

Lawyers

An important finding in the Irish research is that undergoing training in the collaborative process alone had a big impact on the way lawyers approached family-law cases. Ninety-six per cent of those who responded to the nationwide questionnaire noted that the training raised their awareness as to the impact that the tone of their correspondence may have in terms of increasing conflict in a case, and they asserted that they now try to approach cases in a less adversarial way. This was also evident in the research undertaken internationally.

Concerns continue about screening for domestic violence. Arguably, there is a reassurance in the fact that there are two lawyers carrying out this screening rather than one mediator. The difference, however, is that a mediator will have received training in this skill and the lawyers may not. If collaborative practice is to be undertaken by lawyers, particularly in cases where they do not have the additional support of mental health experts, then they need proper training in screening and also in dealing with the emotional issues that may arise for clients.

Critics of collaborative practice have raised concerns about the high level of costs for clients. No doubt in cases where there is a lot of conflict or protracted negotiations, the costs will be high, but this is the situation within the adversarial system also. The research carried out internationally to date, however, does not appear to have found any evidence of exorbitant costs. Clients surveyed and interviewed for the Irish research did not raise this as a concern, with the majority of the view that they saved money by using this process.

While the interdisciplinary model of collaborative practice provides the most holistic approach to handling divorce/separation cases, the evidence suggests that, despite widespread agreement about the potential benefits of the collaborative model, most cases have been settled through the lawyer-only model. A concern is the ability of collaborative lawyers to deal with the wider emotional and other issues involved in the separation process without additional expert assistance. Training is required to ensure that collaborative lawyers are adequately equipped to deal with these issues.

It is clear from the views of the litigators interviewed that there is negativity towards the collaborative process. There is some acceptance of mediation, arguably because regardless of the result achieved in mediation, as these agreements are not binding in law in Ireland, lawyers will continue to have a role, ruling the case in court or litigating if settlement cannot be reached. This is particularly relevant in an Irish context as, if collaborative practice was to be widely used, it may result in a diminution of income for barristers. Ceding an element of control in the case may also deter litigators from engaging. Less obvious reasons may be their fear of exposing their negotiation skills before colleagues and clients. Business can be done faster and similar results achieved by negotiating the way it has always been done, through positional negotiation.

Some lawyers, though seeing the potential in having assistance to enable clients to negotiate and communicate in a less emotionally-fuelled way, have pointed to the lack of interest from clients and the lack of trained experts as stumbling blocks. Apathy from the profession however was the most frequently cited factor and a sense of 'why change the way it has always been done?' The 'automatism' referred to earlier by Cameron is, as she notes, frequently used as 'a defence mechanism that insulates one from self-awareness.'[63]

Although collaborative law has received a less than warm welcome from litigators and some academics alike, the lawyers who use and promote the process, as evidenced by this research and research internationally, are experienced family lawyers, many of whom have concerns about the impact of adversarial negotiation and the courts' process on their clients' family life and ability to co-parent post-separation or divorce. While recognising that it is often a more challenging way to practise, they appear to remain committed to the collaborative process because of the long-term benefits for clients. Only further longitudinal research can fully assess the extent to which these benefits continue in the months and years after separation.

Notes

1 O'Leary, Z., *The Essential Guide to Doing your Research Project* (Sage, 2010); Smith, J., Flowers, P., and Larkin, M., *Interpretative Phenomenological Analysis, Theory, Method and Research* (Sage, 2010); Marshall, C., and Rossman, G., *Designing Qualitative Research* (5th edn, Sage, 2011); Kvale, S., *InterViews: An Introduction to Qualitative Research Interviewing* (Sage, 1996).

2 Smith, J., Flowers, P., and Larkin, M., *Interpretative Phenomenological Analysis, Theory, Method and Research* (Sage, 2010) at 32.

3 Ibid.

4 O'Leary, Z., *The Essential Guide to Doing your Research Project* (Sage, 2010) at 121.

5 Ibid.

6 Kvale, S., *InterViews: An Introduction to Qualitative Research Interviewing* (Sage, 1996) at 2.
7 Marshall, C., and Rossman, G., *Designing Qualitative Research* (5th edn, Sage, 2011) at 144.
8 Pilot interviews were carried out to test the topic guides and changes were made accordingly. For example, the initial topic guide addressed demographic issues at the outset. On testing, it was decided that it was better to build rapport with participants before asking profiling questions.
9 Again, pilot studies were carried out and advice sought from experts in social science research methodologies prior to distributing the questionnaires and surveys.
10 O'Leary, Z., *The Essential Guide to Doing your Research Project* (Sage, 2010) at 129.
11 The Legal Aid Board is a state-run service provided to clients on low incomes (less than €18,000 p.a.) in Ireland.
12 Purposive sampling is employed when non-random samples are chosen, with participants being selected because of their experience of a particular phenomenon.
13 These collaborative lawyers were chosen because of their experience of using the process in practice.
14 O'Leary, Z., *The Essential Guide to Doing your Research Project* (Sage, 2010) at 169.
15 Macfarlane, J., *The Emerging Phenomenon of Collaborative Family Law (CFL): A Qualitative Case Study* (Department of Justice Canada, 2005); Sefton, M., *Collaborative Family Law: A report for Resolution*, Association of Family Lawyers in the UK (2009); Barlow, A., Hunter, R., Smithson, J., & Ewing, J., *Mapping Paths to Family Justice*, (Economic and Social Research Council (ESRC), June 2014); Schwab, W., 'Collaborative Lawyering: A Closer Look at an Emerging Practice' (2004) (4) *Pepperdine Dispute Resolution Law Journal* 351–399. See Chapter 4.
16 The results from this aspect of the quantitative research have been published. See Connie Healy, '"On the plus side, I empathise more with my clients. On the negative side, I empathise more with my clients!" – Training as a Collaborative Lawyer: An Empirical Analysis' (2013) (3) *Irish Journal of Family Law* 70–78.
17 Ibid.
18 Courts Service Annual Report 2012 at 22. Available at http://www.courts.ie/Courts.ie/library3.nsf/(WebFiles)/87BE463114EF96FF80257BA20033953B/$FILE/Courts%20Service%20Annual%20Report%202012.pdf. Last accessed 1 August 2016.
19 Barlow, A., Hunter, R., Smithson, J., & Ewing, J., *Mapping Paths to Family Justice* (Economic and Social Research Council (ESRC), June 2014) at 4. Available at http://socialsciences.exeter.ac.uk/law/research/frs/researchprojects/mappingpathstofamilyjustice/. Last accessed 1 August 2016.
20 This is slightly lower than the settlement rate recorded in the research carried out in the UK.
21 It is not possible to determine from the replies received whether this was both parties instructing specific experts jointly or whether it was, as was evident from the qualitative research, one party seeking the advices of a specific expert to clarify matters of concern to them. This question should have been more clearly stated in the questionnaire.
22 Healy, C., '"On the plus side, I empathise more with my clients. On the negative side, I empathise more with my clients!" – Training as a Collaborative Lawyer: An Empirical Analysis' (2013) (3) *Irish Journal of Family Law* 70–78 at 73.
23 This, again, is in accordance with international research.
24 See section on the views of collaborative lawyers on the disqualification provision, as detailed later in this chapter.
25 Healy, C. '"On the plus side, I empathise more with my clients. On the negative side, I empathise more with my clients!" – Training as a Collaborative Lawyer: An Empirical Analysis' (2013) (3) *Irish Journal of Family Law* 70–78 at 74.
26 Ibid.
27 By three out of 15 respondents.

28 12 out of 25 respondents.

29 According to six out of 25 respondents.

30 By four out of 25 respondents.

31 Davy, E., 'Problems Associated with Collaborative Practice' 1 (2009) *Judicial Studies Institute Journal* 14–18 at 16.

32 Ibid. at 76.

33 The model participation agreement drafted by the ACP relies on Section 9 of the Family Law (Divorce) Act 1996 with respect to privilege. Section 9 of the Act provides: 'An oral or written communication between either of the spouses concerned and a third party for the purpose of seeking assistance to effect a reconciliation or to reach agreement between them on some or all of the terms of a separation or a divorce (whether or not made in the presence or with the knowledge of the other spouse), and any record of such a communication, made or caused to be made by either of the spouses concerned or such a third party, shall not be admissible as evidence in any court'. The issue of the confidentiality of negotiations was challenged in the Supreme Court of British Columbia in the case of *Banerjee v. Bisset* 2009 B.C.L.R. 2d. 1808 at paragraph 19: 'The court, having considered the matter, held that in signing the participation agreements "… the parties agreed to have a confidential process; they agreed to forgo access to the court unless either or both of them withdrew from the collaborative law process; and they agreed that no agreements would be enforceable unless they were agreements in writing. They also, necessarily, agreed to forgo disclosing negotiations which stopped short of a written agreement for the purpose of trying to prove that an oral agreement was made and should be enforced. In other words, they agreed to a different set of rules than apply to normal litigation"'.

34 According to six out of 26 respondents. Lack of trained practitioners was cited by 20% of respondents as causing difficulty for the development of collaborative practice.

35 Cited by five out of 26 respondents.

36 According to five out of 26 respondents.

37 Healy, C., '"On the plus side, I empathise more with my clients. On the negative side, I empathise more with my clients!" – Training as a Collaborative Lawyer: An Empirical Analysis' (2013) (3) *Irish Journal of Family Law* 70–78 at 76.

38 This is consistent with the age profile of parties who have used the collaborative process across the US and the UK.

39 90% had been married for more than ten years.

40 70% of participants had children who were under the age of 18.

41 80% of participants' household income was over €50,000, with 20% indicating that their household income was over €100,000.

42 The Legal Aid Board is a state-run service provided to clients on low incomes (below €18,000 p.a.) in Ireland.

43 Wray, L., and Lloyd, S., *Research regarding Collaborative Practice: A Comparison of Findings from the International Academy of Collaborative Professionals and Resolution* (IACP 10th Annual Forum, October 2010).

44 This is in line with the research carried out by the IACP which indicated that there is no clear referral source. See Wray, L., and Lloyd, S., *Research regarding Collaborative Practice: A Comparison of Findings from the International Academy of Collaborative Professionals and Resolution* (IACP 10th Annual Forum, October 2010).

45 This service is now under the auspices of the Legal Aid Board.

46 Macfarlane, J., *The Emerging Phenomenon of Collaborative Family Law (CFL): A Qualitative Case Study* (Department of Justice Canada, 2005) at 72.

47 Conneely, S., *Family Mediation in Ireland* (Ashgate, 2002).

48 Coulter, C., *Family Law Reporting, Pilot Project.* Available at http://www.courts.ie/Courts.ie/library3.nsf/(WebFiles)/C4FA6C02C7B13A428025738400521CE9/$FILE/Report%20to%20the%20Board%20of%20the%20Courts%20Service.pdf 40. Last accessed 15 July 2016.

49 The impetus is a result of the transposition of the European Mediation Directive, the merger of the Legal Aid Board and the Family Mediation Service and the introduction of pilot mediation schemes.
50 Four female participants indicated that their husbands would have continued in the marriage rather than end it.
51 See the results of IACP research as detailed in Chapter 4.
52 Fisher, R., and Ury, W., Getting to Yes (2nd edn, Random House, 1992). See Chapter 1.
53 Women's Aid, *Submission to the Family Law Reporting Committee* (January 2009) at 5. Available at: www.womensaid.ie. Last accessed 1 July 2016.
54 The national body for collaborative lawyers in Ireland.
55 Cameron, N., *Collaborative Practice: Deepening the Dialogue* (Continuing Legal Education Society of British Columbia, 2004) at 106.
56 This is in accordance with the views expressed by Lowenthal that one cannot take a collaborative approach if one's opponent is to take a competitive one. See Lowenthal, G., 'A General Theory of Negotiation Process, Strategy and Behaviour' (1982) 31 *University of Kansas Law Review* 69–114 at 92.
57 If collaborative practice was to increase in popularity and more cases were settled by solicitors, this would considerably reduce the case-load for barristers and therefore their fee income. The structure of the legal profession in Ireland, as it stands in 2016, is that barristers do not have direct access to the public and therefore even if they trained as collaborative lawyers they could not take on their own cases.
58 'Marital breakdown is acrimonious – it's an acrimonious place to be and I think the acrimony comes from that into the legal process rather than the legal process creating it' – opinion of barrister interviewed.
59 Three barristers expressed this view.
60 Both of these parties had, in fact, tried mediation some time previously. One party had managed to agree access arrangements within the mediation process, but the remaining issues were not resolved. The other party did not find the mediation process helpful.
61 Four years in one case, and eight in another.
62 The impact of time, as noted by Bronfenbrenner, U., 'Ecological systems theory', in Ross Vasta (ed.), *Six Theories of Child Development: Revised Formulations and Current Issues* (Jessica Kingsley Publishers Ltd, 1992) (see Chapter 1).
63 Cameron, N., *Collaborative Practice, Deepening the Dialogue* (The Continuing Legal Education Society of British Columbia, 2004) at 51.

6 In conclusion …

Introduction

This book has outlined the theoretical foundations of alternative dispute resolution and collaborative practice, it has explained and examined the process, the enactment of the Uniform Collaborative Law Act and has presented the results of research undertaken in Canada, the US, England and Wales and Ireland. In completing this work, this chapter will begin by examining another method of dispute resolution born out of collaborative practice, namely, cooperative law. It will explore whether this process has benefits for prospective parties and the response it has received from the legal profession. In doing so, it will review research on the cooperative process undertaken by Lande and Hoffman and the extent to which the results compare with the international findings on collaborative practice.

In concluding, this chapter will examine the *need* for the collaborative process. Is it just what 'good lawyers do anyway', merely 'an evolutionary development of an already existing tendency rather than a seismic paradigm shift'[1]? Would it be more effective, as remarked by one of the barristers interviewed in Ireland, to stop 'duplicating and duplicating' in creating 'new' or perhaps 'different' versions of existing processes and focus on the key elements that need to be addressed regardless of the method used? Following on from the review of the research internationally, this book will conclude with an evidenced-based analysis of collaborative practice through the framework of the key provisions of the UCLA, the impetus or lack thereof towards embracing the benefits of a multidisciplinary approach to the resolution of conflict and the implications of this 'evolution' for clients, practitioners and crucially for the development of legal education.

Cooperative law

This book has focused mainly on collaborative practice, negotiation through lawyers and the courts' process. Reference was also made to 'kitchen table negotiation' and mediation. It was noted in Chapter 1, that theorists like Fuller were keen to stress the importance of maintaining the integrity of each process and argued against combining methods of dispute resolution.[2] Over the years, however, many other forms of dispute resolution have emerged. Many of these are hybrids of existing processes.[3] Hoffman refers to this as the 'cross fertilization of law and dispute resolution', motivated in his opinion mainly by 'economics' and 'ideology'.[4] Similar to the views of Gillers[5] referred to in Chapter 2, Hoffman refers to lawyers developing an interest in processes that they consider legitimate or beneficial in monetary terms. Ostensibly, processes have been altered for the benefit of clients. Nevertheless, some changes have also, by accident or design, removed barriers to lawyers' representation. One such process is cooperative law.

Cooperative law was first developed in Wisconsin in 2003. Since then it has gained popularity in other States across the US and in England and Wales.[6] Cooperative lawyers purport to follow the principles of collaborative practice, *without* the disqualification provision. They have described their approach as a 'reflection of dissatisfaction with certain aspects of both litigation-oriented and Collaborative Practice.'[7] Lawyers and their clients make a commitment to settlement. In some cases, a Cooperative Participation Agreement is signed. Cases are settled within what they describe as a 'culture of civility'.[8] Four-way meetings are held, thus purportedly giving clients the same element of ownership and control that is evident within the collaborative process. Information is shared and parties are encouraged to 'talk candidly'.[9] Again, cooperative lawyers instruct experts jointly. Prospective parties and their lawyers agree to correct each other's mistakes and to refrain from issuing proceedings unless they need to seek directions, or an opinion, from the court. They use 'litigation selectively when it seems appropriate' and '[m]ost say that using litigation usually does not prevent the parties from negotiating cooperatively.'[10] Afterwards, the parties go back to the negotiating table and resume settlement talks.

The way in which cooperative cases are managed seems to vary. At Boston Law Collaborative (where all forms of dispute resolution are offered) cooperative lawyers replace the disqualification provision with a two-step process:

- a 'cooling off' period which can be for any agreed length of time but would typically be for 60 days, followed by
- a requirement that the parties engage in mandatory mediation.[11]

If neither of these additional steps results in settlement, the parties may instruct their original lawyers to act on their behalf in any subsequent court proceedings.

The Cooperative movement points to the advantages of this process for clients. Firstly, their lawyers will not, as they describe it 'abandon' clients if settlement cannot be achieved within the process.[12] Secondly, many of the risks associated with collaborative practice are removed. Clients and lawyers are not prevented from seeking the assistance of the court. This, they believe, furthers settlement rather than being a breach of trust. Importantly, removing the disqualification provision removes the threat of one client being able to 'fire' the other party's lawyer, thereby possibly achieving a strategic advantage. In the opinion of cooperative lawyers, removing the disqualification provision actually encourages more open discussion between the parties because they are not in fear of losing their lawyers.[13]

Research into cooperative law

Unlike the collaborative movement where the International Academy of Collaborative Professionals has been, as noted earlier, instrumental in developing ethical standards, promoting the process and ultimately bringing about the enactment of the Uniform Collaborative Law Act, the same impetus has not been evident in terms of promoting cooperative practice and therefore it is not as well known. Lande's study in 2007 was the first research undertaken into cooperative practice. He interviewed ten lawyers, members of the Divorce Cooperation Institute (DCI) in Wisconsin. In addition, he surveyed all of the members of the DCI group. Some members of DCI were also members of the Collaborative Family Law Council of Wisconsin (CFLCW). As with the research undertaken into collaborative practice, all were experienced family lawyers, many of whom had been in practice for over twenty years. Lande's study is based on the views of these lawyers and their perceptions of cooperative law, and includes what he describes as 'lawyers' perceptions of clients' reactions to it'.[14] In carrying out the study, Lande notes that although he had not planned for lawyers to compare cooperative law with collaborative practice, they tended to do so. This may be because of the ten persons he interviewed, six had also dealt with cases through the collaborative process.

The results of the surveys revealed that cooperative lawyers saw collaborative practice as 'cumbersome', 'rigid' and 'expensive' and in particular viewed the disqualification provision as being problematic.[15] Forty per cent of cooperative lawyers considered the disqualification agreement as being unethical. Particular criticisms of collaborative practice included the view that issues were 'talked to death'[16] and that there was an expectation that experts would be brought into the process as a matter of routine.

The research into cooperative law in Wisconsin shows that settlement rate, similar to that in collaborative practice, is high, with over 90% of cases settling.[17] Cooperative lawyers, however, are less focused on structure. In many cases no participation agreements were signed, there were no four-way meetings held. There is also what he described as a 'less onerous duty of disclosure.'[18] The research revealed that cooperative lawyers, rather than disclose everything as is the expectation in collaborative practice, disclose information they consider to be *relevant* and events or issues that are *certain* to occur. Otherwise, full disclosure is not required unless clients are asked direct questions.

Nevertheless, Lande found that most cooperative lawyers did, in fact, encourage their clients to provide full disclosure. Despite their dissatisfaction with collaborative practice, surprisingly 88% of these lawyers said that they would 'withdraw from the representation if the parties fail to comply with their disclosure obligations.'[19] As a process that purports to remove barriers to lawyers' representation of their clients when settlement cannot be reached, prospective parties need to be fully advised prior to engaging in the cooperative process, that non-disclosure will lead to the withdrawal of the lawyer. Lande recommended that cooperative lawyers should provide 'a clearly-identified process and clear information about it'.[20]

Without this clarity at the outset, collaborative lawyers may be justified, in describing cooperative law, as one collaborative lawyer described it, 'a little too much like a wolf in sheep's clothing'[21] particularly in the light of the extensive efforts made by the IACP to address the issue of informed consent as part of their ethical guidelines and the enactment of the UCLA.

With regard to client involvement in the process, the lawyers interviewed advised that 'parties are substantially involved in making decisions, though this varies depending on the clients' situations and preferences'.[22] Lande, however, found evidence of what he describes as 'shuttle diplomacy' with lawyers discussing the cases on their own and then going back to their respective clients or into joint meetings.[23] This raises concerns that cooperative law therefore may, in fact, be no more than polite ordinary lawyer negotiation.

Those that were described as 'dual members' (members of DCI and CFLCW) were more accepting of the purported benefits of collaborative practice and did not view the disqualification provision as being unethical. The lawyers who were amenable to the use of both processes were of the view that the disqualification provision in collaborative practice is seen as a sign of good faith. Clients, the dual members felt, were more satisfied when they resolved issues through the collaborative process, than if they had used any other process. Of the lawyers surveyed, half were equally satisfied with collaborative practice and cooperative law, 33% were more satisfied with cooperative and 11% were more satisfied with collaborative practice. There was widespread agreement that clients had no difficulty understanding collaborative and cooperative with 96% of lawyers surveyed believing this to be the case. Likewise, there was a similar level of agreement that collaborative practice is not suitable where there are issues of domestic violence. The majority of cooperative lawyers surveyed were in favour of practice groups, similar to those that exist for collaborative lawyers, to facilitate regular meetings to discuss the process and to improve their skills.

The research undertaken therefore highlights the need for informed consent and participation agreements in which the terms of the negotiation process are clearly set out in language that prospective parties can understand. Most significantly, these agreements should specify that cooperative lawyers too will withdraw if disclosure is not complied with, despite the lack of the disqualification provision. While resisting the rules and structure that is part of the collaborative process, the research points to the need for rules in cooperative. This may mean that there will be little to distinguish the two processes. One of the main factors which may undermine both processes is a blurring of the boundaries, with clients being unsure as to the approach being taken. More worryingly, situations may arise where clients are being told that one or other approach is being taken and negotiations progressing as is the practice during ordinary lawyer negotiation with lawyers continuing to represent them at the final hearing.

Lande notes, however, that where the disqualification provision has been the 'barrier to the use of Collaborative Practice, in non-family cases cooperative practice serves as a catalyst for spreading Collaborative *ideals* outside of the family law arena.'[24] Also, for some separating parties their relationship post-separation may be such that they are unable to sit in a room together and cooperative law may be a good option: permitting them to adhere to the principles of good faith, interest-based negotiation in a neutral setting away from the pressure of the courthouse, without the absolute requirement to negotiate in face-to-face meetings from the outset. The process is flexible enough for this to occur if desired, but it would not be rigidly enforced.

Hoffman, one of the leading members of Boston Law Collaborative also undertook research on 199 cases dealt with by their practice between 2004 and 2007. He established that the larger cost of failing to settle within the collaborative process is the cost of trial, or of negotiating up to the point of settlement, not the cost of educating a new lawyer about the case.[25] Hoffman's research identified 'costs, contentiousness and delay' as the key issues clients were seeking to avoid. Bar the difficulties posed by litigation on these counts, he saw little to differentiate between mediation, cooperative practice and collaborative practice.[26]

Thus on concluding his research, Hoffman was keen to stress the need for what he called a 'big tent' philosophy, where clients are advised of and have access to the whole range of dispute resolution processes from the courts to less adversarial means. He acknowledged, as did Barlow, that it was important not to portray the courts as the worst option; the courts are required to determine the law and resolve cases that otherwise could not be resolved.[27] Alternative processes rely on the courts to provide that last port of call, while symbiotically, the courts rely on alternative processes and ordinary lawyer negotiation to remove some of the cases from their lists.[28] Within this recognition, there is a need for many different dispute resolution processes. Hoffman also recognised the difficulties faced by separating parties in trying to select a process that best fits their needs, commenting that the 'choice of a dispute resolution process at the beginning of a case is essentially a judgment call about the future, made at the confusing intersection of law, fact, and emotion.'[29] Having a range of options and lawyers that are willing and capable of providing an objective view of each and how best it may address clients' particular needs is more conducive to settlement rather than a one-size-fits-all approach. In the final analysis, he did not find sufficiently convincing evidence that one process was better than another. What Hoffman did find of relevance, however, was the 'intentions, skill, flexibility, and interpersonal chemistry of the parties and counsel'.[30]

The impact of lawyers as agents in the dispute resolution process

As noted in Chapter 1, therefore, those with whom disputing parties come into contact during the dispute transformation process and the relationship clients form with their legal advisors can have a significant impact on how matters are resolved. Relationships between lawyers are equally important. Throughout the research undertaken into collaborative practice and cooperative law internationally, lawyers were keen to stress the importance of the *attitude* of the lawyer on the opposing side as being a key determinant in the approach taken. Many newly-qualified lawyers learn this lesson early in their careers. 'Playing nicely' in the litigation game can result in adverse consequences for the lawyer and their client if they encounter an opponent that is adversarial in their approach. As a result, lawyers negotiating on behalf of their clients waste money, effort and, something particularly important in the context of family law disputes where there may be children to consider, time, by trying, as Peppet observes to 'hedge against the risk of exploitation', dealing with the 'strategic difficulties of trying to collaborate with an uncertain adversary'.[31] The fear of appearing weak before an opponent or that taking a less than forthright approach, one that may be interpreted as being defeatist from the client's perspective, can be an issue for many lawyers. Arguably, therefore, there is logic to a system in which lawyers agree to 'playing nicely' at the outset. Many of the lawyers interviewed described collaborative practice as putting a structure on something that they had been looking for, where lawyers model positive behaviour to their clients and colleagues. Trust, therefore, is a key factor.

On the other hand, lawyers who are resistant to alternative methods of dispute resolution speak of the primacy of the rights-based systems, lawyers remaining in control and justice being determined by the system rather than focusing on outcomes. Macfarlane describes this adversarial approach as being 'highly seductive but ultimately dissatisfying'[32] and also, as noted earlier, impervious to change. Negotiation within this system is merely an adjunct or by-product of litigation, rather than something which has value in itself and which takes a structured approach. Moving from the adversarial *system* does not sit easily with many litigators who rely on the procedures and rules set out by the Superior courts and legislation. Yet, ironically, it may well be the 'structure' that is present in the collaborative process, that leads to lawyers refusing to engage. The risks for collaborative practice may lie in the fact that it requires more structured up-front preparation time for lawyers, for, as demonstrated in this research and research internationally, and contrary to what the legal profession assert, no greater financial gain. This may mean that the service may simply not be offered to separating couples.

What is clear, however, is that clients, in many cases, will be influenced by what they are advised by their legal representatives as 'experts' and while some clients are researching matters themselves and are less willing to hand the control of their issues completely to a lawyer, unless there is an acceptance of these processes by the legal profession, the whole area of alternative dispute resolution is likely to remain, as described by one practitioner, 'a minority sport'.

Amongst the wider legal profession, there was some limited acceptance of mediation but not of collaborative practice. Both the results of the quantitative research carried out as part of this study and an analysis of the information gleaned from collaborative practitioners who were interviewed highlight *apathy* from the legal profession and a lack of willingness to engage as the main stumbling blocks to the development of collaborative practice. Many lawyers will never be of the mind-set that they are willing to engage in interest-based negotiation or to sit down around a table with clients and give them advice as to where and how to access information and services that may help them to reach a more holistic solution. This is clear through the negativity expressed by some litigators towards the collaborative process.

Impetus too needs to come from the legislature and the Judiciary. In Ireland, for example, draft heads of a Mediation Bill were proposed in 2012. No further action was taken until February 2017 when a draft Mediation Bill was published. Accepting the need for flexibility within these processes, having regulation of the mediation profession, specific training requirements and clarification of issues like confidentiality and privilege would provide an element of reassurance for the public and the legal profession.

The key differences in approach – collaborative practice *v.* ordinary lawyer negotiation or court

The settlement rate for cases through the collaborative process is much the same as for those settled through ordinary lawyer negotiation. The outcomes, similarly, are much the same. So what distinguishes collaborative practice as a method of dispute resolution?

The importance of preparation

Fisher and Ury, in assessing why lawyers continue to resort to positional negotiation, noted that it is easy, it effectively needs very little if any preparation and it is universally understood (see Chapter 1).[33] This accords with the view expressed by litigators interviewed for this research, that, in many respects, the facts are the same in each case – settlement is somewhat of a formula informed by the lawyers' knowledge of their judge.

In contrast, one of the essential elements of the collaborative process, as noted by Webb[34] (see Chapter 2), is that the lawyers contact each other in advance of the first meeting to discuss areas of possible conflict and to devise what has been described as a 'mutual game plan'. By doing this, the lawyers are better placed to deal with particular issues of concern to their clients and to guide clients through the process. The first pre-meeting discussion also gives clients an opportunity to tell their story *as they see it*, and furthermore it is a valuable opportunity for lawyers to explain the key issues of relevance from a legal perspective. When lawyers engage in routine positional negotiation there is a risk that these matters will be overlooked. Information will only be gathered that the *lawyer* believes is relevant to any possible settlement, with less regard for the client's narrative.

One collaborative practitioner highlighted the importance of this preparation as follows:

> What undoes the collaborative process, and what gets under my skin, is where people [collaborative lawyers] don't prepare for the meetings, where people are late for the meetings or where people think the meeting is a case of, 'I can turn up with my papers and we will deal with it when we get there'. Whereas, instead it really is a case of that necessary meeting beforehand, and the common plan of 'What are we doing here?' This is special, this isn't just a court application that I can go in before a judge and I can wing it if I say the

> right things when an issue arises. I have to actually be in command of what I am doing …

Another spoke of the importance of this pre-settlement meeting work that 'you wouldn't normally be doing in litigation at all'. In examining the results of the interviews with litigators, it became clear that a detailed meeting with a client in advance of any settlement negotiations was of importance to some. Whether this happens, however, may depend on the approach of the particular lawyer. In contrast, this preparation is an integral and essential part of the collaborative process.

Managing client expectations

Barlow noted that engaging in the courts' system can be a more passive decision than choosing to use mediation or collaborative practice.[35] She also comments that even though clients engage in the legal process, they do so with 'an active desire to avoid court'.[36] During the research undertaken in Ireland, one of the collaborative lawyers expressed the same view:

> A lot of people think, that is not going to be our case, we are not going to fight it out to the nth degree and only settle on the steps of the court. It is very difficult to say to them, 'Well, here is your chance of mediation or collaboration to actually come to an agreement, and if you can't come to an agreement, well that's the only other route to go'. It [the case] is not going to get that dynamic, that settlement dynamic, until you are literally on the steps of the court, on the road going down to the steps of the court and believe me, that is the way it operates; litigation lawyers and barristers will focus on the case when it is coming up next month.

Therefore, while much emphasis has been placed on the issue of informed consent when choosing the collaborative process, it appears that separating parties are not always fully aware of the implications of proceeding down the litigation route. Lawyers, as noted by Lande, often begin with 'unilaterally-initiated litigation procedures',[37] a policy of litigate first and ask questions later. As part of this litigation, they make unreasonable demands, seeking everything with a view to negotiating a more realistic settlement. This however can raise client expectations such that regardless of the merit of the eventual settlement or court order, they may experience a sense of disappointment. As noted earlier, clients need to be aware that their case may not get the 'settlement dynamic' until it is actually listed for hearing, and by that point considerable damage may have been done to relationships through acrimonious correspondence or pleadings. The reality, as one solicitor described it, is:

> This is the cake. Is the judge going to make it bigger; is he going to increase your husband's salary; is he going to reduce your mortgage; is he going to get the government to increase your child benefit? No. These are the facts.

If a relationship has broken down to the extent that it ends up in court, it may be unrealistic to expect a judge to be able to 'reach a satisfactory solution'. The judge will, on balance, give the parties a fair hearing. In a jurisdiction like Ireland, where divorce is granted on a no-fault basis, the judge will not, however, be interested in what has happened in the relationship to-date and will be concerned solely with making a ruling on issues that the parties have not been in a position to agree. One Irish barrister commented that people:

> have a completely misguided idea of the degree of interest that court will have in their personal life, and I think if they only knew how little interest the court has and what a blunt instrument the court is for dealing with the breakdown of a marriage. I think that would be helpful certainly.

Clients, therefore, may not get an opportunity for the 'thorough presentation' that Fiss envisaged.[38] Solicitors and barristers will determine what is relevant and how the case is presented. The client may have very little input. Part of ensuring informed consent to engage in the courts process requires that these matters be pointed out to prospective parties at the outset and managing client expectations accordingly.

Change in approach by lawyers

Lawyers will know the unwritten rules to solve the mysteries of the legal system. Decisions as to whether and when to initiate negotiations are often made on an ad hoc basis. Positional negotiation frequently involves the strategic use of information to reach settlement with no transparency as to whether pressure was brought to bear on parties to settle. Research indicates that 90% of cases settle. Felstiner and Sarat note that family lawyers are more anxious than most to try and reach settlement rather than go to court.[39] In many instances, the pressure to settle may be understated with no ethical standards in place for lawyers negotiating within the adversarial system.[40] In contrast, the 'pressure', if it arises, in the collaborative process is identifiable as the disqualification provision and can be discussed in advance.

By setting the terms of negotiation out in a participation agreement, collaborative lawyers and their clients agree to higher standards from the outset avoiding this unnecessary posturing, saving additional costs, and avoiding the fear and pressure that is frequently associated with negotiating in the dark, and the on-going threat of a court hearing. As noted earlier, the solicitors and barristers interviewed consistently referred to the impact of the approach taken by 'the other side' in positional negotiations. By engaging in collaborative practice, in contrast, lawyers agree from the outset not to take an adversarial approach but to work with the clients and the lawyer on 'the other side' in an effort to reduce the acrimony and find a solution that is crafted to the particular client's needs. They, as noted by Peppet, agree to, arguably, a higher standard of legal ethics than is required within the adversarial system.[41]

In doing so, they build up, and rely upon, this 'reputation' of being less adversarial. Lawyers purporting to take this approach, but acting in an overtly adversarial or positional manner, will, as noted by Coser (see Chapter 1) be excluded from the 'group': the collaborative community.[42] Setting these parameters gives a certain assurance to lawyers: a commitment by both to take an interests-based approach. In this regard, Schneyer comments that the collaborative law movement has 'quickly developed an infrastructure or "private legal system" to govern the negotiation process that is promising and surpasses anything the mainstream bar has produced'.[43] Separating parties, by engaging in the process, negotiate within this 'infrastructure'.

If of no other benefit and never used by lawyers, training in collaborative practice alone appears to have a significant impact on the way lawyers approach cases. Across all studies, over three-quarters of all lawyers surveyed noticed a change in the way they practice; they think more carefully about the long-term impact of adversarial correspondence, of raising clients' expectations by making excessive claims in court proceedings and are now willing to think more broadly about the family's long-term needs rather than a 'win' for their own client. Information is shared for the purpose of understanding rather than winning,[44] with a view to resolving conflict rather than settling it.[45] Does this mean lawyers are not acting as a zealous advocate for their client? Collaborative lawyers will argue that they continue to advocate for their clients, they just approach this in a different way. The research undertaken internationally supports this view with clients being keen to stress that they always felt that their lawyers were on their side and acting in their best interests.

The collaborative process through the framework of the UCLA?

As a new process, particularly one that has consequences for lawyers, in the event of failure, many concerns were highlighted by the mainstream Bar: the importance of having a clear agreement in place as to how negotiations will be undertaken, clarifying the ethos of the process and the importance for clients and their lawyers of ensuring informed consent to enter the process and capacity to engage; a clear understanding of the disqualification clause and its possible implications financially and emotionally and ensuring that proper safeguards are in place with regard to ethical standards, privilege and confidentiality. These issues were addressed during the enactment of the UCLA.

The process

The research undertaken notes that while there may have been many variations of participation agreements and how the process has been run, collaborative lawyers remain loyal to the good faith ethos of the process, negotiating through four-way meetings and approaching cases in non-adversarial manner. The evidence suggests that they have been successful in this aim. While the numbers of cases reported in each of the studies examined were small, especially when compared to the volume of cases that proceed through the adversarial system and settle at the door of the court, overall, those that took part were satisfied with the process and the outcomes.

Clarity has been gained through the enactment of the UCLA which sets out the requirements for a collaborative participation agreement and a recommended practice that collaborative lawyers sign the agreements simply to confirm their representation of the client rather than as a party to the agreement. This also addresses ethical concerns raised in relation to the lawyers taking on obligations to third parties. The definition given to the process under the Act is also important in ensuring that clients are not offered what is purported to be collaborative practice but is merely polite lawyer negotiation. Collaborative lawyers and practice groups would be wise to review their agreements accordingly.

Informed consent

Concerns have been raised about collaborative lawyers with their belief that this is a better way for prospective families, encouraging clients into the process without them being fully advised. This was commented upon by Barlow and also by Hoffman who note that lawyers tend to promote what fits within their philosophical views or their preferred way of practice. Schwab too noted that lawyers' influence 'appears to figure significantly in client decision making'.[46] Central to the success of collaborative practice is the importance of ensuring that clients enter the process will full knowledge of the process and its unique features. The statutory requirements imposed on lawyers by Section 14 of the UCLA should assist to address this issue in States where the Act has been adopted. No doubt difficulties will remain. Each lawyer's approach in any given case cannot be policed. There remains the risk that lawyers will simply give clients information to 'tick the box' and continue to 'steer' them towards the process that the lawyer is most familiar or comfortable with. Litigators interviewed as part of the Irish research admitted taking this approach to their statutory requirements in relation to mediation – informing clients of the process because they were obliged to do so, rather than because they had any belief in the process. There was a mixed response from clients that were interviewed internationally. Some remember being told about all of the options available, others were not sure. Many said that they did not want to hear about other options as they had already researched the collaborative process themselves or it had been recommended to them by friends.

Screening

The research indicates that there is an accepted view amongst collaborative practitioners that collaborative practice is not suitable where there are on-going issues of domestic violence. At a minimum, there would have to be an acknowledgement of what had happened and a willingness by both parties to move on. The Act does not prevent parties from using in the process, once having been given full information, they make an informed decision and the alleged victim wishes to proceed. Lawyers, too, need to be confident that they have the necessary skills to deal with what may be a high conflict case. In situations where the parties are willing and in a financial position to engage mental health experts or counsellors to address the underlying issues this would be the most holistic solution in an effort to end the cycle of violence. The screening obligations under the Act highlight the importance of assessing capacity, as does the requirement that screening is to continue throughout the process. As Ver Steegh notes, the screening provision in the UCLA is an example that should also be followed within the adversarial courts system.[47] In court situations, if the parties are already living separately and apart, many lawyers and indeed judges may fail to question whether there have been any past issues of domestic violence and crucially, the impact that such pressures may have had on settlement agreements reached. Hiding domestic abuse does not just occur within alternative processes. All lawyers need to undergo training to enable them to recognise and detect underlying issues.

Disqualification provision

Contrary to the critics' claims that the disqualification provision is putting pressure on clients to settle and that it is removing their best alternative to a negotiated settlement, those who contributed to the research internationally were keen to stress that they were fully aware of the implications of the disqualification provision. Most who engage do not do so lightly. They tend to have researched the process themselves and are committed to finding an amicable solution. For some, having the provision in place helped them focus more intently on reaching settlement. Others specifically pointed to the risk for their lawyers too in investing in this process and how they value this commitment. If the negotiations fail, clients have the safety net of court. Lawyers lose a client. Conversely, within the litigation process there is often little, if any, incentive for lawyers to reach settlement; the incentive rather may be to keep a case going to the date of hearing or not attempting settlement until the steps of the courthouse, due to the potential for increased fees.

Does the disqualification provision prejudice and affect lower income clients more severely? Yes, it probably does. The statistics worldwide have shown that it tends to be a wealthier middle-class client that uses the process. However, efforts have been made to address this through the provisions of the UCLA where exceptions to the disqualification provision are made for low-income clients. However, without collaborative practice being offered as part of State legal aid systems in some jurisdictions, this may mean that low-income clients will not be in a position to avail of the process.

A significant risk remains with the disqualification provision: the danger that one client may use the disqualification provision to 'fire' the other party's lawyer. Questions have been raised regarding the ethical issues surrounding the possibility of such an event occurring. The consensus, as endorsed by the ABA in the US is that collaborative practice is a limited representation contract. However, questions remain as to how clients can give advance consent to something that may or may not happen and whether they are prejudiced should their lawyers be dismissed in this way. It is clear that even if the research evidence suggests that the instances of disqualification occurring are rare, clients need to be aware of the risk and fully advised.

Ethical issues

As documented throughout this book, concerns have been raised about whether collaborative practice is ethical. Despite the publishing of the American Bar Association Ethics Opinion and passing of the Uniform Collaborative Law Act, there is a sense of uneasiness in what Murphy refers to as a 'couple as a unit of law-making.'[48] She raised concerns that clients would settle for less than the minimum guaranteed to them through the legislative provisions and the courts. As noted by Wetlaufer, 'ethics is more demanding than law'[49] because it comes from an internal value system rather than an external source. Issues like when to negotiate and when to walk away; the information given by clients to lawyers and given to clients by lawyers during the negotiation process and how lawyers frame the 'best alternative to a negotiated settlement' when advising clients of their options if settlement cannot be achieved, are frequently based on value judgements made by the lawyers or the clients in any given situation. Values are difficult to assess. Much will, as noted by Hoffman, rely on the approach taken by individual lawyers and the type of relationship they form with clients. There has been no evidence found in the research undertaken to date that couples have been involved in law making. Indeed, the evidence is very much to the contrary in that the outcomes achieved in financial terms are almost identical to those achieved as a result of ordinary lawyer negotiation. The difference being that outcomes are more creative, tailored to the individual families' needs and have what Macfarlane referred to as 'value-added', most notably improved communication between the parties, a sense of achievement and empowerment having being actively involved in the settlement and better relationships post-separation.

Section 13 of the Act has reiterated the position that has always been adopted by the collaborative law movement, that lawyers retain their duties to their clients and are obliged to maintain their professional standards in dealing with cases.

Privilege and confidentiality

When tested before the court, it was acknowledged that clients negotiating with the collaborative process do so under a different set of rules.[50] Once these rules are clear at the outset and parties agree, the courts tend not to interfere. Concern has also been raised regarding the binding nature of agreements reached with the benefit of legal advice. Lawyers also represent clients during positional negotiation. Such agreements are therefore also reached with the benefit of legal advice, so in this respect the collaborative process does not differ from the practice in ordinary lawyer negotiation. In some jurisdictions, regardless of the manner in which settlement is reached, the Court will have to give final approval.

The provisions in relation to privilege and confidentiality under the Act take a sensible approach. Privilege is provided for. Parties, however, also have some discretion as to experts' reports etc. and safeguards are in place to prevent these provisions from allowing the introduction of evidence when needed to address issues of abuse, professional negligence, etc.

Barriers to collaborative practice

Examining the results of the research undertaken in this study, the main barriers identified to the development of the collaborative process were: apathy from the legal profession; a perception, fuelled by the mainstream Bar, that collaborative practice is prohibitively expensive and a lack of trained experts (collaborative lawyers and Personal and Family Consultants).

Many lawyers will never be of the mind-set where they are willing to sit down around a table with clients and give them advice as to where and how to access information and services that may help them to reach a more holistic solution. One barrister interviewed commented:

> we just provide a service that suits us. If it suits the customers, all well and good; and if it doesn't, so be it. I think you've got to get customer orientated and they (the profession) need to sit down and they need to say, 'Listen what's the best thing for our customers?'

Change can be difficult. Lawyers work in a profession steeped in tradition and the importance of the rule of law. Though a small study, the research presented here points to the benefits of having undergone training in collaborative law or mediation in helping lawyers reflect more on what may have become routine practices with the adversarial system.

This research, and research internationally, challenges the view that collaborative practice is prohibitively expensive; most clients who used the process were of the view that they saved both time and money. Where there is increased conflict, costs will be higher, regardless of the process used. The findings accord with there being benefits associated with taking a more focused approach to negotiating marital breakdown and engaging independent experts. The evidence did not back up the assertion, as alleged, that there were cases with 'two, if not three, accountants employed', or that the process costs 'thousands like tens of thousands and all it did was delay the case for a year' as commented by one of the Irish barristers interviewed.

Finally, training additional collaborative lawyers will help to ensure that this option will be available to clients who may choose to use it. Difficulties that have arisen to date are that one party may consult a collaborative lawyer and be in favour of taking this approach but the lawyer consulted by the other party may not be collaboratively trained. Similarly, further training is needed for Personal and Family Consultants, financial experts and child specialists if the multidisciplinary model is to flourish and provide holistic solutions for clients. In addition, this training needs to take an interdisciplinary approach encouraging lawyers to work constructively with these other professions for the benefit of their clients, if collaborative practitioners are going to fully embrace the comprehensive law approach and the benefits of understanding and adopting a therapeutic approach to practice. Culturally, there is also some work to be done in removing the negative association with seeking help with emotional issues, particularly in the Irish and English context. Participants in the US and Canada were more open to the benefits of the multidisciplinary approach. For some Irish participants, they advised that it is only in hindsight that they see the benefits that this approach would have achieved, noting however that they would have resisted it at the time.

Addressing the barriers through a change in the way lawyers are taught: impact on legal education

Law has a tendency to be taught in what Meyer and Land have described as a 'fragmented fashion.'[51] Central to this is a strong emphasis on the adversarial system and the rule of law. While this is of vital importance, as is the continuing role of the courts, legal education would benefit from a more open broad-based approach.

Developing 'skills' is one of the aims of the comprehensive law movement and of those that promote a therapeutic jurisprudence approach. Earlier exposure to alternative ways of 'thinking like a lawyer' which incorporate an understanding of the role of conflict and the importance of considering the wider sociological and ecological implications for clients and their families, should begin as part of third level or university education. Conflict, as noted in Chapter 1, is not always a negative force and should not be perceived as such. This is particularly important in family law where clients' emotions are also involved especially when dealing with cases where there may have been issues of domestic violence. To represent their client to the best of their ability, understanding the dynamics of conflict and being able to recognise factors that may suggest an underlying issue of domestic violence, may be as much of a benefit to lawyers as concentrating on how to become a zealous advocate, particularly with the overwhelming evidence that over 90% of cases settle before hearing.

With the impetus towards more holistic solutions, clients seeking more autonomy and a participative role in negotiating settlement of their cases, it is clear that law students should be introduced to working in a multidisciplinary manner and be exposed to the benefits of considering another viewpoint. Macfarlane refers to the need for what she describes as 'conflict resolution advocacy'.[52] She notes that while:

> adversarial advocacy tends to see settlement as capitulation, conflict resolution advocacy is committed to evaluating the pros, cons, and the alternatives of any settlement option, which includes an evaluation of the legal, cognitive, and emotional dimensions because all are part of how clients appraise settlement.[53]

This approach also necessitates more intensive training and guidance for lawyers on *how* to engage in interest-based rather than positional negotiation. Interest-based negotiation, as outlined in Chapter 1, concentrates on how to find shared interests and opportunities for mutual gain, with the parties having more control over the process itself and the outcome. This approach also necessitates lawyers having a better understanding of the context in which the parties are negotiating.

Finally, law students and lawyers should be taught how to engage in reflective practice.[54] When interviewing solicitors and barristers working within the adversarial system, many were keen to stress that they take a reasoned approach to settlement, pointing instead to a colleague who takes a much more 'adversarial' stance. When interviewing this alleged 'adversarial' colleague, it was found that they also believed that *they* were reasonable but others were not. Initially, this raised questions as to whether there was an element of social desirability bias evident in the findings – a belief perhaps, that this is what they *should* say. Having analysed the interviews further, however, it is evident that each one genuinely believed that they were, in fact, being reasonable. This may well have been true. However, this approach possibly changes somewhat once they were engaged in battle with colleagues – the expected and automatic behaviour within the adversarial system. There is a need for the legal profession to reflect on what Menkel-Meadow referred to as the 'purpose' of the case from the client's perspective. What will enable the lawyer to assist their client reach the best possible settlement for them? For some, this will be a court battle. As noted both by clients and lawyers interviewed, in many cases, this is an 'easier', 'more familiar' option. For others, the best option may, as Hoffman concluded, depend on the 'intentions, skill, flexibility, and interpersonal chemistry of the parties and counsel'.[55]

Adapting the courts' system

As noted, rather than there being substantial differences in outcomes between those achieved within the courts' process and collaborative practice, the research indicates that the results are remarkably similar in financial terms. The differences in the collaborative approach have already been noted, most significantly addressing the issues earlier in the dispute, preparation for negotiations and a change in approach by lawyers. Could this be achieved within the courts' system such that there would be no need for processes like collaborative practice, or as commented by one of the barristers interviewed 'duplicating and duplicating'? Objectively, yes, these principles could be applied. Attempts have been made to encourage earlier engagement with the issues in a case through case management systems within the courts' process. Solicitors and barristers interviewed were, however, of the view that these were generally a 'waste of time', with one barrister pointing out that they had been designed by administration without any consultation with practitioners. Could lawyers be simply trusted not to act in an adversarial way? The evidence suggests that many will revert to an adversarial mind-set. Would lawyers be happy to work on a more collaborative basis with coaches or mental health professions? Perhaps, but again the tendency to date has been towards finding specialists that support their client's view of the case, sometimes without bringing any objectivity to bear. One lawyer referred to one client 'working' with the psychologist in building a case against the other party but saw their representation of the client as facilitating this approach. All is possible within the courts' system, but this approach has not been and is not likely to be embraced by those that remain adversarial in their outlook.

Conclusion

Many may question the validity of the studies undertaken. Most of the sample sizes were small, due mainly to the lower up-take on collaborative practice compared to the courts' system. There were no control groups. Examining human lived experiences is not a purely scientific experiment. The goal of these case studies, for the most part, was analytic rather than statistical in nature.[56] In the final analysis, clients' views as to advantages of one process over another, are, as noted by Hoffman 'largely situational' and dependent on the facts in each specific case: the personalities, issues to be resolved and their relationship with those to whom they turn for advice. Further longitudinal research into collaborative practice will be required to asses if there are long term benefits.

Murphy, in highlighting concerns about theories of justice and private law-making being undertaken by couples within the collaborative process leading, potentially, to the vulnerable getting less than they may be entitled to by law, refers to an analogy of what her mother taught her – that everyone, regardless of their place in the family, whether they were male or female, were entitled to a share in the hamburger.[57] To end, therefore, with a lesson my mother, also a Murphy, taught me – 'It is not what you say, but *how* you say it'. Taking a less adversarial approach regardless of the process used, can only be of benefit to separating parties and their families.

Notes

1 Wright, K., 'The evolving role of the family lawyer: the impact of collaborative law on family law practice' (2011) 23 *Child and Family Law Quarterly* 370–392, 380.
2 Fuller, L.L., *The Principles of Social Order: Selected Essays of Lon L. Fuller*, Winston, K., (ed.) (Bloomsbury, 1981).
3 Adversarial Collaboration; Mediative Collaboration; Arbitrative Mediation; Mediative Arbitration; Litigative Arbitration; Mediative Litigation; Medicollab – using mediators as case manager.
4 Hoffman, D.A., 'Colliding Worlds of Dispute Resolution: Towards a Unified Field Theory of ADR' (2008) *Journal of Dispute Resolution* 11–44, 17.
5 Gillers, S., 'How to Make Rules for Lawyers: The Professional Responsibility of the Legal Profession' (2013) 40 *Pepperdine Law Review* 365–422, 377.
6 Started by the Divorce Cooperation Institute in Wisconsin in 2003. Also a number of lawyers in Boston have been offering the process since 2005.
7 Lande, J., 'Practical Insights from an Empirical Study of Cooperative Lawyers in Wisconsin' (2008) *Journal of Dispute Resolution* 203–266, 206.
8 Ibid. at 215.
9 Ibid. at 242.
10 Ibid.

11 Hoffman, D.A., 'Colliding Worlds of Dispute Resolution: Towards a Unified Field Theory of ADR' (2008) *Journal of Dispute Resolution* 11–44, 15.
12 Lande, J., 'Practical Insights from an Empirical Study of Cooperative Lawyers in Wisconsin' (2008) *Journal of Dispute Resolution* 203–266, 218.
13 Ibid. at 215.
14 Ibid. at 211.
15 Ibid. at 217.
16 Ibid. at 226.
17 Ibid. at 203.
18 Ibid. at 246.
19 Ibid. 88% of the respondents to the survey said that they would withdraw from representing the client.
20 Ibid. at 258.
21 Hoffman, D.A., 'Colliding Worlds of Dispute Resolution: Towards a Unified Field Theory of ADR' (2008) *Journal of Dispute Resolution* 11–44, 16.
22 Lande, J., 'Practical Insights from an Empirical Study of Cooperative Lawyers in Wisconsin' (2008) *Journal of Dispute Resolution* 203–266, at 254.
23 Ibid. at 240.
24 Ibid. at 259.
25 Hoffman, D.A., 'Colliding Worlds of Dispute Resolution: Towards a Unified Field Theory of ADR' (2008) *Journal of Dispute Resolution* 11–44, 33.
26 Ibid. at 34.
27 Barlow, A., Hunter, R., Smithson, J., and Ewing, J., *Mapping Paths to Family Justice* (Economic and Social Research Council (ESRC), June 2014) at 16. Available at http://socialsciences.exeter.ac.uk/law/research/frs/researchprojects/mappingpathstofamilyjustice/. Last accessed 1 August 2016.
28 Hoffman, D.A., 'Colliding Worlds of Dispute Resolution: Towards a Unified Field Theory of ADR' (2008) *Journal of Dispute Resolution* 11–44, 39.
29 Ibid. at 36.
30 Ibid. at 35.
31 Peppet, S., 'Lawyers' Bargaining Ethics, Contract, and Collaboration: The End of the Legal Profession and the Beginning of Professional Pluralism' 90 *Iowa Law Review* 475–538, 484.
32 Macfarlane, J., *The New Lawyer: How Settlement is Transforming the Practice of law* (UBC Press, 2008) at 64.
33 Fisher, R., and Ury, W., *Getting to Yes*(2nd edn, Random House 1992) at 157.
34 Webb, S., 'Collaborative Law: A Practitioner's Perspective on its History and Current Practice' (2008) 21 *Journal of the American Academy of Matrimonial Lawyers* 155–169 at 160.
35 Barlow, A., Hunter, R., Smithson, J. and Ewing, J., *Mapping Paths to Family Justice* (ESRC, June 2014) at 4.
36 Ibid.
37 Lande, J., 'Practical Insights from an Empirical Study of Cooperative Lawyers in Wisconsin' (2008) *Journal of Dispute Resolution* 203–266, 251.
38 Fiss, O., 'Against Settlement' (1986) 93 (6) *Yale Law Journal*, 1073–1090.
39 Sarat, A. and Felstiner, W., *Divorce Lawyers and their Clients* (Oxford University Press, 1995).
40 Wetlaufer, G., 'The Ethics of Lying in Negotiations' (1990) 75 *Iowa Law Review* 1219–1273.
41 Peppet, S., 'Lawyers' Bargaining Ethics, Contract, and Collaboration: The End of the Legal Profession and the Beginning of Professional Pluralism' 90 *Iowa Law Review* 475–538, 484.
42 Coser, L., *The Functions of Social Conflict* (The Free Press, 1956).
43 Schneyer, T., 'The Organized Bar and the Collaborative Law Movement: A Study in Professional Change' (2008) 50 *Arizona Law Review* 289–336, 334.

44 Macfarlane, J., *The New Lawyer: How Settlement is Transforming the Practice of Law* (UBC Press, 2008) at 78.
45 Rubin, J.Z., 'The Nature of Conflict and Negotiation' in Breslin, W., and Rubin, J. (eds), *Negotiation Theory & Practice*, (The Program on Negotiation, Harvard Law School, 1999).
46 Schwab, W., 'Collaborative Lawyering: A Closer Look at an Emerging Practice' (2004) 4 *Pepperdine Dispute Resolution Law Journal* 351–399, 378. Of the clients surveyed, 20% ranked 'lawyer's recommendation' as the primary factor for their choice, while another 24% identified it as their second most important consideration.
47 Ver Steegh, N., 'The Uniform Collaborative Law Act and Intimate Partner Violence: A Roadmap for Collaborative (and Non-Collaborative) Lawyers' (2009–2010) 38 *Hofstra Law Review* 699–755.
48 Murphy, R., 'Is the turn toward collaborative law a turn away from justice?' (2004) 42 (3) *Family Court Review* 460–470, 466
49 Wetlaufer, G., 'The Ethics of Lying in Negotiations' (1990) 75 *Iowa Law Review* 1219–1273, 1234–35.
50 *Banerjee v. Bisset* 2009 B.C.L.R. 2d. 1808.
51 Meyer, J., and Land, R., 'Threshold Concepts and Troublesome Knowledge (3): Implications for Course Design and Evaluation' in C. Rust (ed.) *Improving Student Learning: Diversity and Inclusivity* (Oxford Centre for Staff and Learning Development, 2005) at 2–3.
52 Macfarlane, J., *The New Lawyer: How Settlement is Transforming the Practice of Law* (UBC Press, 2008) at 111.
53 Ibid.
54 Schön, D., *The Reflective Practitioner: How Professionals Think in Action* (Temple Smith 1983).
55 Hoffman, D.A., 'Colliding Worlds of Dispute Resolution: Towards a Unified Field Theory of ADR' (2008) *Journal of Dispute Resolution* 11–44, at 35.
56 Yin, R., *Case Study Research: Design and Methods* (5th edn) (Sage Publications, 2014).
57 Murphy, R., 'Is the turn toward collaborative law a turn away from justice?' (2004) 42 (3) *Family Court Review* 460–470, 461.

Bibliography

Arrigo, B.A., 'The Ethics of Therapeutic Jurisprudence: A Critical and Theoretical Enquiry of Law, Psychology and Crime' (2004) 11(1) *Psychiatry, Psychology and Law* 23–43.

Babb, B., and Wexler, D., 'Therapeutic Jurisprudence' (2005) University of Baltimore Legal Studies Research Paper No. 2014–2013.

Barlow, A., Hunter, R., Smithson, J. and Ewing, J., *Mapping Paths to Family Justice* (ESRC, June 2014).

Bederman, D.J., *Customs as a Source of Law* (Cambridge: Cambridge University Press, 2010).

Berger, M.J., 'A Comparative Study of British Barristers and American Legal Practice and Education' (1983–1984) 5 *Northwestern Journal of International Law and Business* 540–584.

Berger, Y., 'Relationship Transformation, in Search of a "Roadmap" for Separating Couples', Workshop given at the Third European Conference on Collaboration entitled 'Challenging Conflict' Bad Aibling, 11 June 2010.

Bottemley, A., *Feminist Perspectives on the Foundational Subjects of Law* (London: Cavendish, 1996).

Boulle, L., and Kelly, K., *Mediation: Principles, Process, Practice* (New South Wales: Butterworths, 1998).

Boyarin, Y., 'Generating "Win-Win" Results: Negotiating Conflicts in the Drafting of Process if the Uniform Collaborative Law Act' (2009–2010) 38 *Hofstra Law Review* 495–536.

Bronfenbrenner, U., 'Ecological systems theory', in Ross Vasta (ed.), *Six Theories of Child Development: Revised Formulations and Current Issues* (London: Jessica Kingsley Publishers Ltd, 1992).

Brooks, S., and Madden, R., (eds) *Relationship-centered Lawyering: Social Science Theory for Transforming Legal Practice* (Durham NC: Carolina Academic Press, 2010).

Bryan, P., '"Collaborative Divorce", Meaningful Reform or Another Quick Fix?' (1999) 5(4) *Psychology, Public Policy and Law* 1001–1017.

Bush, J., and Folger, R., *The Promise of Mediation: Responding to Conflict through Empowerment and Recognition* (San Francisco: Jossey-Bass, 1994).

Cameron, N., *Collaborative Practice: Deepening the Dialogue* (Continuing Legal Education Society of British Columbia, 2004).

Centre for Effective Dispute Resolution (CEDR). *The CEDR Mediator Handbook* (Centre for Effective Dispute Resolution, 2004; 4th edn).

Cochran, Robert F., 'Legal Ethics and Collaborative Practice Ethics' (2009) 38 *Hofstra Law Review* 537–567.

Combs, G., and Freedman, J., 'Narrative, Poststructuralism, and Social Justice: Current Practices in Narrative Therapy' (2012) 40(7) *The Counseling Psychologist* 1033–1060.

Conneely, S., *Family Mediation in Ireland* (Dartmouth: Ashgate, 2002).

Coser, L., *The Functions of Social Conflict* (New York: Free Press, 1956).

Coser, L.A., 'The Termination of Conflict' (Dec., 1961), 5(4) *The Journal of Conflict Resolution* 347–353.

Coulter, C., *Family Law Matters* No. (1) (Brunswick Press, Spring2007).

Coulter, C., *Family Law Reporting Pilot Project; Report to the Board of the Court Service* (Courts Service of Ireland, 2007).

Cox, G., and Wray, L.K., 'Comparing Difficult with Very Difficult Terminated and Settled Collaborative Cases' available at https://www.collaborativepractice.com/media/2818/Comparing_Difficult_Very_Difficult_Terminated_Settled_Cases_2011_08_29.pdf.

Daicoff, S., 'Law as a healing profession: The comprehensive law movement' (2005) *Pepperdine Dispute Resolution Law Journal* NYLS Clinical Research Institute Paper No. 05/06–12, 1–61.

Daicoff, S., 'Families in Circle Process: Restorative Justice in Family Law' (2015) 53(3) *Family Court Review* 427–438.

Daicoff, S., 'The Comprehensive Law Movement' (2002–2004) 19 *Touro Law Review* 825–846.

Daicoff, S., 'The Role of Therapeutic Jurisprudence within the Comprehensive Law Movement', in *Practicing Therapeutic Jurisprudence: Law as a Helping Profession*, Stolle, Dennis P., Winick, B.J., and Wexler, D.B. (eds) (Durham NC: Carolina Academic Press, 2000).

Daigle, C., 'The Neutral Financial Professional: A Unique Opportunity, a Singular Responsibility' (2005) 7(1) *The Collaborative Review* 11–15.

Davis, A. M., 'An Interview with Mary Parker Follett' (1989) 5(3) *Negotiation Journal* 223–235.

Davis, G., Cretney, S., and Collins, J., *Simple Quarrels: Negotiating Money and Property Disputes on Divorce* (Oxford: Clarendon Press, 1994).

Davy, E., 'Problems Associated with Collaborative Practice' (2009) 1 *Judicial Studies Institute Journal* 14–18.

Delgado, R., Dunn, C., Brown, P., and Lee, H., 'Fairness and Formality: Minimizing the Risk of Prejudice in Alternative Dispute Resolution' (1985) 6 *Wisconsin Law Review* 1359–1404.

Deutsch, M., *The Handbook of Conflict Resolution: Theory and Practice* (San Francisco: Jossey-Bass, 2000).

Diduck, A., 'Family Law and Responsibility', in Bridgeman, J., Keating, H., and Lind, C., (eds), *Responsibility, Law and Family* (Aldershot: Ashgate, 2008).

Diesfeld, K., and McKenna, B., 'The Unintended Impact of the Therapeutic Intentions of the New Zealand Mental Health Review Tribunal? Therapeutic Jurisprudence Perspectives' (2007) 14 *Journal of Law and Medicine* 566–574.

Douzinas, C., *Law and Justice in Postmodernity* (Cambridge: Cambridge University Press, 2015).

Drew, M., 'Lawyer Malpractice and Domestic Violence: Are We Revictimizing Our Clients?' (2005) 39 (1) *Family Law Quarterly* 7–25.

Edwards, H., and White, J., *The Lawyer as Negotiator: Problems, Readings and Materials* (Eagan: West Publishing Co., 1977).

Eekelaar, J., Maclean, M., and Beinart, S., *Family Lawyers: The Divorce Work of Solicitors* (Oxford: Hart Publishing, 2000).

Fairman, C.M., 'A Proposed Model Rule for Collaborative Law,' (2005) 21 *Ohio State Journal on Dispute Resolution* 73–122.

Felstiner, W., Abel, R., and Sarat, A., 'The Emergence and Transformation of Disputes: Naming, Blaming, Claiming…' (1980–1981) 15(3–4) *Law and Society* 631–654.

Fisher, R., and Ury, W., *Getting to Yes* (2nd edn, New York: Random House, 1992).

Fiss, O., 'Against Settlement' (1986) 93(6) *Yale Law Journal*, 1073–1090.

Freckelton, I., 'Therapeutic Jurisprudence Misunderstood and Misrepresented: The Price and Risks of Influence' (2008) 30 *Thomas Jefferson Law Review*, 575–596.

Freud, S., *A General Introduction to Psychoanalysis* (New York: Garden City Publishing Co., 1938).

Fuller, L.L., 'Mediation – Its Forms and Functions' (1971) 44 *Southern California Law Review* 305–339.

Fuller, L.L., *The Principles of Social Order: Selected Essays of Lon L. Fuller*, Winston, K., (ed.) (Oxford: Bloomsbury, 1981).

Galanter, M., 'Worlds of Deals: Using Negotiation to Teach about Legal Process' (1984) 34 *Journal of Legal Education* 268–276.

Gamache, S., 'Collaborative Practice: A New Opportunity to Address Children's Best Interest in Divorce' (2005) 65 (4) *Louisiana Law Review* 1455–1485.

Gamache, S., 'The Role of the Child Specialist' in Cameron, N., (ed.), *Collaborative Practice, Deepening the Dialogue* (Vancouver: The Continuing Legal Education Society of British Columbia, 2004) 189–213.

Gardner Brown, D., 'The Role of the Financial Specialist' in Cameron, N., (ed.), *Collaborative Practice, Deepening the Dialogue* (Vancouver: The Continuing Legal Education Society of British Columbia, 2004) 223–232.

Gehani, R., and Gehani, R., 'Mary Parker Follett's Constructive Conflict: A "Psychological Foundation of Business Administration" for Innovative Global Enterprises' (2007) 30 *International Journal of Public Administration* 387–404.

George, R., *Ideas and Debates in Family Law* (Oxford: Hart, 2012).

Gerami, A., 'Bridging the Theory-and-Practice Gap: Mediator Power in Practice' (2009) 26(4) *Conflict Resolution Quarterly* 433–451.

Gillers, S., 'How to Make Rules for Lawyers: The Professional Responsibility of the Legal Profession' (2013) 40 *Pepperdine Law Review* 365–422.

Goldberg, S., *Judging for the 21st Century: A Problem-solving Approach* (National Judicial Institute of Ottawa, 2005).

Greco, A., 'Professional Fees Associated with Collaborative Divorce Resolution: The Evidence to Date' (2006) 12(3) *Journal of Legal Economics* 75–88.

Gribben, S., 'Mediation in Family Law Disputes' (1992) 6 *Australian Journal of Family Law* 126.

Grillo, T., 'The Mediation Alternative: Process Dangers for Women' (1991) 100 *Yale Law Review* 1545–1610.

Griswold, E.N., Edited text of speech given by Dean Griswold of Harvard Law School available at (1956) 37 Chicago Bar Record 199.

Gulliver, P.H., *Disputes and Negotiations: A Cross Cultural Perspective* (New York: Academic Press, 1979).

Hart, H.M. Jr., and Sacks, A.M., Preface to the 1958 'Tentative Edition' of Hart, H.M., and Sacks, A.M., *The Legal Process: Basic Problems in the Making and Application of Law*, Eskridge, W.M. Jr. and Frickey, F.P., (eds) (New York: Foundation Press, 1994).

Hazard, G., 'Rules of Ethics: The Drafting Task' (1981) 36 *Record of the Association of the Bar of the City of New York* 77–97.

Healy, C., '"On the plus side, I empathise more with my clients. On the negative side, I empathise more with my clients!" – Training as a Collaborative Lawyer: An Empirical Analysis' (2013) 3 *Irish Journal of Family Law* 70–78.

Healy, C., 'American and Irish Perspectives on Collaborative Practice' (2011) 4 *Irish Journal of Family Law* 98–108.

Healy, C., 'Collaborative Practice: An Interdisciplinary Approach to the Resolution of Conflict in Family Law Matters' in Boele-Woelki, K., and Dethloff, N., (eds) *Family Law and Culture in Europe, Developments, Challenges and Opportunities* (Antwerpen-Oxford: Intersentia, 2014) 119–134.

Healy, C., 'Dispute Resolution through Collaborative Practice: A Comparative Analysis' (2015) 27(2) *Child and Family Law Quarterly* 173–193.

Healy, C., 'The Child Specialist' (2012) 12(1) *The Collaborative Review* 22–24.

Heavin, H. and Keet, M., '"Skating to Where the Puck Will Be": Exploring Settlement Counsel and Risk Analysis in the Negotiation of Business Disputes' (2013) 76 *Saskatchewan Law Review* 191–211.

Herring, J., *Family Law* (5th edn, Oxford: Pearson, 2011).

Hoffman, D.A., 'Colliding Worlds of Dispute Resolution: Towards a Unified Field Theory of ADR' (2008) *Journal of Dispute Resolution* 11–44.

Keet, M., Wiegers, W., and Morrison, M., 'Client Engagement inside Collaborative Law' (2008) 24 *Canadian Journal of Family Law* 145–204.

Kelly, J.B., 'The Determination of Child Custody, The Future of Children' (1994) 4(1) *Children and Divorce* 130.

King, M., 'Should problem-solving courts be solution-focused courts?' (2011) Monash University Research Paper, Victoria.

Kvale, S., *InterViews: An Introduction to Qualitative Research Interviewing* (Thousand Oaks CA: Sage, 1996).

Lande, J., 'An Empirical Analysis of Collaborative Practice' (2011) 49(2) *Family Court Review* 257–281.

Lande, J., 'Practical Insights from an Empirical Study of Cooperative Lawyers in Wisconsin' (2008) *Journal of Dispute Resolution* 203–266.

Lande, J., 'Principles for Policymaking About Collaborative Law and Other ADR Processes' (2006–2007) 22 *Ohio State Journal on Dispute Resolution* 619–706.

Lande, J., 'Teaching Students to Negotiate Like a Lawyer' (2012) 39 *Washington University Journal of Law and Policy* 109–144.

Lande, J., 'The Promise and Perils of Collaborative Law' (2005–2006) 12 *Dispute Resolution Magazine* 30.

Law Reform Commission of Ireland. Report *Alternative Dispute Resolution: Conciliation and Mediation* (LRC 98–2010) (Dublin, 2010).

Law Society of Ireland. *A Guide to Good Professional Conduct for Solicitors* (3rd edn, Law Society of Ireland, 2013) https://www.lawsociety.ie/Documents/committees/conduct-guide.pdf.

Lehane, N., 'Making Talk Work', in Sweeney, D., and Lloyd, M. (eds), *Mediation in Focus: A Celebration of the Family Mediation Service in Ireland* (Family Mediation Service, 2011) 99–112.

Lowenthal, G.T., 'A General Theory of Negotiation: Process, Strategy and Behaviour' (1982–1983) 31 *University of Kansas Law Review* 69–114.

Macfarlane, J., *The Emerging Phenomenon of Collaborative Family Law (CFL): A Qualitative Case Study* (Department of Justice Canada, 2005).

Macfarlane, J., *The New Lawyer* (University of British Columbia Press, 2008).

Mackenzie, C., *Relational Autonomy: Feminist Perspectives on Autonomy, Agency and the Social Self* (Oxford University Press, 1999).

Maclean, S., *Legal Aid and the Family Justice System* (Legal Aid Board Research Unit, 1998).

Marshall, C., and Rossman, G., *Designing Qualitative Research* (5th edn, Sage, 2011).

Matthews, R.E., 'Negotiation: A pedagogical challenge' (1953) 6 *Journal of Legal Education* 93–101.

Mayer, B., *The Dynamics of Conflict Resolution: A Practitioner's Guide* (San Francisco: Jossey-Bass, 2000).

Mayer, B., *Beyond Neutrality: Confronting the Crisis in Conflict Resolution* (San Francisco: Jossey-Bass, 2004).

Meltsner, M., and Schrag, P. G., *Public Interest Advocacy: Materials for Clinical Legal Education* Chapter 13, *Negotiation* (Boston: Little, Brown and Co., 1997).

Menkel-Meadow, C., 'Ethics in Alternative Dispute Resolution: New Issues, No Answers from the Adversary Conception of Lawyers' Responsibilities,' (1997) 38 *South Texas Law Review* 407–454.

Menkel-Meadow, C., 'Legal Negotiation: A Study of Strategies in Search of a Theory' (1983) 8(4) *American Bar Foundation Research Journal* 905–937.

Menkel-Meadow, C., 'Mothers and Fathers of Invention: The Intellectual Founders of ADR' (2000) 16(1) *Ohio Journal of Dispute Resolution* 1–37.

Menkel-Meadow, C., 'Pursuing Settlement in an Adversary Culture: A Tale of Innovation Co-Opted or "The Law of ADR"' (1991) *Florida State University Law Review* 1–46.

Meyer, J., and Land, R., 'Threshold Concepts and Troublesome Knowledge (3): Implications for Course Design and Evaluation' in Rust, C. (ed.) *Improving Student Learning: Diversity and Inclusivity* (Oxford Centre for Staff and Learning Development, 2005).

Mnookin, R., and Kornhauser, L., 'Bargaining in the Shadow of the Law: The Case of Divorce' (1978–1979) 88 *Yale Law Journal* 950–977.

Mosten, F.S., 'The Future of Collaborative Practice: A Vision for 2030' (2011) 49(2) *Family Court Review* 282–291.

Murphy, R., 'Is the turn toward collaborative law a turn away from justice?' (2004) 42 (3) *Family Court Review* 460–470.

Nader, L., 'Forums for Justice: A Cross Cultural Perspective' (1975) 31(3) *Journal of Social Sciences* 151–170.

O'Leary, Z., *The Essential Guide to Doing your Research Project* (London: Sage, 2010).

Parker Follett, M., *Prophet of Management: A Celebration of Writings from the 1920s*, Graham, P. (ed.) (Cambridge MA: Harvard Business School Press, 1996).

Parker Follett, M., *The New State: Group Organization, the Solution of Popular Government* (University Park PA: Pennsylvania State University Press, 1918/1998).

Parsons, T., 'Racial and Religious Differences as Factors in Group Tension', in Bryson, L., Finkelstein, L. and MacIver, R. (eds) *Approaches to National Utility* (New York: Harper Bros, 1945).

Peppet, S., 'The Ethics of Collaborative Law' (2008) 1 *Journal of Dispute Resolution* 131–161.

Peppet, S., 'Lawyers' Bargaining Ethics, Contract, and Collaboration: The End of the Legal Profession and the Beginning of Professional Pluralism' (2004–2005) 90 *Iowa Law Review* 475–538.

Quinn, M., 'An RSVP to Professor Wexler's Warm Therapeutic Jurisprudence Invitation to the Criminal Defense Bar: Unable to Join You, Already (Somewhat Similarly) Engaged', (2007) 48 *Boston College Law Review* 539–595.

Ratnapala, S., *Jurisprudence* (2nd edn, Cambridge: Cambridge University Press, 2016).

Rawls, J., *Justice as Fairness: A Restatement* (Cambridge MA: Harvard University Press, 2011).

Roussos, P., 'It is Therapy' (2002) 1 *The Collaborative Review, Journal of the International Academy of Collaborative Professionals* 5.

Rubin, J.Z., 'The Nature of Conflict and Negotiation' in Breslin, W., and Rubin, J., (eds), *Negotiation Theory & Practice*, (Cambridge MA: The Program on Negotiation, Harvard Law School, 1999).

Sacks, H., 'Human Relations Training for Law Students and Lawyers' (1959) 11 *Journal of Legal Education* 316–345.

Sales, B.D. and Shuman, D.W., 'The Newly Emerging Mental Health Law', in Sales, B.D. and Shuman, D.W. (eds) *Law Mental Health, and Mental Disorder* (Wadsworth Publishing, 1996).

Sander, F.E.A., 'Varieties of Dispute Processing', Address Delivered at the National Conference on the Causes of Popular Dissatisfaction with the Administration of Justice (Apr. 7–9, 1976), in (1976) 70 *Federal Rules Decisions.*

Sarat, A. and Felstiner, W., *Divorce Lawyers and their Clients* (Oxford University Press, 1995).

Schneyer, T., 'The Organized Bar and the Collaborative Law Movement: A Study in Professional Change' (2008) 50 *Arizona Law Review* 289–336.

Schön, D., *The Reflective Practitioner: How Professionals Think in Action* (Temple Smith 1983).

Schwab, W., 'Collaborative Lawyering: A Closer Look at an Emerging Practice' (2004) 4 *Pepperdine Dispute Resolution Law Journal* 351–399.

Sefton, M., *Collaborative Family Law: A report for Resolution* (Resolution, 2009).

Shephard, A., and Hoffman, D., 'Regulating Collaborative Law: The Uniform Collaborative Law Act Takes Shape' (2010) 17(1) *Dispute Resolution* 26–29.

Shields, R.W., 'On Becoming a Collaborative Professional: From Paradigm Shifting to Transformative Learning Through Critical Reflection and Dialogue' (2008) 2 *Journal of Dispute Resolution* 427–463.

Simmel, G., *Conflict*, Wolff, K.H., *et al.* trans., (New York: Free Press, 1955).

Simon, W., *The Practice of Justice* (Cambridge MA: Harvard University Press, 1988).

Sloin, S.G., 'Message from the President' 2010 11(2) *The Collaborative Review* 5.

Smith, J., Flowers, P., and Larkin, M., *Interpretative Phenomenological Analysis, Theory, Method and Research* (London: Sage, 2010).

Spain, L.R., 'Collaborative Law: A Critical Reflection on Whether a Collaborative Orientation can be Ethically Incorporated into the Practice of Law' (2004) 56(1) *Baylor Law Review* 141–173.

Stansbury, C., Wray, L., and Pence, M., 'Lessons Learned from Drafting the UCLA', Paper delivered at the IACP 11th International Networking and Educational Forum, Washington D.C. 2010.

Tesler, P., *Collaborative Law: Achieving Effective Resolution in Divorce without Litigation* (2nd edn, American Bar Association, 2008).

Tesler, P., and Thompson, P., *Collaborative Divorce: The Revolutionary New Way to Restructure your Family, Resolve Legal Issues, and Move on with Your Life* (New York: Harper Collins, 2007).

Tindall, H., and Smith, J., 'The Uniform Collaborative Law Act as a Teaching Tool' (2009–2010) 38 *Hofstra Law Review* 685–698.

Twining, W., 'Alternative to What? Theories of Litigation, Procedure and Dispute Settlement in Anglo-American Jurisprudence: Some Neglected Classics' (1993) 56 *Modern Law Review* 380–392.

Tyler, T., 'Procedural Justice', in Wexler, D.B. and Winick, B.J. (eds), *Law in a Therapeutic Key: Developments in Therapeutic Jurisprudence* (Durham NC: Carolina Academic Press, 1996) 3–15.

Ver Steegh, N., 'The Uniform Collaborative Law Act and Intimate Partner Violence: A Roadmap for Collaborative (and Non Collaborative) Lawyers' (2009) 38 *Hofstra Law Review* 699–755.

Ward, T., 'Good Lives and the Rehabilitation of Offenders: Promises and Problems' (2002) 7(5) *Aggression and Violent Behaviour* 513–528.

Ward, T., and Stewart, C.A., 'Criminogenic Needs and Human Needs: A Theoretical Model' (2003) 9(2) *Psychology, Crime and Law* 125–143.

Webb, S., 'Collaborative Law: A Practitioner's Perspective on its History and Current Practice' (2008) 21 *Journal of the American Academy of Matrimonial Lawyers* 155–169.

Webb, S., and Ousky, R., *The Collaborative Way to Divorce: The Revolutionary Method that Results in Less Stress, Lower Costs, and Happier Kids – Without Going to Court* (New York: Penguin, 2007).

Wetlaufer, G., 'The Ethics of Lying in Negotiations' (1990) 75 *Iowa Law Review* 1219–1273.

Wexler, D.B., 'Therapeutic Jurisprudence: An Overview', (2000) 17(1) *Thomas M. Cooley Law Review* 125–134.

Wexler, D.B., 'From Theory to Practice and Back Again in Therapeutic Jurisprudence: Now Comes the Hard Part' (2011) *Arizona Legal Studies* Discussion Paper No. 10–12.

Women's Aid, *Submission to the Family Law Reporting Committee* (January 2009), available at: www.womensaid.ie.

Wray, L., and Lloyd, S., *Research regarding Collaborative Practice: A Comparison of Findings from the International Academy of Collaborative Professionals and Resolution* (IACP 10th Annual Forum, October 2010).

Wray, L., *The International Academy of Collaborative Professionals Research Regarding Client Experience* (IACP 11th Annual Forum, Washington D.C., October 2010).

Wright, K., 'The evolving role of the family lawyer: the impact of collaborative law on family law practice' (2011) 23 *Child and Family Law Quarterly* 370–392.

Yin, R., *Case Study Research: Design and Methods* (5th edn, Thousand Oaks: Sage Publications, 2014).

Zartman, W., and Berman, M., *The Practical Negotiator* (New Haven: Yale University Press, 1992).

Index

For Product Safety Concerns and Information please contact our EU representative GPSR@taylorandfrancis.com
Taylor & Francis Verlag GmbH, Kaufingerstraße 24, 80331 München, Germany

www.ingramcontent.com/pod-product-compliance
Ingram Content Group UK Ltd.
Pitfield, Milton Keynes, MK11 3LW, UK
UKHW011015180926
475701UK00004B/756

* 9 7 8 0 3 6 7 8 7 4 9 8 8 *